POLITICS AND POLICY

THE GENESIS AND
THEOLOGY OF SOCIAL STATEMENTS
IN THE LUTHERAN CHURCH IN AMERICA

POLITICS AND POLICY

Christa R. Klein
with
Christian D. von Dehsen

FORTRESS PRESS   MINNEAPOLIS

Library of Congress Cataloging-in-Publication Data

Klein, Christa R.
  Politics and policy.

  1. Church and social problems—Lutheran Church—
History.   2. Lutheran Church in America—Doctrine—
History.   3. Lutheran Church—Doctrines—History.
4. Lutheran Church in America—Doctrines—History—
Sources.   I. Von Dehsen, Christian D.   II. Title.
HN37.L8K55   1989   261.8'088241   88–45242
ISBN 0–8006–0898–4

3518H88   Printed in the United States of America   1–898

CONTENTS

PREFACE

A season of endings and beginnings invites historical reflection. As the Lutheran Church in America completed its allotted quarter of a century and its successor, the Evangelical Lutheran Church in America, is taking shape, the times are ripe to assess the past in preparation for the next steps in American Lutheranism.

This volume treats one legacy of the Lutheran Church in America: the body of nineteen social statements, all adopted during biennial conventions and each dependent upon habits of thought and patterns of organization. The statements were the winnowings of broader deliberations on social issues and had the status of "policy," interpreted both as a required discipline for the corporate structure of the denomination and as guidance for individual members.

During the twenty-five years, two successive agencies had the constitutional mandate to formulate statements and recommend them to conventions. The Board of Social Ministry held this position from 1963 to 1972. Subsequently, the Division for Mission in North America relied upon its Department for Church and Society to prepare items for its Management Committee to recommend to the convention. Dependent on consensus, the statements are inherently political documents. They also represent agreed upon theological perspectives.

I approached this assignment with the desire to know how church leaders, acting through denominational bureaucracy and convention democracy, selected and studied moral and social issues. I also wanted to discern which theological resources they plumbed to make judgments. Moreover, because the Lutheran Church in America spoke less often and with more deliberation on social issues than most other mainline churches, I wanted to view its statements within the sweep of Lutheran history in America and with some reference to the work of other American Christians. To accomplish this analysis I searched the evidence with four factors in mind.

First, I have considered Lutheran social thought as an aspect of Lutheran theology which is always in a reflexive and reciprocal relation to the history of doctrine, to contemporary church practice and to the world of ideas within and beyond academia. What were the concerns and patterns of thought that perdured over these twenty-five years? Where and how were deliberations on social issues conducted within the Lutheran community in North America and with what connections to other circles of conversation? Has the work been faithful to historic concerns of Lutheranism? What other terrains were explored? Are the foundations in place for continued theological reflection on church and society?

Second, I have watched the societal context of statements. What social forces influenced the selection and interpretation of issues? How are they manifest within the statements? Did Lutherans make their own contribution to discussions among Christians, or was their work either derivative or uninformed?

Third, I have considered the experience and viewpoint of the leading Lutherans in the discussion. What were their viewpoints and how did they arrive at them? What was their role in the formulation of a statement? What did they feel to be at stake and how satisfied were they with the results? What do they think in hindsight?

Fourth, how did the denominational structures for the management of discussion and the achievement of consensus work in the case of each statement? There was considerable experimentation and readjustment along the way. Why? What effect did such changes have on the formulation of statements? How did they influence relations among denominational staff members, elected boards, and other leaders, and the church membership? How was consensus achieved and at what cost?

These four themes will be interwoven in the discussion of a history that will proceed chronologically through the biennial conventions. The treatment of the statements thus illustrates the undercurrents of theology, social context, leadership, and church structure.

I have relied primarily on two kinds of sources. First, written documentation in the minutes of the Board of Social Ministry, the Department for Church and Society, the Management Committee and Cabinet of the Division for Mission in North America, the Executive Council, and the biennial conventions of the church. In connection with these items, I have also used relevant drafts and publications authorized by the board or management committee, as the case may be. Second, I have tried to interview, either in person or by telephone, key participants in the formulation and adoption of each statement along with interested outsiders.

Early in my research I became aware that these social statements belonged to a far longer history in American Lutheranism. From the last

quarter of the nineteenth century Lutherans began to act denomination-
ally, that is, collectively through national structures, in response to societal problems. The rise of the inner missions movement, too often and
inappropriately debunked as a side rail to the more central track of the
social gospel movement, deserves more careful consideration. Commitment to inner missions reveals telling features of Lutheran identity, circumstances, and European connection. This work, along with the devotion to the cause of prohibition in some predecessor bodies, gave
Lutherans the experience to approach social problems by other means
at a later time.

The offices of social ministry established in the late 1930s by two of
the LCA's predecessors, the Augustana Synod and the United Lutheran
Church in America, stand as the first stages of contemporary denominational organization of social ministry. Chapter 2 begins with the work
of these two offices and continues through the decades of the 1940s and
1950s, formative times for those leaders who would initiate and fine tune
the processes and substance of the LCA's early social statements.

Since the late 1930s there has been a continuous flow of research about
these times. Nearly a dozen doctoral dissertations completed between
1938 and 1985 explored the responses of Lutherans to social issues,
making this topic, along with immigration and assimilation, a favored
choice among graduate students working on American Lutheran history.
Much of that research is currently stored at University Microfilms in Ann
Arbor, Michigan.

The reasons for this spate of studies are worth pondering. Following
World War II more Lutheran seminary graduates than ever before pursued doctorates in American and European universities. The degree had
become a prerequisite for teaching in church colleges and seminaries, in
part because Lutherans had entered the middle class in sufficient numbers
to be able to afford accredited higher education. Frequently these students
used their doctoral work as an opportunity to examine their own Lutheran
roots in American soil at a time when Lutheran peoples were entering
the mainstream.

Yet Lutheran social responsibility has been a troublesome topic. Most
recognized scholars in the history of American Christianity during the
postwar era had little understanding of or empathy for Lutheran patterns
of church life. In those times Lutherans worldwide were on the spot
because of the capitulation of the *Landeskirchen* to Hitler. Reinhold Niebuhr, Wilhelm Pauck, and Paul Tillich of Union Theological Seminary in
New York, for example, while providing one of the most exciting opportunities for graduate study in America in the late forties through the

early sixties, were also notably critical of Lutheranism while at the same time knowledgeable in renascent Luther studies. The issues raised by these teachers had a lasting impact on such future Lutheran leaders in social ministry as Harold Letts, Rufus Cornelsen, George Forell, and William Lazareth.

In 1957, Sydney Ahlstrom, third generation American Swede and young church historian at Yale University, tried to explain that Lutheranism was best understood "not as something indistinguishably blended in with the luxuriant foliage of American denominationalism but as a tradition living in a real but fruitful state of tension with American church life."[1] The founders and shapers of social policy in the Lutheran Church in America purposefully chose a countervailing approach. Their struggles punctuate this account.

The eight subsequent chapters trace the evolution of the social statements, which are reprinted in the appendix. I had originally expected to focus exclusively on their substance. While content remains central, two observations intervened to suggest that the processes of formulation also deserved close attention. First, in my interviews I was struck by how little major actors said about the full argument in any particular statement. Instead, they remembered debates that tested their own commitments, the mood of the convention which took action, or the relation of the statement to the social context. Second, in June of 1986 the Commission for a New Lutheran Church decided that the social statements of predecessor bodies were to be received as "historical documents," not policy, the same tack taken twenty-five years earlier with the founding of the LCA.[2]

These two facts suggested that for this history to uncover a "usable past," one with meaning for the contemporary church, it must emphasize how the statements were created. An understanding of the way national and ecclesial politics affected the formation of church policy may illumine options for the future. All the statements attempt to get down to the hard and always ambiguous work of discerning how faith informs life in society.

History, for Lutherans, can be an expression of God's law by exposing limitations and pointing to continuing responsibilities. This ordeal is never the final word, but a necessary one for hearing the Word. Lutherans in this denomination worked with self-consciousness and circumspection. Nevertheless, their formulations can only be approximations of the love and justice God promises with the eschaton. That promise frees them to repent of their weaknesses, to draw on their successes, to redouble their efforts, and to work in hope.

This history is also one case study in the experience of American Protestantism. Other denominations struggle with the same social and moral questions and with the resources and structures of their own traditions. Perhaps this volume will contribute to a larger reexamination of the relation between church and society in American culture. Kenneth C. Senft, executive director of the Division for Mission in North America, and Foster R. McCurley, chair of the Church in Society Unit, requested this study. The idea originated with Richard Niebanck, who served for twenty-three years on the staff of Church in Society and its predecessor body, the Board of Social Ministry. I take full responsibility for all interpretations.

My decision to pursue the history prior to the LCA's twenty-five years pushed the deadlines on this book to the limit. I am deeply grateful to Christian D. von Dehsen, who did most of the research on the last fifteen years and provided me with drafts for the last two and one-half chapters. Our conversations came to inform the whole enterprise. Dozens of people consented to interviews. Elizabeth S. Risch helped us with documentary research, especially on the years since 1972. Elisabeth Whitman and Joy Liljegren of the Archives of the Lutheran Church in America provided materials for the earlier years. All those materials are now in the ELCA archives. Gerry Puelle of the Church in Society Unit helped to smooth all ways. The Cabinet of Executives in the Division for Mission in North America reviewed the entire manuscript for the Management Committee. Publication was made possible in part by a grant from the Lutheran Brotherhood. I am indebted to all.

NOTES

1. "The Lutheran Church and American Culture," *The Lutheran Quarterly* 9(1957):326.

2. CNLC Action 86.6.1536, 23 June 1986, adopted as resolution 12 on 29 August 1986 by the three merging bodies. See *Report and Recommendations of the Commission for a New Lutheran Church to The American Lutheran Church, The Association of Evangelical Lutheran Churches, and Lutheran Church in America (Evangelical Lutheran Church in America, 1986)*, 196.

POLITICS AND POLICY

1

CHURCH AND SOCIETY, 1820–1918

The LCA's twenty-five-year record of social statements belongs to the longer history of Lutheran denominational responses to the American social order. Its predecessor church bodies, beginning with the General Synod founded in 1820, pursued various approaches depending upon the social context, the theological and social lenses of their leaders, and the adaptability of church structures. An overview of this past indicates that the character of the church's response to society is neither static nor predetermined. Lutherans in each age have made choices of historic consequence. Moreover, they have often disagreed among themselves.

Two nineteenth-century movements were especially potent in the history of Lutheran social responsibility: temperance and inner missions. The former drew on a broadly based American religious effort with Scandinavian connections. The latter paralleled German and Scandinavian programs and set Lutherans apart from those American Protestants who advocated the Social Gospel, but not from most others who continued to pursue individual conversion to achieve social reform.

Temperance and inner missions have been underrated in recent histories of American Lutheranism, perhaps because they do not fit contemporary conceptions of social reform. Yet these very aspects of their past schooled Lutherans about issues and prepared them to respond in the twentieth century with new structures and forms of collaboration. Although both movements emerged among Lutherans in the first half of the nineteenth century, neither took hold until the second half, after Lutherans had settled their regional, theological, and ethnic differences with each other by founding separate denominations. It should not be surprising that Lutherans who were unable to achieve theological consensus in nineteenth-century America should also fail to reach agreement on how to respond to social issues. Their pieties on such matters tended

1

to follow from their theology, with intervening regional and ethnic variables.

THE GENERAL SYNOD AND
SOCIAL REFORM, 1820–1865

The early years of the first national Lutheran denomination illustrate these difficulties. Between 1820 and 1860, the General Synod had grown to include nearly three-fifths of American Lutheranism. The larger it grew, the more diverse it became and the less able to serve as a forum for significant theological, political, and ethical issues perturbing its members. After the 1860s, when the southern synods and the northern confessionalists left to found their own church bodies, the General Synod, now more homogeneous, would again address issues that had been more prominent in its early years.

Social reform and religious renewal were primary issues for founders and early leaders of the General Synod. Consensus on Lutheran faith and practice had faded by the early nineteenth century at the same time that Lutherans were organizing regional synods as they moved west and south. Jealous of their own powers, the synods were unwilling to delegate more than advisory status to a national body.

In effect, the General Synod was founded to accomplish the projects that district synods could not manage by themselves, namely missionary work, theological education, ministerial aid, and the publication of suggested worship and catechetical materials. The agendas of its biennial conventions were structured around reports from separate societies to accomplish these assignments.

Samuel Simon Schmucker (1799–1874), leading churchman and theologian of the denomination, envisioned a broader goal. For Schmucker, the General Synod provided the structure and means of education for Lutherans to participate in the pan-Protestant movement of renewal and reform among American "Evangelicals," that is, members of denominations with British origin who emphasized an experience of personal conversion, the authority of Scripture, the centrality of the atonement, and holy living. These were the "fundamentals" Schmucker believed Lutherans could agree upon and sustain by affirming them in their own Augsburg Confession. Like other Evangelicals, he was less concerned with the doctrine of the church and the Christian's encounter with the promised Jesus in the sacraments. He took the classic Lutheran positions on these to be both extraneous and divisive.

Evangelicalism found nourishment in a form of millennial eschatology that was foreign to most sixteenth- and seventeenth-century Lutheranism, but had taken root in some radical forms of Lutheran Pietism.[1] Schmucker was at home with the interpretation that anticipated how the work of religious conversion and social reform could hurry Christ's second coming. In this theological system, the work of the gospel easily became the regnant morality of the regenerate. Moreover, the salvation of the world came to depend on the improvement of society through the aggregation of individual conversions.

Schmucker hoped that the new denomination would not only bring order to Lutheranism but also the opportunity to acquaint German-Americans, many of whom were isolated by geography and culture in farming communities, with their coreligionists among other Evangelical Protestants. Then Lutheranism, the mother lode of all Protestantism, might take its rightful place at the center of what he believed to be the contemporary Reformation.[2]

Because the goals for the denomination were above all practical and because Lutheran unity served as the means to that end, the denomination developed procedures for admission that made of it "an inclusive confederation."[3] By the 1850s the General Synod would encompass virtually every theological current among American Lutherans, from the increasingly strict confessionalism of the Pennsylvania Ministerium to the virtually generic Protestantism of the Melanchthon Synod.

Yet, until the mid-1830s, before the General Synod had attracted the oldest regional bodies and before the movement to abolish slavery began to exacerbate sectional tensions in the nation, the atmosphere at conventions allowed for some discussion of major social issues. Nevertheless, no one expected the denomination to carry the major responsibility for the expression of its members' social concerns. There were other more appropriate ways for Christians to work collectively in behalf of reform, ways which would not threaten early consensus in young denominations.

In the same years that Lutherans and other American Protestants were founding new church bodies, they were also organizing pan-Protestant societies to accomplish common goals in education, the American mission field, and social reform. During the course of the two decades surrounding the origins of the General Synod, many of these societies took on a national structure and hired a secretary or two to travel among the local chapters, to edit some kind of newsletter, and to organize an annual convention. Among the more popular were the American Bible Society (1816), the American Education Society (1816) (for the support of young men preparing for the ordained ministry), the American Colonization Society (1817) (to send free Blacks to African colonies), the American

Sunday School Union (1824), the American Tract Society (1825), the American Temperance Society (1826), the American Peace Society (1828), the American Seamen's Friend Society (1828), the General Union for Promoting the Observance of the Christian Sabbath (1828), and the American Antislavery Society (1833).[4]

Leading pastors and laity in the General Synod sponsored chapters and participated in the national organizations. Sometimes they recommended approval of a particular society to the convention of a regional synod to encourage membership and contributions. For example, in 1824 Schmucker spoke to his own Maryland and Virginia Synod in behalf of a proposal to recommend the work of the American Colonization Society.[5] As a movement took on national proportions, it was likely to reach the floor of the General Synod.

By the 1830s, temperance had attained this prominence, especially for many pastors and lay leaders from larger towns and cities where they were in regular contact with "Yankee" Protestants. Recent histories of the movement underscore both the widespread problem of alcoholism, especially as techniques for the manufacture of liquor improved, and the desire of native-born Americans to exercise social control over immigrants, such as Irish Roman Catholics, who drank heavily. As temperance became the symbolic solution to a seemingly intractable set of problems, advocates redefined the term to mean total abstinence from the use of both distilled and fermented beverages.

In 1835 at its eighth convention, the General Synod adopted for the first time a resolution expressing its "deep interest in the progress of the temperance reformation," acknowledging supportive efforts by "the friends of true religion in our church," and recommending "the formation of temperance societies to the people in our connection."[6]

By the 1850s the national movement was becoming prohibitionist, partly in response to the successful passage in Maine in 1851 of a law prohibiting the manufacture and sale of liquor. In 1853, the General Synod in convention called intemperance the "great evil" for "seriously retarding the progress of Christ's Kingdom, and bringing incalculable evils on society," and urged its members to cooperate with others to extend the principles of the Maine liquor law throughout the land.[7]

After that convention, temperance was curiously absent from the floor until 1864. Silence on the issue probably became the solution employed by watchful leaders who recognized the synod's increasing fragility. They hoped to prevent schism, not only over matters of social ethics but also over interpretations of the Lutheran Confessions.

4

The Pennsylvania Ministerium, oldest and largest of the regional bodies, had rejoined the General Synod in 1853 after thirty years, on the proviso that the denomination not require of its member synods "assent to anything conflicting with the old and long established faith of the Evangelical Lutheran church."[8] Such a declaration of confessional norms was a sign of the times, after decades in which most Lutherans had ignored or misrepresented them. Beginning in the 1840s, members of the Pennsylvania Ministerium and others in the General Synod were rediscovering the full body of Lutheran confessional writings. In addition, many among the newly arrived German immigrants had experienced the confessional awakening in their homelands.

For the first time, eastern Lutheranism had the makings of a more comprehensive theology by which to assess Schmucker's minimalism, along with the absolutism of American Evangelical reform movements. In addition, the moderate social use of alcohol, a cultural norm among German immigrants and German-Americans in the towns and countryside of the Ministerium, gave these Lutherans another perspective.

Divided views on slavery and the speed of its abolition added tinder to the fires of discord in the mid-forties. Lutherans perceived the dangers of the antislavery movement for church unity. The Presbyterians, Methodists, and Baptists were already divided over the issue. Moreover, Americans, including Schmucker, who attended the 1846 London meeting of the Evangelical Alliance, had difficulty representing their denominations in the face of British attempts to eliminate slaveholders from membership in any international ecumenical organization.[9]

Schmucker, himself unequivocal in calling slavery sin, was stymied on the appropriate political formula for its eradication. He drew back from the Colonization Society because he did not believe that free or freed Blacks should be forced to emigrate. He was also critical of abolitionist William Garrison's brand of immediatism which ignored political realities. Within the General Synod he and others agreed for the sake of denominational unity to remain silent on this issue.[10] The North Carolina delegation to the General Synod's Pittsburgh convention in 1859 testified to the effectiveness of the gentlemen's agreement in their report home of the "uniform kindness" they received from "the brethren and citizens generally."[11]

The abolitionists were also suspect to the new guardians of the Lutheran Confessions. Where they witnessed a firm commitment to this cause among Lutherans, they also noted few if any confessional commitments. The Franckean Synod of New York, which separated from the

Hartwick Synod over the issue in 1837, was the primary case in point. Along with its reformist platform, the declaration of faith in its constitution offered no allegiance either to the Augsburg Confession or Luther's Small Catechism. Its 1864 application for membership in the General Synod revealed a division on theological and social issues that leaders had been hoping to mask.

The General Synod's program for Lutheran unity had been eroding for a decade. By the mid-fifties, the synods with a stricter interpretation of the Lutheran Confessions were gaining power, and Samuel Simon Schmucker's original vision of an Americanized modification in faith and practice no longer held sway. When he countered by proposing—at first anonymously—a "Definite Platform," including a list of errors in the Augsburg Confession, as a statement of faith required of ordinands in member synods, he brought the debate to a head.

"Americanists," as his supporters were called, rejected Augsburg's approval of private confession and absolution and of the ceremonies of the mass, its affirmation of baptismal regeneration and of the real presence of Christ in the Lord's Supper, and—in a nineteenth-century reading—its denial of the divine obligation of the Christian Sabbath.

On the last point, Schmucker's understanding of Christian social action found expression. Active in the Evangelical Protestant "Sabbatarian" movement which began in opposition to the federal government's transportation of mail on Sundays, Schmucker shared with most contemporary Protestants a desire for legal protection of Sunday observance and the requirement of pious activities by Christians. He had been appalled during his 1846 trip to the Continent by the Sunday recreation he observed even among German Christians. Confessionalists, many of whom favored pious Sunday observances, noted that the Augsburg Confession, Article 28, did not oppose Sunday observance, but rather contended for evangelical freedom in its manner. The Americanists were far more willing to turn to the government to enforce Christian behavior than were the confessionalists, who wished to guard against the confusion of the church's message with legalism.

Although the Definite Platform of 1855 never came to the floor of the General Synod's convention, it proved to be a watershed for Lutherans in the East and beyond. One early outcome was the formation of the Augustana Synod in 1860 by Swedes and Norwegians distrustful of doctrine and practice in the Synod of Northern Illinois, a member of the General Synod. Their name (Latin for the Augsburg Confession) stated their position and marked the departure early leaders had made from American Protestant Evangelicalism.

Their ties with that movement had come quite naturally. Lars Esbjorn, Augustana's chief mover, had come to America in 1849 with the support of the Congregationalist American Home Missionary Society as a missionary to the Scandinavians. In the 1830s and 1840s he had been active in the temperance movement introduced in Sweden by British and American revivalists. Intoxication had become a social problem of major dimensions in a poor farming country where produce was more conveniently and profitably marketed in its distilled form. The vision of pan-Protestant cooperation in America painted during those years did not match the competition he discovered between denominations for the allegiance of the Swedes. Others joined his pilgrimage for Lutheran identity and conversion to a thoroughgoing confessionalism in the early 1850s. The Definite Platform provoked the decision to break with the Synod of Northern Illinois. Confessionalism was grafted to the piety of Swedish revivalism, including temperance.[12]

The southern synods were the next to leave. All parties in Lutheranism were present among them, although their sectional loyalties had made them increasingly critical of the northern Protestant reform movements. The temperance press also tended to be antislavery, and Lutherans in the South as much as elsewhere reflected the practices and beliefs of their region. These synods were not eager to break ecclesiastical ties with northern Lutherans, but they all affirmed secession. The General Synod, meeting in a postponed convention in 1862, condemned it unequivocally. In 1863, the General Synod of the Evangelical Lutheran Church in the Confederate States of America (after the war called the General Synod, South) was founded.[13]

Where Lutherans did take a firm stand in opposition to slavery, their morality was buttressed by cultural experience. For example, the young Republican party with its clear opposition to the extension of slavery and to the compromises favored by the Whigs, attracted a considerable following among Norwegian and Swedish immigrants.[14] The Augustana Synod, located primarily in the upper Midwest, had little difficulty in assuming an antislavery stance from the outset. Its sense of justice had also been sharpened by the memory of liberalization movements within the Swedish social order.

The Norwegian Synod was divided along lay and clergy lines on the issues because of links with the Missouri Synod. Seated in a border state and adverse to public pronouncements on social issues, Missouri engaged in theological debate through conventions and in its theological journals about the citizen's, not the denomination's, relation to the state. Like other southern church bodies, it eschewed the belief that the structure

7

of slavery *per se* was sinful, while also holding that its American form was evidence of God's judgment and punishment for sin. Within the structure, they pointed to new opportunities for the work of the gospel to bring both master and slave to a new relationship based on Christian love.

The clergy of the Norwegian Synod, who had a close relation to Missouri and had been sharing the facilities of Concordia Seminary in St. Louis, tended to follow Missouri's position. This alignment provoked a crisis in convention when lay delegates, whose sympathy for slaves was fed by their own experience of class oppression in Norway, pressed for and succeeded in breaking the seminary link with Missouri.

With the departures of the Augustana Synod and the southern synods from the General Synod, the eastern synods were left with their own theological differences. The debate over the admission of the Franckean Synod, with its abolitionist history and its diluted declaration of faith, revealed deep-seated opposition in the Pennsylvania Ministerium. By 1866, the rupture was complete and the critics of the General Synod had issued a call for another kind of Lutheran unity based on subscription to the Augsburg Confession. After the General Council was founded in 1867, the General Synod represented no more than one-fifth of all Lutherans.

In the aftermath of this splintering, Lutheran unity at all costs was eliminated as the goal of denominationalism. This freed Lutherans institutionally to pursue theological and social concerns for the first time in two decades. Regrettably, concern for emancipated slaves was no lasting priority among the LCA's predecessor bodies. They shared the culturally imbued racism of other Protestants that helped sow the seeds for the emergence of full-scale segregation in the last quarter of the nineteenth century. Neither the abolitionist movement nor the victor's Reconstruction sustained interest in working out the political and social ramifications of emancipation. Among Lutherans, the Missouri Synod alone made an effort to provide for the education of Black pastors in behalf of separate Black Lutheran congregations newly formed in North Carolina and Alabama. Because the work was defined as a "mission," Blacks gained no political equality within the denomination.[15] Lutherans were far more conscious in those years of the needs of European immigrants.

INNER MISSIONS AND LUTHERAN DIVERSITY AFTER 1866

At the same time that some American Lutherans were fixing their vision on the confessional revival in Germany, they also noticed the volunteer beginnings of the inner mission movement to enlist Christians in the work of religious and social renewal. In 1846 William A. Passavant visited the founding institutions of the inner mission movements in Germany, including Kaiserswerth on the Rhine, and returned with a passionate commitment to such work in America. In January of 1848 he described the scope of inner missions in the first number of his new journal, *The Missionary*, with a list covering every imaginable aspect of the church's efforts—devotional, educational, welfare, aesthetic, musical, and liturgical.

Passavant's initial feverish efforts, particularly in the founding of hospitals and orphanages and the introduction of the deaconess movement from Kaiserswerth, occurred as his Pittsburgh Synod was being organized and before the splintering of the General Synod. Thus his call to action circulated widely. In time, the movement came to be associated with the general confessional awakening among Lutherans.

American Lutherans had borrowed an idea from the Continent that fit the pattern of voluntary associations in a new land. In German states, especially in the wake of the revolutions of 1848, the inner mission movement took a more explicit political cast in support of monarchy and state churches, and received favored status by governments. Proponent Johann H. Wichern (1808–1881) explicitly countered Marx and claimed that this movement would revive "the holy orders of life in church and state, whereby a people called Christian can be gathered to become truly Christian people within these orders." He argued that God's kingdom manifested itself in church and state through the work of "charitable institutions."[16]

In the absence of thoroughgoing research on American inner missions,[17] it is difficult to clarify precisely the meaning of "holy orders" and the "kingdom of God" for Lutherans in America. Apparently, the American version of the movement was at first largely apolitical. Religious indifference and family hardship, not socialism, defined the concern of Lutheran leaders in America. With volunteer societies they jury-rigged institutions to provide for the poor, orphaned, infirm, and elderly throughout the late nineteenth century. Everywhere they turned, immigrants from Lutheran homelands were in need. The biography of Erland Carlsson, for example, recounts the tragedies and familial disarray experienced by Swedes who came through Chicago during the cholera epidemic of 1854–55.[18]

Immigrant numbers challenged all existing churches and charitable societies. The steady stream of northern Europeans that had begun in the 1820s peaked in the 1880s when nearly 1.5 million Germans, 177,000

Norwegians, 392,000 Swedes, and 88,000 Danes entered.[19] Most were peasants. Half the Germans and at least 90 percent of the Scandinavians were nominally Lutheran. Hundreds of thousands more would arrive before World War I to make missionary and charitable work among their own kind the compelling Lutheran responsibility for more than half a century.

Inner mission societies flourished in all Lutheran bodies and planted institutions, especially where immigrants settled. In 1890, Lutherans from all church bodies were supporting thirty-two orphanages, eleven hospitals, eight immigrant missions, six deaconess homes, one seamen's mission and one home for the deaf and dumb. By 1913, they sponsored sixty-one orphanages, forty-two hospitals, thirty-six homes for the aged, twenty-one immigrant and seamen's missions, nine deaconess mother houses, five homes for the epileptic, crippled, and feeble-minded, and thirteen hospices.[20]

When these monumental efforts are viewed in the context of immigration and the effort to renew Lutheranism, inner missions can be understood as a massive Lutheran achievement in social service and evangelism. When these same efforts are placed in the context of other American Christian efforts, Lutherans appear to be on a parallel course with most other Evangelical Protestants and Roman Catholics. For example, they shared with the major revivalist movements of the day an urgent sense of people's material needs, as well as a profound concern for their recognition of God's saving grace.[21]

Nevertheless, with few exceptions Lutherans set themselves apart from a significant minority movement, the Social Gospel, which aimed at reforming social structures and not just binding victims' wounds. From the late 1870s through the 1920s, leading Protestants within the Baptist, Episcopalian, Congregational, and Methodist communions developed a working theology that depended on a corporate interpretation of sin and the possibility of its eradication through collective social reform. Many of the farsighted reforms advocated were in fact instituted when Progressives gained national political power during the first quarter of the twentieth century.

Advocates of the Social Gospel deplored the virtually unregulated economy of the United States for allowing the business sector to treat labor—men, women, and children, many of them immigrants—as a commodity and thereby to contribute to the increasingly wretched living conditions of the urban poor. They viewed the conflict between capital and labor as the central problem of industrial society and the one for which Christians, therefore, bore the most responsibility. Millennial thought supplied

10

the reigning vision—the coming kingdom of God on earth. Walter Rauschenbusch, the major theologian of the Social Gospel, expressed this hope in his first book, *Christianity and the Social Crisis*, in 1907:

Since the Reformation began to free the mind and to direct the force of religion toward morality, there has been a perceptible increase of speed. . . . The swiftness of evolution in our own country proves the immense latent perfectibility in human nature.

Perhaps these nineteen centuries of Christian influence have been a long preliminary stage of growth, and now the flower and fruit are almost here. If at this juncture we can rally sufficient religious faith and moral strength to snap the bonds of evil and turn the present unparalleled economic and intellectual resources of humanity to the harmonious development of a true social life, the generations yet unborn will mark this as that great day of the Lord for which the ages waited, and count us blessed for sharing in the apostolate that proclaimed it.[22]

Deeply suspicious of the optimistic theology of the Social Gospel, Lutherans were also uncomfortable with the requirement that church bodies participate directly in social reform. In fact, Lutherans were singled out by the German-born Rauschenbusch for public reprimand first in 1905 and more thoroughly in his later volume, *Christianizing the Social Order*. Lutherans, ranking third in numbers among Protestants, "isolated by their use of the German and Scandinavian languages" and supporting "beautiful institutional charities," were left "unstimulated, uninstructed, and even sterilized against social enthusiasms" because "their ministry is faithful to the older doctrinal issues of the Reformation and declines on principle to let the Church concern itself with social questions." He would have preferred them to transmit

the mature results of social experience and thought of the German Church, just as the Episcopalians have transmitted the impulses of the Anglican Church. But thus far Lutheranism has buried its ten talents in a tablecloth of dogmatic theory and kept its people from that share in the social awakening which is their duty and their right.[23]

When T. E. Schmauk, president of the General Council and a seminary professor who wrote regularly on social issues, answered one of Rauschenbusch's critiques in a personal letter, he spoke for many confessionalists. He suggested the perimeters within which even the more socially aware Lutherans preferred to work:

We do believe in a vigorous and thorough treatment of social questions by Christians in the State, but we believe that this work should be done by them as citizens, and not as Christians. We do not believe it to be the province of the Church to enter as a Church upon the problems of society or of the body politic.[24]

Elsewhere he wrote that according to the philosophy of the Social Gospel, Christianity has value "only when it serves the community":

> The real aim of the Church, according to this view, degenerates into social and political betterment, and into civic righteousness. The individual, with his immortal life, is depressed for the benefit of the common social state, and the Church's chief use and end is found in the local uplift it gives to every specific locality, and to the higher grade of state and national issues. Christianity does not seek to change society first, and thus remove sin by the pressure of social environment. Christianity seeks to eliminate sin through justification and regeneration, and thus to reform society by the new and inner life of the individual.[25]

Members of the General Synod could follow the literature of the social gospel movement by reading their own journals. Nevertheless, conventional economic views dominated editorials until the end of the century when labor attracted an increasingly sympathetic hearing. In the General Council, not only was the Social Gospel given less coverage in the church press but, before the turn of century, there was hardly any discussion of social issues. Later the ways and means of inner missions were described as the solution to the troubles of laborers.[26]

Throughout the period before World War I, Lutherans expressed a spectrum of opinions ranging from conservative to more liberal. Yet there were limits beyond which they would not go. In the words of Reginald Dietz, historian of eastern Lutheranism:

> Liberals and conservatives alike agreed that personal salvation was the church's basic mission. Liberals [among the Lutherans] were simply a bit more venturesome in staking out for the church in society a somewhat broader area of responsibility for judgment, rebuke, criticism, guidance, and education. All agreed that whatever public action was to be taken to deal with the specific ills was the responsibility not of the church but of individual Christians as citizens, workers and employers. The church as such must eschew the roles of political lobby and reform movement.[27]

Dietz based his conclusions primarily on the writings of church leaders and captured the reigning theological perspective. Nevertheless, the convention minutes of the General Synod suggest a slightly altered thesis. On the issue of temperance, the General Synod learned how to take a corporate activist stance. From 1866 to 1917, this issue dwarfed all other social concerns in the Synod. Three responses demonstrate forms of activity which would become more common in the mid-twentieth century.

First, the General Synod was drawn into corporate public advocacy. Second, it organized a committee with funding from the general treasury and eventually hired an administrator. Third, it developed links to a political lobby and came into the orbit of churches which founded the Federal Council of Churches in 1908. Temperance more than the Social Gospel accomplished this shift.

The General Synod regularly passed convention resolutions adding to public testimony on temperance legislation. Its first stand in behalf of law enforcement occurred in 1868 when the convention deplored "the license which so many of our legislators seem disposed to give on the sale of liquor on the Sabbath."[28] In 1897 it advocated the legislation favored by the Women's Christian Temperance Union on educational material for public schools which supplied "scientific temperance instruction."[29]

Throughout the period, the General Synod sent official delegates to meetings of national voluntary societies on the issue. The National Temperance Convention was the favored organization from the 1860s through the 1880s. These Lutherans were even more supportive of the Anti-Saloon League founded in 1893, since the League allied itself with no particular political party.[30] Its platform was to eliminate the saloon and to promote popular local option through education. By 1918, with the help of this technique and platform, two-thirds of the U.S. population lived in the 90 percent of the United States that was dry.

As political activity on this issue mounted in American society, the General Synod organized to follow the movement more closely. Prior to 1881 either the General Synod's president or its Committee on Resolutions brought the issue to the convention's attention. In that year, the General Synod created an *ad hoc* committee on temperance. This committee reported regularly on the national movement and on legislative victories. During these same years, Sunday School and catechetical materials advocated temperance. In 1899 a permanent committee of two years' duration was established. The secretary of this committee happened also to be in charge of the legislative work of the Anti-Saloon League in Washington, D.C. In 1913, $500 was appropriated by the convention for the League's work.[31]

At the 1915 convention, the committee posed a rhetorical question: "Has the time come for our church to do something in its own name and in its own way to advance the cause of temperance?"[32] That convention recommended the appointment of a secretary of temperance, "whose duty it shall be to have charge of the temperance work of the General Synod, to present the cause to our churches and Sunday Schools."[33] Included in the report at the following convention was an announcement that the general secretary charged with this task had also become an associate secretary of the Federal Council of Churches' Commission on Temperance.[34]

Although voices were raised in behalf of the Federal Council's social gospel platform within the General Synod, the Synod itself kept a low profile. Edwin Heyl Delk, revered pastor of St. Matthew's Church in Philadelphia and a member of the council's Commission on the Church and Social Service, became nationally prominent for his work with Washington Gladden, a Baptist leader in the movement.[35] The Synod offered no resolutions of support for the council's Social Creed, revised in 1912. The creed called the churches to advocate the improvement of working conditions and to support the principle of conciliation and arbitration in industrial dissensions.[36] Instead, the 1913 convention's Committee on Resolutions defended the General Synod's record by claiming that the church was the inspiration of all charities and all humanitarian agencies and movements. It also stated that the church's best contribution to the work of social uplift was "by holding itself strictly to the faithful preaching of the Gospel, and to the work of bringing the individual members of society to a saving knowledge of Jesus Christ, and to a consecrated life of service in and for his kingdom."[37] Temperance apparently was more in line with this theology of individual conversion.

Within the Augustana Synod, temperance was also the most prominent social issue. Beginning in 1880 resolutions stating the Synod's position began to appear. Conventions held in 1904 and 1909 adopted resolutions in support of the Anti-Saloon League and called for total abstinence from the use of liquor.[38] Southern Lutherans were not so stringent in their views. In 1872 the General Synod, South, passed a resolution opposing the indiscriminate manufacture and sale of intoxicating liquor as a beverage, but not against drinking itself. More frequently, writers in the church press called for the moderate use of liquor, not total abstinence.[39]

While the temperance issue sparked corporate social action in the General and Augustana Synods, inner missions played a similar role for the General Council. The 1905 convention included a discussion of fourteen theses on "the Inner Mission," the preferred term in the Council, and the recommendation that a permanent committee be established. The 1907 convention heard the first report of the Committee on Inner Mission and adopted its recommendations, including provisions for instruction in the seminary and for the appointment of a general secretary.[40] By 1911 the

General Synod had followed suit and in 1915 granted the committee board status.[41]

Leaders of the General Council were fully aware of other churches' approval of the Social Gospel but could not lend their support. Most members of the Federal Council had established denominational committees or boards to handle corporate social concern. In its 1915 convention, the General Council set forth six theses contrasting the Inner Mission with the Council's statement on social service. Three theses illustrate the General Council's views. First, the Social Gospel functioned as a humanitarian, civic, and ethical movement to change the structures of society; whereas the Inner Mission was both humanitarian and redemptive, seeking to change both the inner and outer life. Second, because the Social Gospel was directed toward society, it was considered "socialistic or communistic," whereas the Inner Mission treated the individual as the primary unit. Third, since the Social Gospel was more concerned about justice and law, it related particularly to the state; whereas the Inner Mission, because of its concern for mercy and love was more related to the church.[42]

The concern for personal morality—promoted by law in the case of prohibition—which characterized the General Synod, and the commitment to inner missions adopted by both the Synod and the General Council were indicative of the social response of other Lutherans in America. The more theologically conservative German bodies resonated to inner missions, but, like the General Council, abhorred the "legalism" of prohibition. Scandinavian groups, for whom temperance was a solution to a severe social problem in their homeland and a mark of the Christian life, adopted a stance more like the General Synod, although they may have been less politically active. The Augustana Synod embodied the double thrust of temperance and inner missions.

Undergirding both concerns lay the expanding structures of denominational Lutheranism. Eastern Lutherans were creating the structures to express their social views. In so doing, their organizations paralleled those developed by denominations of British derivation that favored the Social Gospel. The expression of social responsibility at the national level had become possible organizationally. Often overlooked, the key factor encouraging such expansion derived from increased financial support.[43] During these same years, American denominations had begun to coopt successful fund-raising techniques used in interdenominational missionary campaigns.

The General Synod was apparently the first Lutheran body to adopt a form of systematic finance. Soon after the success of the Laymen's Missionary Movement, organized in 1906 to support the increasing number

15

of youth volunteering for the mission field, the General Synod began to advocate its techniques. Publicity, duplex envelopes, and every-member visitation gradually became standard in the congregations. The General Council and United Synod of the South followed this lead and discovered that giving increased dramatically.[44] After World War I, the foreign-language Lutheran bodies would adopt similar approaches. Lutherans were embarked on denominational courses that would abet mergers among them and promote discourse with non-Lutheran bodies on a range of social issues.

As the General Synod prepared to merge with the General Council and United Synod of the South to form the United Lutheran Church in America, its 1917 convention petitioned the new church to create "a standing committee on temperance or a board on temperance and social service."[45] The new denomination would opt for a committee for its first two decades and also a board, separately incorporated, of inner missions. The stage had been set for a corporate structuring of social ministry within twentieth-century Lutheranism.[46]

NOTES

1. See James L. Haney, Jr., "The Religious Heritage and Education of Samuel Simon Schmucker: A Study in the Rise of 'American Lutheranism' " (Ph.D. diss., Yale University, 1968).

2. See, e.g., Samuel Simon Schmucker, *The American Lutheran Church*, 5th ed. (Philadelphia: E. W. Miller, 1852).

3. For a discussion of the General Synod's approach to Lutheran unity, see John H. Tietjen, *Which Way to Lutheran Unity?* (St. Louis: Clayton Publishing House, reprint, 1975), 13-38.

4. Winthrop S. Hudson, *Religion in America*, 2d ed. (New York: Charles Scribner's Sons, 1973), 152-53; Robert T. Handy, *A History of the Churches in the United States and Canada* (New York and Oxford: Oxford University Press, 1976), 182-83.

5. Paul P. Kuenning, "American Lutheran Pietism: Activist and Abolitionist" (Ph.D. diss., Marquette University, 1985), 227.

6. *Proceedings of the Eighth Convention of the General Synod of the Evangelical Lutheran Church in the United States, 1835,* 15. Further references to the minutes of the General Synod and to those of other Lutheran church bodies will be cited as *Minutes . . . (year)*. See also Larry Lee Lehman, "Lutherans and the Movement for Temperance (1827–1859)" (B.D. thesis, Lutheran Theological Seminary, Gettysburg, 1961).

7. General Synod, *Minutes . . . 1853*, 47.

8. General Synod, *Minutes . . . 1864*, 12, 17, 19.

9. Abdel Ross Wentz, *Pioneer in Christian Unity: Samuel Simon Schmucker* (Philadelphia: Fortress Press, 1969), 290-91.

10. Kuenning, "American Lutheran Pietism," 208-88.

11. H. George Anderson, *Lutheranism in the Southeastern States 1860–1886* (Paris: Mouton, 1969), 23.

12. See Sam Ronnegard, *Prairie Shepherd: Lars Paul Esbjorn and the Beginnings of the Augustana Lutheran Church*, trans. G. Everett Arden (Rock Island, Ill.: Augustana Book Concern, 1952).

13. See Anderson, *Lutheranism in the Southeastern States.*

14. E. Clifford Nelson, ed., *The Lutherans in North America* (Philadelphia: Fortress Press, 1975), 238-40.

15. See Richard C. Dickinson, *Roses and Thorns: The Centennial Edition of Black Lutheran Mission and Ministry in the Lutheran Church—Missouri Synod* (St. Louis: Concordia Publishing House, 1977).

16. Wichern in his 1856 editorial introduction to *Fliegende Blatter* (trans. "Fly-Leaves"), quoted in John E. Groh, *Nineteenth-Century German Protestantism: The Church as Social Model* (Washington, D.C.: The University Press of America, 1982), 311; see also Gerald Christianson, "J. H. Wichern and the Rise of the Lutheran Social Institution," *The Lutheran Quarterly* 19 (November 1967):357-70.

17. For a descriptive account see J. F. Ohl, *The Inner Mission: A Handbook for Christian Workers* (Philadelphia: General Council Publication House, 1913).

18. Emory K. Lindquist, *Shepherd of an Immigrant People: The Story of Erland Carlsson* (Rock Island, Ill.: Augustana Historical Society, 1978).

19. Leonard Dinnerstein and David M. Reimers, *Ethnic Americans: A History of Immigration and Assimilation* (New York: Harper & Row, 1975), 164-65.

20. W. M. Kopenhaver, ed., *The Lutheran Church Almanac* (Philadelphia: General Council Publication Board, 1916), 77-81.

21. See, e.g., Norris Magnuson, *Salvation in the Slums: Evangelical Social Work, 1865–1920* (Metuchen, N.J.: The Scarecrow Press, and The American Theological Library Association, 1977).

22. Walter Rauschenbusch, *Christianity and the Social Crisis* (New York: Macmillan Co., 1907), 422.

23. Walter Rauschenbusch, *Christianizing the Social Order* (New York: The Macmillan Company , 1913), 24-25.

24. Letter quoted in George W. Sandt, *Theodore Emanuel Schmauk* (Philadelphia: United Lutheran Publication House, 1921), 279.

25. Ibid., 278-79.

26. Reginald Dietz, "Eastern Lutheranism in American Society and American Christianity 1870–1914" (Ph.D. diss., University of Pennsylvania, 1958), 194-201. Dietz's interpretation is more carefully nuanced than Harold H. Lentz, "The History of the Social Gospel in the General Synod of the Lutheran Church in America, 1867–1918" (Ph.D. diss., Yale University, 1943).

27. Dietz, "Eastern Lutheranism," 255-56.

28. General Synod, *Minutes . . . 1868*, 27.

29. General Synod, *Minutes . . . 1897*, 38.

30. Albert Urban Gesler, "Official Pronouncements of the United Lutheran Church in America Relating to Certain Moral and Social Problems" (Ph.D. diss., University of Pittsburgh, 1941), 29.

31. Ibid., 21-36.

32. General Synod, *Minutes . . . 1915*, 69.

33. Ibid., 70.

34. Gesler, "Official Pronouncements of the ULCA," 39.

35. Nelson, ed., *Lutherans in North America*, 386. J. H. W. Stuckenberg (1835–1903), a pastor who had graduated from the seminary at Wittenberg, Ohio, had earlier gained a reputation as a leading sociologist in the social gospel movement but had largely removed himself from Lutheran circles by that time. See Dietz, "Eastern Lutheranism," 212-18.

36. The creed was drafted and first adopted by the Methodist Episcopal Church in 1908, whereupon it was adopted at the founding convention of the Federal Council in 1908 and enlarged in 1912. It is reprinted in H. Shelton Smith, Robert T. Handy, and Lefferts A. Loetscher, *American Christianity*, vol. 2 (New York: Charles Scribner's Sons, 1963), 394-97.

37. General Synod, *Minutes . . . 1913*, 55.

38. G. Everett Arden, *Augustana Heritage* (Rock Island, Ill.: Augustana Book Concern, 1963), 370.

39. Anderson, *Lutheranism in the Southeastern States*, 148-49.

40. *Documentary History of the General Council of the Evangelical Lutheran Church in North America* (Philadelphia: General Council Publication House, 1912), 320, 395-98.

41. General Synod, *Minutes . . . 1911*, 79; *Minutes . . . 1915*, 27-31.

42. Lloyd Svendsbye summarizes these theses in "The History of a Developing Social Responsibility among Lutherans in America from 1930 to 1960" (Th.D. diss., Union Theological Seminary, 1967), 30-31.

43. See Ben Primer, *Protestants and American Business Methods* (UMI: Research Press, 1979).

44. Nelson, ed., *Lutherans in North America*, 369.

45. General Synod, *Minutes . . . 1917*, 112.

46. Louis Weeks, who is working on a study of Presbyterian social thought and denominationalism, suggested the importance of these themes in an interview with the author, Louisville, Ky., 11 June 1986.

2

FOUNDATIONS, 1918–1962

The years between the opening of World War I in 1914 and 1920 accelerated dramatic changes for American Lutherans. The onset of war in Europe had reduced the flow of immigration to a trickle, while at the same time the xenophobic mood in this country pressed Lutheran ethnics toward assimilation. Meanwhile, the four-hundredth anniversary of the Reformation in 1917 elevated theological self-consciousness and prompted widespread public celebrations of the Lutheran tradition. The anniversary also occasioned the birth of two new denominations which incorporated smaller bodies. Three Norwegian groups joined to form the Norwegian Lutheran Church in America in 1917, and the more Americanized German Lutherans of the General Synod, United Synod of the South, and the General Council merged in the United Lutheran Church in America in 1918. Ever larger denominations would characterize Lutheran organization throughout the twentieth century.

By the 1920s, Lutherans were laying and testing foundations for their corporate life that would enable them to respond to national and international developments. Like other Protestants, they borrowed bureaucratic structures from the business community to handle their growing national work. At the same time, they dug deeper than ever before within their own tradition to consider its implications for social ethics. Nevertheless, not until the renaissance in Luther studies reached American shores after World War II would the social ethic they were building gain visibility.

FACING THE WORLD, 1918–1939

World War I had caught Lutherans up short. Although they were hardly alone among American Christians in their confused response to international conflict, they took to heart its violent lesson, a wretched paradox

19

of the century. While modernization depended on international stability for the sake of industrial interdependence, technological development, and the organization and control of mass violence, it also exacerbated tribal nationalism and militarism. State security and protracted warfare had emerged as prominent national values.[1]

American Lutherans could not avoid such a world. At first they chose to face it by ministering among themselves and among their coreligionists abroad. A dozen Lutheran bodies had banded together during the war through the National Lutheran Commission for Soldiers' and Sailors' Welfare to provide wartime service to American Lutherans and united representation before the national government. In 1918, out of this first major inter-Lutheran cooperation came the National Lutheran Council, an organization that would continue for nearly fifty years. Although differences over the importance of doctrinal uniformity kept member churches from full cooperation, the council did make its mark primarily in two areas: 1) research and publicity on the state of American Lutheranism, and 2) the funneling of aid to the ravaged Lutheran churches of Europe and their mission fields.[2]

The council staff gained considerable exposure to the challenges facing Lutheranism in France, Czechoslovakia, Rumania, Finland, Germany, Poland, Austria, the Baltic states, and Russia. Staff members represented the missionary interests of Lutherans before governments, the Versailles Peace Conference, the International Missionary Council, and European missionary societies. Through all of these activities, Lutherans gained new self-awareness and experience within fractured international Lutheranism. Friendships developed during three Lutheran world conventions held in Europe: Eisenach in 1923, Copenhagen in 1929, and Paris in 1934. Plans to meet in Philadelphia in 1940 were thwarted by war. Those Americans who had been involved saw a larger world of social and political ferment. They returned frustrated with the clichés of the past and eager to rethink Lutheran social ethics.

In postwar America, the United Lutheran Church was the first Lutheran body to organize for the study of social issues. At the instigation of the General Synod, one of its predecessors, the new denomination created a standing committee on temperance in 1918.[3] At the same convention, meeting during the week in which the armistice was signed, delegates adopted a statement critical of "national aggrandizement" and "unbridled commercialism" and urged that the weak and smaller nations "be given free, full and unhampered opportunity to develop their own national life."[4]

In 1920, after the passage of the eighteenth amendment prohibiting the manufacture, sale, or transportation of alcoholic beverages, the church convention adopted the recommendation of the Committee on Temperance to create in its place a Committee on Moral and Social Welfare. Its responsibility was to provide "a thorough study of moral, social, and industrial problems." No other Lutheran body would so order itself until the late 1930s.[5] The United Lutheran Church now had a second agency, besides its incorporated Inner Mission Board, to consider the church's role in the social order. The church approached these tasks deliberately and self-consciously, in full awareness of the ways of other Protestant bodies.[6]

By 1930 the Committee on Moral and Social Welfare had worked out positions on two issues that would surface repeatedly among Lutherans for the next five decades: marriage and war. This first round of discussion focused on marriage and divorce and an interpretation of Article 16 of the Augsburg Confession on justifiable war and military service.[7] Two statements were presented to the convention which together constituted the committee's report. Debate on each was limited to one hour. In each case, the concluding resolutions were adopted first. The introductory report on marriage and divorce was adopted; the one on Article 16 was "received." The subject matter of these statements, along with the painstaking exegesis from the Bible and the Lutheran Confessions, the sketching of the contemporary situation, and the aim to provide principles to guide pastors and people were all rudiments of a style pursued later in the Lutheran Church in America.

In the statement "Marriage and Divorce," the committee explicated positions taken by the General Council in 1903 and the General Synod in 1907, while also taking into account contemporary biblical scholarship and the increasing use of desertion as legal grounds for divorce. In the 1920s massive shifts in social mores had been spurred by postwar disillusion, the new status of women, the popularization of Freudian thought, the increasing use of the automobile, Prohibition, and the portrayal of sexuality in the film and magazine industries.[8] Together, such forces heightened expectations in the relations between men and women. The continued spiraling of the divorce rate in the United States and the varying responses of Christian church bodies occasioned the statement. From one divorce for every seventeen marriages in 1870, the rate had increased to one in every nine in 1921 and stood at nearly one in every six in 1930.[9] The rate would continue to increase.

The ULCA's position distinguished between public opinion, which condoned the social pattern and therefore prevented the enactment of stricter marriage and divorce laws, and the church's responsibility. The church, according to the statement, had two areas of accountability: (1) to increase the resolve of the clergy to judge which marriages they could in good conscience perform as officials of the state; and (2) to safeguard church members against abandoning valued standards of behavior.

The statement begins with the reigning Lutheran interpretation of marriage as both an institution established by God for the sake of social order and individual development and, for Christians, an opportunity for the oneness of "perfect freedom," gained when husbands and wives submit themselves to each other, as in the mystical union of Christ and his bride, the church.

Implicit in the document is the assumption that if the state would not look after the institution of marriage properly, then the church must make its standards all the clearer, particularly about the remarriage of divorced persons. Since American Protestant and Catholic churches had not reached consensus and because the claim of desertion could be abused as grounds for divorce, the ULCA had to state its own teaching.

After a review of New Testament sources, the statement argues that even as Paul had to apply Christ's teaching to particular circumstances, so does the church in every age. The challenge in contemporary times is to determine the meaning of desertion "not merely from the legal but from the spiritual point of view" to clarify when the marriage bond has been "utterly forsaken." Churches operate with "mistaken zeal" when they "refuse to recognize the effects of malicious desertion upon the marriage relation."

In the seven resolutions which constitute the statement itself, the ULCA specifies the meaning of marriage and the role of the pastor as officiant. Because pastors are accountable not only to the state but also to God, they ought not perform any marriages, if in light of discernible facts they are not "in accord with divine requirements. Divorce itself stands condemned, and yet occurs in a sinful world. The ULCA reaffirms the position of its founding bodies, held by the "leading thinkers of the Lutheran Church,"

> that the marriage bond is effectually dissolved by the sins of adultery and malicious desertion, and that, when a divorce has been legally granted for either of these causes, the innocent party is free to marry again.

This position, first formulated in the early years of the twentieth century, would stand until the mid-fifties, when the church had become less certain of an "innocent party" in destroyed marriages.

The circumstances of world war and efforts for peace reform prompted the second half of the committee's report in 1930. The specific occasion

22

for a statement was a memorial submitted two years earlier at the convention in Erie by Edwin Heyl Delk. Active in the Federal Council of Churches, Delk had been writing on issues of Lutheran social responsibility since the early years of the twentieth century as a member of the General Synod. He was familiar with the Federal Council's indefatigable work to secure government ratification of the Versailles Treaty and membership in the League of Nations.

Delk's resolutions reflected the strength of the peace movement in postwar America. In 1921, nine nations including the United States attended the Washington Conference and achieved some agreements on limiting naval armaments. Other major Protestant bodies had gone on record favoring unilateral disarmament and opposing compulsory military training in public schools or land grant colleges. The World Court had offered new possibilities, as would the Kellogg-Briand Pact of 1929 between France and America outlawing aggressive war.

Standing by themselves, the 1928 resolutions summoned the church to affirm the agenda for peace favored in the midstream of Protestant liberalism.[10] Resolutions 3 and 4 convey the tone:

3. We further believe that through the growth of public confidence in the agencies and instruments for international peace the way can be opened, under the providence of God, for the substitution of peaceful processes of adjudication and arbitration in place of armed conflict in the settlement of international disputes.

4. We therefore resolve to call upon the whole Christian Church to further the realization of this great hope by bringing the Gospel of our Lord Jesus Christ to bear upon the hearts of men, that they may learn to love peace and pursue it in a spirit of patient forgiveness and willing self-sacrifice after the example of our Lord Jesus Christ.[11]

Action on the resolutions was deferred until the 1930 convention after the Committee on Moral and Social Welfare had checked whether or not they were consistent with the Augsburg Confession's Article 16 on civil affairs. The committee's report begins by setting the historical context of Article 16, written as a counterpoint both to the Anabaptist tradition, which forbade any relation between the Christian and the state, and to the monastic tradition, which undervalued the role of the family. Arguing for the continuing value of Article 16, the committee cited the classical Lutheran position that family, state, and church constitute the three "divine institutions within which the Christian life must realize itself." The various duties inherent in each institution shape "the Christian conception of ethical righteousness.

Since Article 16 affirmed the right of Christians to serve as soldiers in just wars, did it also commit "our church irrevocably to the war-system" as a means for settling international disputes? Could military service continue to be "regarded as a Christian duty, in view of the new conscience on war"?

The committee answered its own questions by invoking the justifiable end of all war and soldiering: the preservation of the state. Thus engagement in just wars and service as soldiers were simply illustrative historical examples of the ways and means available for resolving international disputes in the sixteenth century. The 1930 report envisioned a new age when "under the providence of God and through the preaching of the Gospel . . . , armed conflict will no longer be necessary to safeguard the integrity of the State; when other means and agencies better adapted to this end will have been devised." Then, acting in the spirit of Article 16, Christians would have the duty "to oppose the war-spirit and support the efforts for a permanent peace."

In the next stage of its argument, the committee limited the province of church action. The church "has nothing to do with the specific form which the agencies for peace shall assume," although "the movement for peace by arbitration and adjudication now seems to be the most effective way." The church, after "instructing and quickening" the conscience of the Christian in the duties of "civic righteousness," could not tell a Christian how to support such a movement, a matter for the individual conscience under Christian freedom.

Military service "had become a matter of conscience," not something on which the church could legislate for the individual. The church could offer only the general principle that the state as an institution with its origins in God is worth defending and that under certain circumstances the Christian might have that duty, even at the cost of life. Yet the church could define those circumstances no more specifically than to say that such a war had to be "just" so far as human reason could discern. At any given moment in history the Christian, using reason, had to decide whether bearing arms was justifiable. Nearly forty years later, the same argument became the nub of the LCA's position on conscientious objection.

Finally, the committee wrestled with the Lutheran teaching of two ethics—one of the state, the other of God's kingdom. In the latter, war has no place, since only the constraining power of love could regulate conduct. Nevertheless, the state has the "function to administer justice in a sinful world, and to this end it bears the sword" and is governed by

24

the principle of legal justice. Just at this point and because legal justice is relative, the committee argued that the church could heighten people's sense of justice and thereby make the justification for war "at the bar of public opinion" more difficult. Once the public refused to sanction a war, "the more telling victory for peace will have been won."

This interpretation of Article 16, which prefaces the five resolutions submitted by Pastor Delk, reflects both a new confidence in international means for achieving permanent peace and the more traditional belief that the state, God's means for ordering human life, must be preserved by its citizens, even at the cost of war. To resolve the tension between these two commitments, both the individual Christian and the church are assigned responsibilities. Christian citizens are expected to make individual choices about the merits of both peace agencies and any particular call to arms. The church has the opportunity through education for "civil righteousness" to heighten the individual's sense of justice and thereby turn public opinion against war. This approach would become a trademark of subsequent statements passed in the ULCA, although optimism about the possibilities and agencies of permanent peace would be tempered.

At the next convention in 1932 the ULCA adopted another report from the committee which revealed that members were not of one mind about the theological basis for their work. Their report outlining the social tasks of the church ignored the emphasis on civil righteousness that had been so pronounced in the interpretation of Article 16 and in the discussion of marriage. Instead, the report relied solely upon the repentance of Christians for the renewal of the social order. The church had the means at hand to be the "conscience of the world" through preaching, administration of the sacraments, teaching, witnessing, and ministrations of mercy. Intended to create a framework for the future, the report was outdated before the decade's end. Its tenor approached the utopian:

> The execution of His plan, by the use of His means, through His approved measures would so exalt piety, and so invigorate and promote Christian brotherhood, and so develop Christian stewardship that an incorruptible citizenship would control the destinies of the state, wealth would become the servant of all, the conflict between labor and capital would cease, sex immorality with its diseases would disappear, divorce courts would be closed, leisure would be used for the enrichment of personality instead of indulgences in dissipations, the under-privileged would find open doors of opportunity, and this would be like another world. This all depends upon the faithfulness of the Church, which needs only actually to enlist, in active endeavor, everyone it has enrolled into nominal membership. No new program needs to be

set up. No new machinery needs to be added. The great need is spiritual impulse.[12]

The committee was also blinded to the diminished force of Protestantism in American culture. Nor were they yet aware of potent critiques of liberal Protestant activism emerging in its very midst. Reinhold Niebuhr had just published *Moral Man and Immoral Society* and thereby launched his quest for more substantial theological and political analysis to undergird action. Lutherans continued to count on citizen activity, inspired by religious faith. Yet they could not stem a growing desire among Lutherans for "new machinery" to tackle social questions raised by the continuing economic crisis of depression and international instability.

The National Lutheran Council, with both the ULCA and the Augustana Synod holding membership, acted first. In 1933, it established a Committee on Social Trends. The committee's very existence, more than its limited accomplishments, pointed to the increasing efforts among Lutherans to find the ways and means to study and respond to social and political issues. Under its aegis, the council would adopt four resolutions in the next decade. Members reached consensus in opposing the liquor industry, in supporting "cleaner" motion pictures, in condemning the causes of war, and lastly in calling for the churches to favor a position of neutrality in World War II, to pray for peace, and to be loyal to the nation but to avoid excessive nationalism.[13]

In 1934 a smaller organization, the American Lutheran Conference, made up of most midwestern Lutheran bodies except the Missouri Synod, established the Commission on Social Relations at the urging of leaders in the Augustana Synod. With strong leadership but no possibility of legislating the political behavior of its member churches, the commission became a safe forum on controversial social issues. By discussion and a conference journal, midwestern denominational leaders were kept abreast of social issues.[14]

In 1936 the Augustana Synod established a Commission on Morals and Social Problems, similar to the committee which the ULCA had initiated in 1922. In 1937 this commission was granted permanent standing, but no staff. A. D. Mattson, professor of ethics at the Synod's sole seminary, chaired the commission for the next twenty-five years. Gregory Lee Jackson, his biographer, emphasizes Mattson's unique position of influence among American Lutherans as teacher and drafter of social pronouncements.[15]

The ULCA, meanwhile, voted in its 1938 convention to combine its three agencies of outreach into one incorporated board, an act that historian Lloyd Svendsbye admires as an expression of the "wholeness of their theological position."[16] On the one hand, such consolidation can be interpreted as a recovery of Johann Wichern's broad conception of the church's "inner mission" (see p. 9). On the other hand, the desire to rationalize overlapping agencies was also at work. The Committee on Moral and Social Welfare was merged with the Committee on Evangelism and the Board of Inner Missions to form the new Board of Social Missions. Governed by elected trustees, this board was the direct precursor of the LCA's Board of Social Ministry. Although its Department of Social Action would be kept weak until the first full-time staff person, Harold C. Letts, was appointed in 1947, C. Franklin Koch, the board's executive director, provided some leadership and documented mounting requests to provide study literature and position statements on social questions.[17]

The establishment of these structures in two federations of Lutheran bodies and in two denominations signified growing agreement that more was required of the church in American society than could be delivered through traditional inner missions channels. Inner missions had provided Lutherans with focused avenues to service within American society, a buffer against the problematic church-state issue, and a means to express the clear identity of the church as exponent of the gospel. Nevertheless, society looked more complex to Lutherans in the 1930s than it had even a decade before. Economic depression, for example, had revealed major weaknesses in the institutions of private industry and government. As Lutherans moved outside their ethnic and religious circles, they began to view citizenship as a more demanding matter and to expect greater help from their church in sorting out issues and in responding in light of faith.

Increasingly comfortable with using denominational structures to effect corporate commitments, Lutherans moved, as they had earlier with inner missions, to establish offices and consign oversight to resident "experts." Through these new bureaucratic arrangements, the churches would now regularize the processes of study and education on issues along with the drafting of social statements. The rudiments of contemporary policy making were in place, although the language of "policy" would not emerge until the 1950s.

LUTHERANS AND SOCIAL ETHICS, 1940–1962

New structures indicated the increased engagement of Lutherans in the American mainstream. Although Lutherans were expressing a church-wide sense of responsibility for American life, they were hesitant about the implications of their theological tradition for ethical judgments about the social order. Their uncertainty belonged to a larger conversation occurring in American Protestantism over the adequacy of theological paradigms devised in the late nineteenth century to justify the churches' engagement in social action. With the maturing of American neo-orthodoxy in its attack on the politics and theology of Protestant liberalism, Lutherans discovered kindred spirits outside their own circles and were no longer free to remain aloof from the fray. Criticism was insufficient. The times called for reconstruction. Where would Lutherans stand?[18]

The church leaders who promoted this discussion were both excited about the possibilities and burdened with a missionary impulse to bring others along in the quest. As the years passed, they built far-reaching networks that linked them to each other and to other Protestant centers of reflection and activism. Lutherans searched for a responsible mix of religion and politics and appropriate relations between church and state. Their decisions about the adequacy of their own tradition and what to expect from the American social order would have far-reaching consequences. Differences among them would persist to the present day.

The following sketches illustrate some points of contact between Lutherans and the larger discussion within American and European Protestantism. On the whole, these links suggest that the twenty-five years prior to the founding of the LCA stand as the most fertile period in Lutheran social thought thus far in this century. During these years Lutheran teachers and denominational leaders working in church-related schools developed the theological principles for social analysis that would guide the work done within the Lutheran Church in America and other Lutheran bodies. They also drew upon the opportunities available at Union Theological Seminary in New York and explored the work of a generation of European historians and theologians who were reexamining the Protestant Reformation. The constellation of issues, theologians, and institutions undergirded all that followed. When orbits changed, as they had by the 1970s, the approach developed within the LCA attracted more dissent.

A. D. Mattson and the Augustana Synod

In his person and through his positions as seminary professor and chair of the Commission on Morals and Social Problems, Alvin Daniel Mattson (1895–1970) became the dominant voice on social ethics in the Augustana Synod. Other leaders such as Edgar Carlson, who also worked at developing a Lutheran approach to ethics, never had the same platform.

Mattson formulated his opinions early out of his own experience on a railroad gang and his reading of Rauschenbusch while in seminary. He went on to spend three semesters at Yale Divinity School from 1926 through 1928, where he developed close ties to faculty advocates of the Social Gospel and later served on the board of their Religion and Labor Foundation. These ties introduced him to labor negotiations and to union organization in the American South, and enabled him to travel twice to the Soviet Union.

His own commitments, while offbeat in Lutheran circles, were characteristic of the leftism within the mainstream of liberal Protestantism in his day: he was critical of the excesses of capitalism, supportive of the organizing rights of labor, concerned for the uniqueness of personality and the importance of democracy, and committed to pacifism. He formulated his positions early when there was a major vacuum in Lutheran social thought, but as an activist he was not particularly concerned for their coherence within the Lutheran tradition. He withstood the onslaught of American neo-orthodoxy and remained distant from the renaissance in Luther studies. On the whole, he followed Rauschenbusch in domesticating the concepts and vocabulary of theology to the field of politics or, more precisely, to that of social morality. He tended to identify the goal of politics—equality and justice—with the kingdom of God, sharing with Rauschenbusch an analysis of the church which viewed a required "prophetic" role of the church as antithetical to its "priestly" satisfaction with the *status quo*.

Mattson hoped to revitalize Lutheran social ethics by infusing the impulse of the revived but chastened social gospel movement of the 1920s and 1930s. He conceptualized the kingdom of God, the hallmark of his analysis, as the realm of human history in which God is at work accomplishing his purposes. In his book *Christian Social Consciousness* (1957), he would characterize the kingdom as "the very energy of God pressing in upon human affairs." The kingdom, like faith, came as a "gift," when God impressed people into his service. Drawing upon the prophets of the Old Testament, the ethical teachings of the New, and the political options of his times, Mattson explicated God's will for human affairs. Progress toward those ideals was possible, if fulfillment was not. He relied heavily on the motive of service as the means to escape the evils of competitive capitalism and war.

Although in his writing he made some use of the distinction between the work of church and state, his students at Augustana Seminary between 1931 and 1965 graduated without an introduction to Luther's conception of God's dual reign in creation and through redemption. Matt-son was too impressed with Lutheran inaction in the past to find that tradition of present use.[19] His legacy to the more than one thousand students who passed through his classroom heightened their sensitivity to issues of social injustice while also leaving them with the riddle of determining what constitutes God's will or manifests the kingdom in the struggle for justice.

Under Mattson's leadership, the commission set about drafting "pro-nouncements." Its first, offered five years after the repeal of Prohibition ended what Herbert Hoover had labeled the "noble experiment," urged that pastors and denominational programs and publications continue instructing people in the "evils of intemperance," and that all members "use their best efforts, through whatever legitimate and proper channels that may present themselves, to wipe out the present liquor traffic."[20] Temperance had dwarfed all other social issues in the twelve conferences of the Synod throughout the early 1930s.[21]

The Synod spoke from its longstanding view of liquor traffic "as a destroyer of souls and therefore, as an enemy of the church." In a social reinterpretation of that tradition, the statement went on to say that "the Synod has been justified in this attitude, because the liquor traffic chal-lenges the church with grave social problems in its heartless waste of human resources and human life." In 1956 the Synod would oppose increased advertising and consumption and would endorse the work of Alcoholics Anonymous.[22]

Although many within the tradition may have assumed that the 1937 statement implied total abstinence, that was not its wording. The ULCA, always divided between those active in the temperance movement and those opposed to such "legalism," equivocated similarly by passing res-olutions in 1920 and 1922 which urged compliance with the law, and in 1936 and 1948 which pressed for the publication of educational materials on temperance and the "scientifically demonstrated" effects of alcohol.[23] The increase in the 1980s of both chemical abuse and public awareness of its complexity suggest renewed attention to Lutherans' previous strug-gle with this issue.

The commission plowed new ground for Augustana with statements on labor and on war, both topics at the 1937 Oxford Conference on Life and Work, at which Reinhold Niebuhr's somber presence and view of human possibility marked the up and coming generation. Although it took two conventions in the Synod to reach an agreement on a parallel statement on labor, in 1939 delegates adopted the position reached at

Oxford on the dignity of labor and the rights of workers. Augustana's statement also favored union organization for collective bargaining, improved working conditions, a six-day work week, and abolition of child labor.[24]

Throughout the 1930s, voices were raised against the specter of war. Those at the forefront of the effort to increase social consciousness within the Synod, such as A. D. Mattson, Edgar Carlson, and E. E. Ryden, who was editor of *The Lutheran Companion*, were also committed to peace reform. In its 1939 statement, Augustana again relied on definitions established at the Oxford Conference: "War is a particular demonstration of the power of sin in this world, and a defiance of the righteousness of God as revealed in Jesus Christ and Him crucified." The convention then opposed the sale of war materials to aggressor nations and, for the first time, instructed its members to "acquaint their Senators and Representatives in Congress concerning our position."[25] In 1941, Augustana became the first Lutheran body officially to ask the government for exemption from all forms of combatant military service for members of the Synod who were conscientious objectors.[26]

In 1942, with "heaviness of heart," the Synod recognized the stark realities of World War II and urged its members "to be on guard lest the sanction of the Church be given to anything which is contrary to the spirit of Christ." After the excesses of patriotism during World War I, church members were urged to seek the maintenance of civil and religious liberties in wartime and to show generosity toward the suffering, including prisoners. They were to support the chaplaincy in the armed services and "to work for justice and good will among groups and nations."[27] Pacifism, isolationism, and a somber nationalism in the wake of Japan's attack on Pearl Harbor combined to sustain antiwar sentiment even after war was declared.[28] There was also a persistent strain of piety which counted personal holiness as removal from occasions of sin, of which war was one. From the late 1930s, Augustana was actively engaged at the national level in responding to the contemporary world. Mattson's former students would bring into the new LCA his restless dissatisfaction with Lutheranism's past record of uninvolvement and an eagerness to enhance the work of social advocacy.

The ULCA in the Orbit of Union Seminary

In the ULCA the groundwork for social ethical concern was more dispersed. In the postwar years teachers at the seminaries at Philadelphia and Gettysburg were especially influential. At Philadelphia, theologian

Martin Heinecken's Kierkegaardean concern for how faith expresses itself in love and historian Theodore Tappert's close attention to the meaning of the gospel fueled interest in social ethics among students. Meanwhile, at Gettysburg, German émigré Bertha Paulssen in courses on "Christian sociology and psychology" introduced her students to hard-nosed social and political analysis, neo-orthodox theology, and field work in Lutheran social service institutions and agencies. Knowledgeable in the developing social sciences, she gave her students standards for discerning the effectiveness of social ministry and the reach of Lutheran social responsibility.[29]

Union Theological Seminary in New York served as a catalyst for future leaders in social ministry in both the ULCA and the LCA. As an interdenominational school at the forefront in the development of American neo-orthodoxy, Union captured national attention as two of its professors, Reinhold Niebuhr (1892–1971) and Paul Tillich (1886–1965), established positions of dissent within Protestant liberalism.

The school became a hospitable way station for Lutherans at odds with the Social Gospel who were rethinking their own tradition. Niebuhr served as professor of "applied Christianity" from 1930 to 1960. Tillich taught philosophical theology from 1933–1955. Later, Wilhelm Pauck, influential in bringing the full force of Continental Luther studies to America, added to the mix as church historian from 1953 to 1967. These three, singly and in concert, all to one degree or another personally alienated from Lutheranism, addressed their Lutheran students with the challenges of postliberal social thought and the demands of contemporary Luther scholarship. Four individuals who helped to shape the agenda for social ethics in the ULCA and later the LCA, spent formative years in Union's precincts: Harold Letts, Rufus Cornelsen, George Forell, and William Lazareth. All had studied at the Philadelphia Seminary at Mt. Airy as well.

Letts and Cornelsen both stood on the beachhead of the ULCA's social ethics in the 1930s and would later serve as staff to the Board of Social Missions beginning in 1947 and 1957, respectively. Each would leave the denomination to work for a time with the National Council of Churches of Christ in the USA. Letts would then return to the staff of the LCA, while Cornelsen would become executive director of the Philadelphia Council of Churches. Both men regarded theology as central to the quest for increasing Lutheran responsibility for the social order.

Their backgrounds illustrate the magnetic and formative power of Union Seminary's theological ferment. Letts, a graduate of Colgate College, recalls taking as many courses with Niebuhr as possible when he came at the recommendation of his college chaplain to Union in 1933. He took an extra year to complete his divinity degree in order to work at Union's settlement house. He also commuted to the Mt. Airy seminary once a week to satisfy denominational ordination requirements.[30]

Cornelsen did not come to Union as a Lutheran. Raised a Mennonite in Oklahoma, he completed his divinity degree at Union after two years of study in a Southern Baptist seminary where he began reading Niebuhr. At Union, Tillich became his mentor and introduced him to Luther studies. He also began attending Holy Trinity Lutheran Church in Manhattan, where Paul Scherer's preaching enabled him to clarify his own theological position. In 1941–42 he spent a year of graduate study at Philadelphia Seminary prior to his ordination in the ULCA. While there, he helped arrange for Niebuhr to visit the campus.[31]

Niebuhr's name would become familiar to Lutherans beyond academic circles when, at editor Elson Ruff's request, he began writing for *The Lutheran*. During the late 1940s through the 1950s he wrote some eighty columns.[32] By then, Lutheran self-consciousness over the German church's acquiescence to Hitler and the new threat posed by atomic weaponry had increased the stakes for a Lutheran social ethic.

Both Letts and Cornelsen served parishes after seminary and joined a monthly gathering of young metropolitan area pastors known as the "Timotheans," initiated in the early 1940s by Paul White of the ULCA's New York Synod. The Timotheans, who met monthly for lunch with the formal agenda of discussing papers they had written, provided an opportunity for an informal discussion of social ethics. Harold Haas, a New Jersey pastor who would become the executive of the ULCA's Board of Social Missions and later of the LCA's Board of Social Ministry, was also among their number. Haas was a graduate of Philadelphia Seminary who had studied with Bertha Paulssen when she first arrived and taught at Wagner College. He pursued sociology at the University of Pennsylvania and wrote his doctoral dissertation at Drew University on Lutheran social concern in the ULCA before 1948.

Other members of the circle included Donald Heiges, chaplain at Columbia, George Forell, graduate student at Union, Albert Stauderman, future editor of *The Lutheran*, and Richard Niebanck, a recent graduate of Mt. Airy and future staff member of the Board of Social Ministry. A number of Timotheans also collaborated on the Social Missions Committee of the New York Synod.[33]

Letts recalls his interview in 1946 with ULCA president Franklin Clark Fry for the new position of secretary for social action with the Board of

Social Missions. Fry asked whether he really believed that Lutheran theology supported social action. Letts recalls answering that it did, but that "it hasn't been illuminated or clarified."[34] Fry and Letts had named a concern that would become a scholarly project. In addition to Letts's many new responsibilities as the first secretary for social action, he was also charged in 1948 with overseeing a fourteen-member commission made up of seminary professors, pastors, and church executives gathered to develop an explicitly Lutheran approach to Christian social responsibility. Their task was to produce a book that would "bring together and clarify the full teachings of Scripture on this subject, the witness of our confessions hereto, and all the pertinent pronouncements of the U.L.C.A." as a way of schooling Lutherans on the "grounds for social action."[35]

After eight years of deliberations, the three-volume collection of essays, *Christian Social Responsibility*, appeared. The essayists were among the ULCA's scholarly fathers and up and coming sons. Among them were Karl Hertz, sociologist at Wittenberg College and Hamma Divinity School, along with T. A. Kantonen, systematic theologian; Charles W. Kegley and Howard Hong, philosophers teaching respectively at Wagner and St. Olaf colleges; Franklin Sherman, doctoral candidate and Chicago pastor; Martin Heinecken, systematics professor, Theodore Tappert, church historian, and William Lazareth, instructor in theology and ethics, all from the Philadelphia Seminary; Jerald C. Brauer, dean of the Federated Theological Faculties at the University of Chicago; E. Theodore Bachmann, church history and missions professor at Pacific Seminary; Joseph Sittler, systematics professor at Chicago Seminary; Rufus Cornelsen, pastor in New Brunswick; Harold Haas, executive secretary for the Board of Social Missions; and Harold Letts. Eight other commissioners had been part of the deliberations: E. E. Glack, C. Franklin Koch, Harold H. Lentz, Bertha Paulssen, Sten Rodhe, Carl C. Rasmussen, John Schmidt, and Russell D. Snyder.[36]

William Lazareth, a younger member of the commission, recently recalled the origins of his own commitment to articulate a Lutheran approach to social issues. He views the preceding generation, and Heinecken, Kantonen, and Sittler in particular, as struggling courageously for an "alternative to the biblicistic scholasticism of their teachers without giving up confessionalism." He believes his own generation had to avoid the "theological hernia" one courted by trying to live with one foot in the Luther renaissance and the other in Barthian neo-orthodoxy with its "analogical and relatively simplistic" ethical solutions.

Lazareth himself considered the alternatives during the year he spent in Tübingen with Helmut Thielicke. (Later, Lazareth would edit his *Theological Foundations* and *The Political Ethics*.) Lazareth returned to Mt. Airy seminary and then attended Union Seminary for graduate studies with Pauck, Tillich, and Niebuhr from 1953 to 1956. Those three he found enmeshed in an intense "love-hate relationship with Lutheranism" that sharpened his own quest. He next spent a year at the University of Lund with Gustav Aulén and Gustav Wingren and returned convinced that American Lutherans had no cultural model for social ethics in either German or Scandinavian sources.[37] His singular focus on the dilemma, along with President Fry's respect for his concerns, contributed to his increasing influence in the years ahead.

Essays in *Christian Social Responsibility* set the course and defined some of the debates that would characterize the work of the LCA. The arrangement of the books was in itself significant, foreshadowing as it did the "descriptive," "normative," and "regulative" progression favored in the LCA's studies and statements. The first book, *Existence Today*, defined the times with essays on the state of Western civilization, the character of contemporary anxiety, and mistaken theological responses. The second, *The Lutheran Heritage*, covered changing emphases in the Lutheran tradition since the Reformation. The final volume, *Life in Community*, considered the shape of Christian ethics and applications to economic, political, familial, and ecclesial issues. The authors struggled to reinterpret foundational teachings about the created orders, the two realms or kingdoms, law and gospel, faith active in love, Christian vocation, and the poles of faith and life.

The series was a timely and valuable tool for the education of the church. The third assembly of the Lutheran World Federation in Minneapolis in 1957 assured the Americans that their work contributed to the international conversation on social ethics.[38] Because the books surveyed the contemporary terrain of Lutheran social ethics and presented current historical judgments about the Lutheran tradition, they became useful for college and seminary teaching. Their content was also taken on the road in more than two dozen conferences where some twelve hundred pastors and two hundred lay people gathered for discussions.[39] Furthermore, the issues identified by the commission continued to shape the work of the Board of Social Missions and its successor, the LCA's Board of Social Ministry.

Two essays in particular illustrate contemporary debates about ethics that have perdured among Lutherans. In the third volume, Joseph Sittler's "The Structure of Christian Ethics" breaks with a propositional approach that he saw as contributing to legalism and calls for an "evangelical vitality." William Lazareth's "Christian Faith and Culture" categorizes Christian experience according to the work of the Trinity in propositional form in order to clarify how Lutherans can function as ethical beings in a pluralistic culture without making social improvement dependent on conversion.

The process of producing these volumes had a lasting impact on the church. For example, the statement on nuclear weapons presented by the Board of Social Missions to the 1960 convention demonstrates greater sophistication in both its political and theological analysis than the report offered to the church in 1930 on the Augsburg Confession, peace and war. The rhythm of argument moves from a description of the world situation to theological assertions and back to particular responses to the nuclear crisis. The bases for social action derive from God's sovereignty over all nations as well as the call to Christians for service. At a time when armaments remained "a basic element in international diplomacy" and nuclear armaments threatened "mutual annihilation," this church body voted to affirm that possession of such weapons "in peace may serve to deter aggression," to warn against abstract solutions, and to assert "that decisions must be made humbly and responsibly as each new situation arises."[40] The specifically Christian contribution to the political pursuit of peace lay not in religious conversion, but in a profound sense of responsibility originating in Christ's redemptive love.

Other Centers of Discussion

Renewed concern for social ethics among Lutherans was of course not limited among Lutherans to the Augustana Synod or ULCA. Discussion had surfaced in other sectors. The National Lutheran Council and the American Lutheran Conference have already been mentioned. In 1948 the (former) American Lutheran Church changed the name of its Board of Charities to Board for Christian Social Action. Sociologist Carl F. Reuss, its new part-time staff person, led the denomination in a style of response that emphasized social analysis and depended for its theology on quotations from the Bible and references to God's providence and the Christian's moral accountability. According to historian Lloyd Svendsbye, the church body's "official theological leadership" remained "fairly aloof" from the growing movement favoring involvement in social issues.[41]

In the same era, experience was its own tutorial in social ethics as the postwar generation of students explored a vulnerable world. In 1947, the American Section of the Lutheran World Convention approved using college and seminary student volunteers to staff a program of services to Lutheran refugees in Europe. Seminarians Kenneth Senft, from Gettysburg, and William Lazareth, from Philadelphia, were among the sixteen to join the program.[42] A generation gained exposure to the church's role in international relations. The 1954 Assembly of the World Council of Churches in Evanston, Illinois, brought the world of Christians to the United States with reports on "The Responsible Society in a World Perspective," "Christians in the Struggle for World Community," and "The Churches amid Racial and Ethnic Tensions."[43]

The web of interdenominational student organizations and their international conferences provided other avenues of learning for future Lutheran leaders. Lawyer William Ellis, member of the LCA's Board of Social Ministry and the Executive Council, recalls how, while he was on assignment with the YMCA in the World Student Congress, the challenge of student communism in the late 1940s provoked his quest for a Christian position and his reading of Niebuhr and Tillich.[44] He joined Herluf Jensen, then of the American Evangelical Lutheran Church (Grundtvigian Danes) in student work in the 1950s. Jensen, who would serve on the staff of the LCA's Board of Social Ministry and later as Bishop of the New Jersey Synod, was General Secretary of the United Student Christian Council and its successor under the National Council of Churches, the National Student Christian Federation. Jensen recalls his immersion in the civil rights movement as students developed sit-ins throughout the South in the early 1960s.[45] Doubtless, there are comparable stories among others who came of age in the postwar period.

Valparaiso University, related to but financially independent of the Missouri Synod, might seem an unlikely place for the emergence of an annual inter-Lutheran seminar on social ethics. And yet, President O. P. Kretzmann's convening of scholars interested in the field had lasting repercussions for the Lutheran church bodies. In its most active years, from 1947 to 1959, the seminar annually attracted up to three dozen participants—mostly theologians—from such varied institutions as his own, the University of Chicago, Princeton Seminary, and such Lutheran seminaries as Augustana, Concordia (St. Louis), Hamma, Capitol, Luther, Gettysburg, and Maywood. Otto Piper, émigré from Bavaria and New Testament professor at Princeton, served as moderator. His students—George Forell, who completed his master's degree at Princeton, and Warren Quanbeck—were part of the group. Forell would finish his graduate work at Union and make the interpretation of Luther's social ethics the center of his scholarship.[46]

The implications of Luther scholarship and the uneven record of the European state churches during the war made church-state relations figure deeply in the seminar's deliberations. The group met for a dozen years before issuing the book *God and Caesar,* based on papers they had discussed.[47] The published essayists include George Forell, Arthur Carl Piepkorn, Jaroslav Pelikan, Walter Bauer, Ernest Schwiebert, Paul Bretscher, and Otto Piper. A second inter-Lutheran center of discussion, overlapping in membership with the seminar, added to the number of individuals who shared these concerns. The Lutheran Theological Study Group which met at the DeKoven Foundation in Racine, Wisconsin, from 1945–66 devoted itself primarily to discussions of systematic theology."[48]

When the ULCA's Board of Social Missions determined to make a special study of church and state relations, theologians were already primed on the topic. After a conference in the spring of 1961, the board was authorized to appoint a Commission on Church and State in a Pluralistic Society, including Lutherans from the American Lutheran Church and the Lutheran Church–Missouri Synod. Four of its nine members had participated in the Valparaiso seminar. The new commission carried forward a discussion begun decades earlier that would continue in the Lutheran Church in America. Its membership included two laymen, Paul G. Kauper, a law professor at the University of Michigan, and J. Martin Klotsche, provost at the University of Wisconsin, along with theologians George Forell, William Lazareth, Conrad Bergendoff of Augustana, Arthur Carl Piepkorn of Missouri, Warren Quanbeck of the American Lutheran Church, Theodore Tappert of Philadelphia Seminary, and William Villaume of Waterloo Lutheran University. Rufus Cornelsen provided staff assistance.[49]

Traditions for the LCA

By the time the Joint Committee on Lutheran Unity met to plan the structure of the new church, institutional patterns of social responsibility had emerged in the two dominant bodies, the ULCA and the Augustana Synod. Augustana was probably the more thoroughly pervaded by a sense of responsibility, while the ULCA was the more structured for the study of issues at the national level. Bureaucratic experience and the direction of Franklin Clark Fry gave the ULCA's pattern more weight in the new church. Conrad Bergendoff gave the new board its name, the Board of Social Ministry.[50]

Carryover went beyond the legal charter adapted from the old Board of Social Missions. The merger of direct social services, rooted in the inner missions movement, with social action had been prefigured in the creation of the Board of Social Missions and was preserved, even though the Joint Commission had originally proposed that supervision of social services be assigned to the National Lutheran Council. Evangelism was dropped out of the mix and linked programmatically, but as a separate commission, with stewardship, a widespread practice in Protestantism in the 1950s.[51] The bylaws of the LCA Constitution provided for two departments within the Board of Social Ministry: Social Missions, "devoted to the church's ministry directly to persons," and Social Action, concerned with "matters of the church amidst the structures of society."[52]

More telling was the retention of the men who had directed the work of the earlier Board of Social Missions. Harold Haas, executive director since 1957, would continue in the same job for the Board of Social Ministry until 1966. Alfred Stone, who had chaired the board since 1958, held the same position on the new board until 1966.[53] Rufus Cornelsen would also continue as a staff member until 1965.

These and other leaders of the new church were also active in the committees of the young National Council of Churches of Christ in the USA, which provided ongoing educational opportunities for the LCA's staff. The executive of its Division of Christian Life and Work, C. Arild Olsen, with a background in the American Evangelical Lutheran Church, was assisted by Harold C. Letts, while Haas served on the executive committee.

The board's leaders drew upon resources developed earlier. The *Christian Social Responsibility* volumes had established traditions of thought. A study process had been tried in which experts within the church were assembled to make judgments on both theological underpinings and social issues. The social statements passed in convention, especially from the mid-1950s, reflected that process. In the new denomination there would be greater reliance on the pertinent expertise of lay women and men through study commissions. The theological approach based on historical Lutheran resources and tried first in the United Lutheran Church became institutionalized in the Lutheran Church in America. Lazareth, a young seminary professor of theology and ethics in the 1950s, would become one of the most influential voices, first as a board member and later as the staff director of the unit charged with drafting social statements.

The ways and means for the corporate expression of social ministry were well-rooted by 1962. The authority behind social statements was more centralized. The former board had on occasion issued its own position statements.[54] Under the new church's constitution, only the convention, and in emergency, the Executive Council, could adopt social statements. The Executive Council interpreted this to mean that synods were not to adopt positions on national issues, but to act only on regional matters, a judgment that proved unenforceable as events of the 1960s heightened social consciousness.[55] Also, by the closing years of the ULCA, the language of *social policy* had filtered in, "by osmosis" and probably from the National Council of Churches, according to Harold Haas, to describe the status of social statements as both teachings for the guidance of the church and documents governing the denomination's internal ordering and external witness. The language matched the experience of church staff members who, in an increasingly corporatized culture, were called upon to present the denomination's "position" on social issues.[56]

NOTES

1. See Charles DeBenedetti, *The Peace Reform in American History* (Bloomington: Indiana University Press, 1980).

2. Nelson, ed., *Lutherans in North America*, 403-14.

3. ULCA, *Minutes . . . 1918*, 112.

4. Ibid., 9-10.

5. Svendsbye, "Developing Social Responsibility among Lutherans," 47.

6. For a full account see Harold Haas, "The Social Thinking of the United Lutheran Church in America, 1918–1948" (Ph.D. diss., Drew University, 1953).

7. Quotations from these two items which follow are taken from ULCA, *Minutes . . . 1930*, 103-17.

8. See, e.g., Frederick Lewis Allen, *Only Yesterday* (New York: Harper & Brothers, 1931).

9. Haas, "Social Thinking of the ULCA," 229-30.

10. See Donald B. Meyer's criticism of the "liberalization" of the ULCA in the 1930s in *The Protestant Search for Political Realism, 1919–1941* (Berkeley and Los Angeles: University of California Press, 1960), 344-45.

11. ULCA, *Minutes . . . 1930*, 115.

12. ULCA, *Minutes . . . 1932*, 417.

13. Svendsbye, "Developing Social Responsibility among Lutherans," 55-57.

14. Gregory Lee Jackson, "The Impact of Alvin Daniel Mattson upon the Social Consciousness of the Augustana Synod" (Ph.D. diss., University of Notre Dame, 1982), 105-106.

15. Ibid., 107.

16. Svendsbye, "Developing Social Responsibility among Lutherans," 176.

17. Ibid., 349.

18. The term *social ethics* does not have a technical, academic meaning in this commentary, but refers, as in common parlance, to the concern to define and to determine a course of moral action on societal problems.

19. Jackson, "Mattson," 71-90; Svendsbye, "Developing Social Responsibility Among Lutherans," 289-97.

20. "Social Pronouncements of the Augustana Lutheran Church, 1937–1962," (multilithed by the Board of Social Ministry, LCA), 27-38.

21. Svendsbye, "Developing Social Responsibility among Lutherans," 120.

22. Arden, *Augustana Heritage*, 371.

23. *Social Statements of the United Lutheran Church in America 1918–1962*, (Board of Social Missions, ULCA), 88-89.

24. "Social Pronouncements of Augustana," 11.

25. Ibid., 19; see also Svendsbye, "Developing Social Responsibility among Lutherans," 128-41.

26. "Social Pronouncements of Augustana," 19.

27. Ibid., 19-20.

28. Svendsbye, "Developing Social Responsibility among Lutherans," 134.

29. These characterizations have been culled from recollections of former students.

30. Harold Letts, interview with author, Asheville, N.C., 29 April 1986.

31. Rufus Cornelsen, interview with author, Swarthmore, Pa., 21 February 1986.

32. Svendsbye, "Developing Social Responsibility among Lutherans," 482.

33. Cornelsen, interview with author, 21 February 1986; Harold Haas, telephone interview with author, 8 June 1987.

34. Letts, interview with author, 29 April 1986.

35. This task was assigned to them in 1948 by the Commission of Faith and Life which Fry had appointed. Harold Letts, ed., *Christian Social Responsibility*, vol. 1 (Philadelphia: Muhlenberg Press, 1957), v-vi.

36. Ibid., vi.

37. William Lazareth, interview with author, New York, 4 April 1986.

38. Haas, telephone interview with author, 8 June 1987.

39. Svendsbye, "Developing Social Responsibility among Lutherans," 387.

40. ULCA, *Minutes . . . 1960*, 1027.

41. Svendsbye, "Developing Social Responsibility among Lutherans," 238-39, 284-87.

42. E. Clifford Nelson, *The Rise of World Lutheranism* (Philadelphia: Fortress Press, 1982), 362-63.

43. The Second Assembly of the World Council of Churches, 1954, *The Evanston Report* (New York: Harper & Brothers, 1955).

44. William Ellis, interview with author, New York, 17 April 1986.

45. Herluf Jensen, interview with author, Trenton, N.J., 7 May 1986.

46. George Forell, telephone interview with author, 4 April 1987.

47. Warren Quanbeck, ed., *God and Caesar: A Christian Approach to Social Ethics*, (Minneapolis: Augsburg Publishing House, 1959).

48. "Lutheran Theological Study Group," Record Group 26, the Archives of Cooperative Lutheranism, Evangelical Lutheran Church in America, Chicago.

49. *Church and State: A Lutheran Perspective* (Board of Social Ministry, LCA, 1963), i-iii. Hereafter in citations the board will be abbreviated "BSM."

50. Some Augustana negotiators, A. D. Mattson among them, were suspicious that the board structure might suppress social action. Harold Haas, interviews

with author, Camp Hill, Pa., 6 September 1985; York, Pa., 17 February 1987. Memo from Haas in the author's possession, 3 November 1987.

51. Johannes Knudsen, *The Formation of the Lutheran Church in America* (Philadelphia: Fortress Press, 1978), 86ff.

52. Constitution of the Lutheran Church in America, Article III, Section 3.

53. Alfred Stone, telephone interview with author, 11 February 1987.

54. Rufus Cornelsen, "Foreword," *Social Statements of the ULCA*, 10-11.

55. Harold Haas, "Staff Memorandum," No. 1, 28 February 1963 (BSM files, LCA, ELCA Archives).

56. Harold Haas, telephone interview with author, 9 July 1987.

3

CORPORATE MEMORY AND POLICY IN THE LCA, 1962–1964

The new Lutheran Church in America was constituted in convention on July 1, 1962. Although its boards met twice before the year's end, their incorporations officially took effect on January 1, 1963, none too soon in times demanding moral leadership from the churches. In that same month came the clarion call from the National Conference on Religion and Race, a gathering of Protestant, Roman Catholic, and Jewish leaders, that congregations and denominations become beacons in the nation for integration and the pursuit of racial justice.[1]

The church was fortunate to have had a corporate memory grounded in the prior efforts of the United Lutheran Church in America and the Augustana Synod. The American Lutheran Evangelical Church (Danish) and the Finnish Evangelical Lutheran Church (Suomi Synod) had added committed leaders to the mix. Franklin Clark Fry, LCA president, Harold Haas, executive director of the Board of Social Ministry, and others were continuing a conversation about the nature and institutional expression of *Lutheran* social responsibility. In the sixties this would be no mere academic exercise. American politics had raised the ante on social reform.

Historians now recognize that the election of John F. Kennedy in 1960 initiated a resurgence of political liberalism that had not dominated the American landscape since Franklin Delano Roosevelt's first term in the early 1930s. This liberalism was different—more tamed, and not in direct contact with the lives of American blue-collar workers. In keeping with the affluence of the age, it was a "corporate liberalism," intended to make American political and economic systems more effective. Nevertheless, one issue aroused passion—the desire to achieve legal and political equality for southern Blacks.

Life in the American South underwent dramatic adjustments in the years between 1930 and 1960. Massive changes in agriculture, including the end of the once-dominant cotton farming, drove nearly two-thirds of the South's farm population away from the countryside. Under the old system, most Blacks were either landless tenants or domestic servants. White supremacy depended on a population that could be easily policed, kept semiliterate, and humiliated by enforced racial segregation. Now there were cracks everywhere in the culture as urban Blacks earned more money, gained education, and were able to escape surveillance. Black Southerners who grew up after World War II knew the possibilities of another life. The three million southern Blacks who joined the massive migration to northern cities altered the makeup of the Democratic party in the North and added pressures for social change.

The churches could not remain immune from the growing momentum for civil rights. In 1954 in the case of *Brown* v. *Board of Education of Topeka*, the U.S. Supreme Court ruled that legally enforced school segregation was unconstitutional. In 1956, the Reverend Martin Luther King, Jr., led a successful boycott of segregated buses in Montgomery, Alabama, while preaching Christian nonviolence as the means to America's renewal. In 1957, President Dwight D. Eisenhower sent the U.S. Army to Little Rock, Arkansas, to enforce the court-ordered desegregation of Central High School. In 1960, militant Black students directed sit-ins, mobilizing fifty thousand people and desegregating public facilities in 140 cities and towns, primarily in the upper South.[2]

The Lutheran churches struggled to find their public voices. In the ULCA there had been differences dating to the late 1940s within and between the Board of Social Missions and the Executive Board over the issuing of a statement on race relations. Southern members of both bodies were uncomfortable with the prospect. Pressures from the majority on the Board of Social Missions finally prevailed, and a remarkably comprehensive statement was adopted jointly in 1951 and then reported to the 1952 convention. But when the Board of Social Missions went to the 1956 convention with a statement endorsing the 1954 decision of the Supreme Court, consensus was not won without concessions. The Court's decision was not explicitly affirmed, although the 1951 statement was. Congregations were "encouraged" to contribute to the solution of the controversy over school desegregation "by demonstrating in their own corporate lives the possibility of integration." Moreover, all parties to the controversy were expected "to follow and uphold due process of law, and to maintain public order."[3]

By contrast, the Augustana Synod passed a resolution in its 1956 convention directly supportive of the Supreme Court decision and more demanding of its members, who lived primarily in the North, to work to end discrimination in housing, real estate transactions, and employment. Congregations were urged to stay in "changing" neighborhoods, and members were challenged not to abandon parishes that were integrating. In 1958 the church adopted a set of resolutions written as a statement of faith. "We believe . . . that since the Church is created by the Holy Spirit, the decisive factor in its policies and practices is not the will of men as conditioned by social, economic, or cultural patterns but rather the eternal will of God."[4]

By April of 1963, at its third meeting, the new Board of Social Ministry had adopted the staff's proposal that the social statements of predecessor bodies be neither refined nor reaffirmed, but instead "be given primary consideration" in fulfilling the board's constitutional mandate to "formulate statements on moral and social questions for consideration by conventions of this church." Augustana's Commission on Social Action had forced the decision by proposing that Augustana's pronouncements speak for the LCA, except where they conflicted with statements of other bodies to the merger. The board also voted to send each congregation a "basic social ministry library" which included the social statements of the ULCA, Augustana, and the National Council of Churches.[5]

The staff anticipated that race relations and economic affairs were two issues requiring official responses by the church and was authorized by the board to hold "seminars, consultations or conferences, looking foward to the formulation of new social statements."[6] Participants in the National Conference on Religion and Race had discussed such issues for the churches as appeals to the consciences of individual believers, the correction of abuses within religious institutions, and the corporate role of religious institutions as moral leaders within society.[7]

During the spring of 1963 demonstrators were taking to the streets of the South, while moral support for civil rights was mounting in the North. King had mastered these dynamics and chose locations for demonstrations where media coverage would fan the Northern conscience. When he defied a court order against further protests in Birmingham, Alabama, in April of 1963, he was jailed and wrote his eloquent "Letter from the Birmingham Jail" in defense of demonstrations, nonviolent protest and civil disobedience. The next month, as King involved more of the Black community, including children, in protests, the city's Commissioner of Public Safety, Bull Connor, lost all restraint and loosed dogs, clubs, and fire hoses on the marchers. Media coverage assured a national outpouring of sympathy, and, historian Allen Matusow claims, "a mass constituency for civil rights for the first time since Reconstruction."[8] In June, Kennedy sent a Civil Rights Bill to Congress. In August, two hundred thousand people—including Haas and Cedric Tilberg, officials representing the board—joined in the March on Washington.

The LCA was on the spot. At the end of June, the Executive Council exercised its prerogative of adopting resolutions, but only in anticipation of convention action the following year and in the tradition of the ULCA's 1952 and the Augustana Synod's 1956 statements. The resolution called for a complete program of self-examination and renewal to end discriminatory practices in the church and for members to support community efforts in behalf of reconciliation between the races and legislative efforts to bring equal opportunities and access in the political, economic, and social order. President Fry was requested and authorized to issue a pastoral letter.

On July 8 Franklin Clark Fry issued his letter to all LCA pastors. He denied that either his missive or the Executive Council's action derived in any simple way from the current crisis. Rather, he affirmed that "spiritual roots" for a Christian's position on race rest in God's works of creation and redemption, that all people are equal, and that racial distinctions are "an affront to the Lord and a sign of deviation from Him." He claimed that Christians lacked "will," not mind or heart, in the matter of seeking reconciliation and corrective legislation. He anticipated that his prodding would "taste too much for some like staid Lutheran conservatism." "I trust the power of Law and Gospel. The Lord trusts you," he concluded.

In September the staff released a study report to the church, including the Executive Council's resolution, the president's letter, and excerpts from prior statements by Augustana, the ULCA, and some LCA synods. In October the board convened a consultation on racial issues that included a discussion of the ends and means of a social statement. Haas recalls that the question was not primarily one of what to say but of how to say it.[9] Herluf Jensen tried his hand at a draft that was modeled on a letter from the National Student Christian Federation about civil disobedience. It did not garner support.[10]

"RACE RELATIONS"

When the Board of Social Ministry met from November 19 through 21, days immediately preceding Kennedy's assassination, Charles Bergstrom, chair of its Social Action department, reported that a statement on race relations would be ready for the board's review the following February, the last meeting before the convention. The subcommittee charged with the task was made up entirely of board members: Joseph Sittler, William Ellis, Clarence C. Stoughton, who was a previous president of Wagner College and Wittenberg University, and George Whittecar, president of the North Carolina Synod.[11] Whittecar would move for the adoption of the statement at the Pittsburgh convention.

Sittler was chiefly responsible for the format of the proposed statement based on the Prayer of the Church, an approach unique among the denomination's nineteen statements and a "pedagogical device," as Haas remembers. Haas probably wrote the statement's policy sections and, with staff member Richard Niebanck, handled the editing.[12]

The draft adopted by the board in February after seven hours of discussion[13] began with an assessment of the times, the naming of discrimination as implicitly heretical, and an appeal to the Prayer of the Church as a test to the integrity of the supplicant's witness: "Unless we mean what we say, and live as men who intend to do what we mean, the holy gravity of our prayer itself condemns us."

The explication of these points is then illustrated by excerpts from four petitions selected from the Prayer of the Church. Sittler was drawing upon language increasingly familiar to Lutherans, since this prayer had assumed a central position in the new common Liturgy of the *Service Book and Hymnal* (1958) as part of the Offertory rites, which followed upon the sermon and looked forward to the reception of the Sacrament.[14] The petitions Sittler chose plead for the unity of the church, the preservation of the government—held accountable to God's will, the conformity of Christians in the mind of Christ, and the bestowal of these requests for the sake of Jesus who died and rose again.

The third and final section of the statement covers church policy and acknowledges its more ephemeral nature. There follow then seven "elements" in the LCA's "call to action." The term *institutional racism* had not yet been coined, and yet the concept informed the sense of corporate responsibility expressed. The statement speaks of "institutional disobedience" and invokes a new activist principle for Lutheran church life. Unlike previous statements by the ULCA and the Augustana Synod, these policy affirmations were meant to be normative not only for church members and their congregations, but also for the national denomination, its synods, and its affiliated institutions and agencies.

The draft also broke new ground by specifying the conditions necessary for civil disobedience, not only by individual church members but also by official representatives of the denomination. No other section would receive greater attention or be more fully revised at the 1964 convention.

Today, the doxological form of the statement is recalled with some ambivalence by some former board members. William Ellis, who served on the drafting subcommittee, recollects that he "wouldn't have written that kind of statement. I would have approached it [the race issue] more directly. Yet, the format Sittler gave it provided an enduring quality." [15] Betty R. Amstutz recalls the potency of the format: "You can't fight prayer." [16]

Indeed, the use of petitions from the Prayer of the Church had the advantage of loading language familiar to churchgoers with the vivid imagery of a multiracial church, a government accountable to God for securing justice for all its citizens, and individuals reprieved from the hold of racist convictions by the work of Christ. Presumably once the images were set, congregants could no longer pray without recalling the matter of race relations.

But should a prayer of thanksgiving and adoration to God also serve to condemn the white supplicant for his or her moral failings? In the words of the draft, to be modified both by the board and the convention, "To stand before God and pray that he will 'take away . . . hatred and prejudice,' and then as a praying church to discriminate among men . . . is an act of devout blasphemy." This was the issue troubling board member William Lazareth. When social ethics are done in a "doxological context," he pondered recently, "how does one characterize those who disagree?" [17] Can sinners pray without further condemning themselves? Are church disciplinary proceedings indicated for such duplicity? Lazareth's theological misgivings about the format today are rooted in differences between his and Sittler's approaches to social ethics already evident in their essays in the 1957 trilogy *Christian Social Responsibility*.

In his essay "The Structure of Christian Ethics," Sittler envisions an ethical "dynamic" in which believers respond to the gifts and tasks set before them through God's triune work in their particular historical circumstances. They are enabled to respond by faith:

> Faith is the name for the new God-relationship whereby the will of God who himself establishes the relationship is made actual. And that will is love. Faith active in love is alone faith, and love is the function of faith horizontally just as prayer is the function of faith vertically. [18]

Faith must discern among the facts of a situation and then act upon what it has discerned:

> There is, to be sure, no human fact in which sin is not involved. But within some structures of fact there are alive, free and operative forces of grace,

48

insights of elemental justice, re-creating energies of love. It is a fact that the Negro community in American life has been exploited, contemptuously handled, overtly insulted by public law. It is also a fact that within American public life, concerned man [sic] and institutions have been free to combat injustice, illumine ignorance, plead and work for equality of treatment.[19]

Sittler's concern is for the integrity and therefore the responsiveness of Christian faith, i.e., for lived faith. He dislikes guidelines which could trammel the inventiveness of Christian love in particular circumstances.

Lazareth, in his essay "Christian Faith and Culture," is concerned with how such ethical wisdom emerges. For him the framework of Christian ethics does not lie within the individual response to God's action through faith, but rather in the way God has structured human community. The Christian simultaneously belongs to the community of faith, the church, and the community of life, human society. The judgments Christians make are influenced by three realities—God's sovereignty, God's rule through creation, and the particular witness of Christians, individually and in concert:

> First, there is no sphere of life which is a law unto itself, autonomous of the absolute sovereignty of God, however free it must remain from ecclesiastical domination. Secondly, that all men, even apart from Christ, are capable of a high degree of social justice in the building of a peaceful and humane society in which the Christian offers his critical co-operation and responsible participation. Thirdly, that it is primarily in and through the personal and corporate witness of his faithful followers in their civic vocations, as well as their church worship, that Christ's lordship—however hidden in its servant form—is made manifest in our communal life in contemporary society.[20]

From 1963 to 1967 Sittler and Lazareth sat together on the Board of Social Ministry. Their disagreements remained an undercurrent and, as some members recall, a form of education for the rest of the board.[21] Lazareth, whose approach to social ethics would eventually become predominant, said in a recent interview that he thought that Sittler's theological reflections on the Prayer of the Church were consonant with the "cosmic Christology" which Sittler had been developing as a delegate on the Faith and Order Commission of the World Council of Churches through his exposure to Roman Catholicism and Eastern Orthodoxy. This troubled Lazareth, who wanted an ethic that would illumine the common ground for both Christians and non-Christians living together in a pluralistic society.[22]

For his part, Sittler describes his position as deeply affected by "classic Catholic natural law doctrine." In September of 1985 he said:

I was never entrapped by the effort to make the 16th-century bifurcation between law and gospel a permanent structure. The forces that have determined ethical reflection are vigorously present outside that format. The organic character by which ethical issues are stated defies this cookie-cutter two kingdoms thing.[23]

Both Sittler and Lazareth have recorded their memories of the review of the drafted statement by board members and President Fry in February of 1964. Recollections center around Fry's scrupulosity. "Fry-mood [sic] exegesis," wrote Sittler, was accompanied by his rhythmic finger-tapping, varying according to his "excitement, or anger, or impatience, or frustration or affirmative exultation."[24] Lazareth recalls Fry's "grueling critique of every phrase of that statement," which contained "two significant innovations for social ethical thinking on American Lutheran soil: corporate church involvement in social action and moral justification for civil disobedience to unjust laws":

He spared no words in posing every biblical, theological, legal, social and political counter-argument that he could muster. A few weeks later the entire statement was adopted in substance by the church, not least of all because it had already survived its most exacting "ordeal by fire."[25]

Ellis recalls that Fry had already made clear to him in a private conversation that the church could not press forward on the issue of race relations by simply condemning and abandoning the South. Fry showed Ellis a file of correspondence from southern pastors and lay members who bore the burdens of conscience over racial injustice. And so it was that the language of the original draft was clarified at that meeting in ways that have contributed to the endurance of the statement. Fry exerted both the power of his office and of his personality to ensure that the statement was theologically consistent in its opposition to racism, but not unnecessarily inflammatory. Because the board itself contained a variety of viewpoints, his aggressiveness uncovered a range of concerns.[26]

One significant change in the introductory paragraph was the insertion of a single word, *injurious*, to modify "discrimination based on race." "Injurious discrimination," Fry contended, according to Lazareth's recollections of the hour-long debate on the sentence, was the appropriate modification from a biblical point of view. God was no respecter of persons, but distinguished among individuals in choosing prophets and among nations in the selection of Israel. Fry's insistence upon "injurious" proved prescient in light of subsequent affirmative action legislation.[27]

50

Another change was to substitute "unbiblical" for "heretical" in describing the views of God and man implicit in racial discrimination. Thus began the second paragraph of the statement. In the next sentence, where the church is called upon to oppose "heresy," the noun is replaced by the phrase "such false views." Lazareth recalls proposing these changes in order to preserve the traditional meaning of "heresy" as wrong doctrine.[28] By definition, heresy is explicit, not "implicit" as described in the sentence. Lazareth and others did not want the term's meaning diminished.

For the most part, other changes compressed language and added clarity. Nevertheless, two paragraphs were altered substantially. First, under the petition asking for the mind of Christ, the second sentence received close attention. For Christians to continue, after asking God to take away hatred and prejudice, "to discriminate among men on the basis of an heretical doctrine of God and of man, is an act of devout blasphemy." The change was to substitute "on any such sinful basis" for the allusion to heresy and to remove the adjective "devout" as unnecessarily inflammatory. "Blasphemy" would not survive the convention.

The final paragraph covered civil disobedience and would be substantially rewritten three times, first at this review and twice at the convention. A comparison among the versions illustrates the evolution of a position that was reaffirmed by the three merging churches in August of 1986 and at the constituting convention of the Evangelical Lutheran Church in America as one of four perduring positions on the church's relation to civil affairs. The original draft read:

The church, its agencies, synods and congregations, including their representatives, should be free to resist civil authority when governmental processes are not realistically adequate to redress wrongs and correct unjust laws.

The revision at the February meeting of the board was more explicit:

When other methods to bring about change have failed, the church, its congregations, synods, agencies and institutions, including their representatives, should be free to take part in public "demonstration" or similar measures of civil disobedience designed to focus attention on unjust laws or social customs and to effect the redress of wrong therein, so long as such demonstrations, etc., are conducted peaceably.

The revision itself was put aside at the convention when Lazareth offered a substitute motion which clarified, elaborated, and provided theological grounding. The first feature of the substitute motion was to distinguish between participation in legal, peaceable demonstrations and in civil disobedience, a distinction which had been overlooked in previous attempts and evidence that demonstrations *per se* were not yet part of the "repertoire of collective action" agreed upon within the LCA.[29]

The second element stipulated the conditions for such disobedience, should legal recourse be unavailable or inadequate to achieve reform: willingness to accept the penalty, willingness to focus the protest against the specific grievance, and willingness to act nonviolently with prayer and in consultation with other Christians. The third section was a direct allusion to Article 16 of the Augsburg Confession as the normative teaching for the church on the issue. With this reference, Lazareth widened the statement's doctrinal basis beyond the theology implicit in the Prayer of the Church.

Debate at the July 1964 convention, during the same week that Congress passed the Civil Rights Bill, centered around the first portion of the section on civil disobedience and indicated that some delegates were not of a mind to have the church represented officially in such action, but rather to confine the option to "individual members of congregations." Others were not satisfied that the section sufficiently expressed a Lutheran respect for the law of the land. Finally there was a motion to refer the entire section for redrafting to a subcommittee. President Fry appointed Carl M. Anderson and three members of the board, Franklin Jensen, William Lazareth, and George R. Whittecar to report back the following day.[30]

The new draft, after debate, recognized "the church, its congregations, synods, agencies and institutions, including their representatives, as well as individual members" "as free to" engage in lawful demonstrations and other efforts to change laws or customs in conflict with the U.S. Constitution or "the moral law of God." The three stipulations for civil disobedience, action taken only after all other means are exhausted, were set in a separate paragraph.[31] (See Appendix, "Race Relations," Section 7.)

Two other points in "Race Relations" were heavily debated. Amendments on the church's monitoring of its own business practices eliminated specific recommendations on contractors, investors, and suppliers for the general principle that the church "should support its concern for racial justice in all its business involvements and give critical scrutiny to its own employment practices."

In the major discussion of the statement's theological section controversy centered on the use of the term *an act of blasphemy* to describe the continuation of discrimination in a praying church. The substitution which passed the convention, "a contradiction to this prayer," modified

Sittler's intent, but was in line with the board's own effort to maintain a strict definition of "heresy." Blasphemy would have to be more an explicit rejection of God than one implied in racial discrimination.[32] The majority at the convention tried not to give unnecessary offense to southern Lutherans while also maintaining a commitment of the faith to integration and racial justice.[33]

Debate over this statement had sprawled over three of the four days of the Pittsburgh convention, including its last moments. All in all, passage of the statement demonstrated readiness within the church body to respond aggressively to racial injustice by cleaning its own house. Both elected and appointed leaders within the LCA had been prepared to argue the merits of their case before the delegates. Their success launched the denomination on a course of implementation that would govern the church throughout its years.

After its adoption and in the final session of the convention on the morning of July 9, a resolution supporting the Civil Rights Act of 1964 was moved as a "special order" and passed with little discussion. By it, the denomination recorded its "appreciation" for the work of national elected leaders and private citizens on its behalf, urged compliance "in letter and spirit," and called upon its members "to take the lead in their communities to encourage obedience to this legislation and to undergird by prayer and action those whose duty it is to enforce it."[34] This resolution would be printed for distribution with the statement.

"MARRIAGE AND FAMILY"

The Pittsburgh convention was asked to take action on two other social statements, both of which passed summarily. "Marriage and Family," originally passed at the 1956 convention of the ULCA, was offered by the board—at the behest of President Fry—to provide interim guidelines for pastors and people before the church body could formulate its own position.[35]

Former staff members recall that the remarriage of New York Governor Nelson B. Rockefeller to a divorcée under the cloud of scandal in May of 1962 reminded Fry of the urgent need for church policy. Rockefeller's campaign appearances for the presidency with his new wife in 1964 helped to keep this issue before the public.[36] At first the staff drafted a proposed statement for the board's consideration in 1963. At its November meeting, the board directed the staff to seek the counsel of seminary professors Martin Heinecken in Philadelphia and Arnold Carlson in Rock Island to consider the adequacy of the staff proposal in comparison with the previous ULCA pronouncement.[37]

Haas recalls that the ULCA's statement was favored for its compre-
hensiveness over the Augustana Synod's statements of 1939 on divorce
and 1954 on reproduction, both of which were specific in addressing
issues but lacked a developed theological framework.[38] In February of
1964 the board voted to recommend the ULCA's statement to the summer's convention and requested the Executive Council to approve distribution of the statement and also the ULCA background study to delegates. The board also called for a fresh study and position statement for
the 1966 convention "to take into specific consideration the sociological
and psychological dynamics of present-day marriage and to speak to them
theologically."

The board chose not to appoint a special commission to work on the
next statement, but to seek the advice of "competent persons" in the
fields of sociology, psychology, law, medicine, and systematic theology.
They also recorded their concern that other sectors of the church be
represented by the inclusion of a parish pastor, "at least one housewife,"
and an unmarried woman.[39]

The statement adopted in Pittsburgh bears the marks of the discussions
which led up to the publication of *Christian Social Responsibility* in 1957.
Harold Haas, who wrote the chapter "Christian Faith and Family Life,"
was the guiding spirit behind the statement which condenses his argument and draws upon his language. The 1956 statement proper had
consisted of thirteen summary propositions which followed from *A Study
on Marriage and Family Life*. The motion for its adoption in 1956 named
the superceded portions of the 1930 statement: the three paragraphs on
divorce, valid reasons for divorce, and the remarriage of the divorced.[40]
The 1956 statement affirms the position given in 1930 that marriage is
one of the God-given orders of creation. Its study guide recasts language
about human fulfillment through marriage in terms of an "I-Thou" relationship and the "disclosure of selfhood," recalling contemporary writings of Martin Buber and Paul Tillich.

In an age in which divorce was measured to have increased to one in
every four marriages, "400% in fifty years," it is not surprising that Haas
should note the inadequacy of "the prevailing romantic notion that marriage is based solely on love." Instead, "that which should hold the two
together and nurture the love that brought them together in the first place
is fidelity, i.e., faithfulness in that relationship which has indebted them
to each other forever and made them one flesh."[41]

After establishing that marriage is God-given and "binds one man and
one woman in a lifelong union of the most intimate fellowship of body

and life," the statement describes sexual relations as God's purpose to bring "husband and wife into full unity so that they may enrich and be a blessing to each other."[42] (See Appendix, "Marriage and Family.") "Continence outside of marriage and fidelity within marriage are binding on all."

In the case of divorce, guilt is assigned to no one party, nor is there any attempt to list acceptable reasons. Moreover, where Christians fail at marriage, the church is said to share in the complicity. The role of the church then is to "seek to lead all concerned to repentance and forgiveness," and if the reconstitution of the marriage is "impossible or unwise in the light of Christian love and concern for the welfare of all," then the church should not abandon either party. The statement then provides considerations for the clergy on the marriage of the divorced.

Because the new statement placed a far greater onus on church leaders to discern motives and to seek repentance and reformation, it is not surprising that four of the remaining propositions cover the training of counselors, the education of the laity, including youth; and the role of synods in promoting "the highest standards of pastoral practice." In time, the increasing divorce rate among the clergy themselves would complicate the individualizing of divorce counseling.

Passage of the statement occurred in anticipation of a new one in two years. Yet the formulation of a statement on sex, marriage, and the family proved far more difficult and time-consuming than expected. Moreover, when it was finally placed before the Minneapolis convention six years later, delegates were deeply divided in their ethical judgments.

"PRAYER AND BIBLE READING
IN THE PUBLIC SCHOOLS"

Harold Haas and Cedric Tilberg recall their surprise at the convention's ready adoption of the proposed position on prayer and Bible reading in the public schools. When Pastor Frank K. Efird presented the Executive Council's report and moved for the convention's endorsement, there was not even discussion.[43] Expecting contention, Rufus Cornelsen, who had drafted part of the statement, was prepared to be grilled from the floor. Yet the dynamics of the convention apportioned energy elsewhere, despite earlier rumblings.

The issue had first emerged at the constituting convention in 1962 in response to the Supreme Court decision on the prayer adopted by the New York State Regents for public schools. Joseph Rinderknecht, a lawyer from Toledo, and pastors George Haynes and Albert Buhl submitted a resolution voicing regret that the Court ruled the use of "a noncompulsory nonsectarian prayer in the public schools to be in violation of the First Amendment" and asking the church to admonish its people as Christian citizens "to vote for and support" those "believers in the Almighty God" who recognize the nation's historic dependence upon him. With 140 dissenting, the convention voted, upon recommendation of the Committee on Reference and Counsel, to refer the resolution "more appropriately" to the Executive Council "for any action it may wish to take."[44] The Kentucky-Tennessee delegation offered a similar proposal, also referred to the Council.[45]

Letters addressed to President Fry in subsequent months indicated strong opposition to the Court's decision and anxiety about its meaning for religious expression in public places. Fry, always respectful of this fear, did not mask his own dissent. The following sentences from a letter written on July 9, 1962, are characteristic: "As for me, I have no great affection for prayers written by public officials (New York State Board of Regents) and addressed to a blurry God, which is what the Supreme Court specifically ruled out."[46]

President Fry sought the advice of the newly constituted Board of Social Ministry at its first meeting in July and received the suggestion that whether or not the Council rendered an opinion, since there were still pending decisions of the Supreme Court on Bible reading and the use of the Lord's Prayer in schools, and since the matter belonged in the broader context of church and state, this issue might be referred to the board for study by its Commission on Church and State Relations in a Pluralistic Society. The Executive Council agreed.[47]

The double track of a response from the Executive Council and from the commission was thus put into motion. In June of 1963, following the Supreme Court's ban on the devotional use of the Bible and Lord's Prayer in public schools in the Schempp and Engel cases, and preceding the tidal wave of support for a constitutional amendment to allow such practices, President Fry issued a statement that the Council adopted as its own by converting his "I's" to "we's."[48] The amended statement would become the first part of the one adopted at the 1964 convention. Fry's argument built directly on the work of the Commission on Church and State.

The commission was a direct carryover from the ULCA. Authorized by the Executive Board in July of 1961, the commission grew out of a meeting of scholars convened earlier that year by the Board of Social Missions. The election of a Roman Catholic to the presidency of the

United States, along with continuing debates over the use of public funds in church schools and the problems in social welfare, stirred up Lutheran concern to reevaluate its own position. School prayer was then added to the mix.

The nine-member commission was purposefully inter-Lutheran: Conrad Bergendoff, George Forell, Paul Kauper (of the ALC, professor of law at the University of Michigan and author of the study report on the subject at hand), J. Martin Klotsche, William Lazareth, Arthur Carl Piepkorn (of LC-MS), Warren Quanbeck (of ALC), Theodore Tappert, and William Villaume. Newly authorized by the new church, the commission met twice in 1963 and produced a small volume of essays, *Church and State: a Lutheran Perspective*, to provide historical perspective on the exercise of religion in North America, an analysis of contemporary religious pluralism and of constitutional issues, and an "evangelical response," including the biblical witness and ethical guidelines.[49]

Paul Kauper was invited to analyze the issue and completed his essay on the legal, social, and psychological issues involved in the Court's decisions the month before President Fry issued his statement. By July, Kauper's work was widely circulated as the board's first staff study report. He began with the judgment that religion was not the great loser in the Court decisions, since the use of a nonsectarian prayer, of Bible reading without comment, or of the Lord's Prayer in school settings for vague religious or moralistic reasons denigrated the specificity of the Christian faith. Nevertheless, Kauper acknowledged the best intentions behind these exercises of "cultivating a respect for our nation's religious heritage, instilling respect for prayer and for the teachings of the Bible and contributing thereby to the value served by religion in the community."[50]

Virtually quoting Kauper, President Fry noted in his statement that when Christians insist on "common denominator" religious exercises or instructions, there is the great risk "of diluting our faith and contributing to a vague religiosity which identifies religion with patriotism and becomes a national folk religion."

Kauper proceeded to analyze the Court's reasoning and to call into question its broad interpretation of the prohibition of the government's establishment of religion in the Constitution's First Amendment, its inconsistency in allowing other forms of religious expression, and the abstraction in its appeal to a principle of "neutrality" in matters religious.

President Fry shared Kauper's sense of appreciation that the Court's decisions recognized religious pluralism. He noted in his memorandum this "watershed": "It opens an era in which Christianity is kept separate from the state in a way that was foreign and would have been repugnant to the minds of our ancestors." It signals that the United States "is past the place where underlying Christian culture and beliefs are assumed in its life" and "intensifies the task of the church" and increases its need for strength "to stand alone" in society. It also calls "for greater depth of conviction" among all Christians.

Kauper was willing to sustain the Supreme Court's decision on two grounds: first, that the religious value of prayer and Bible reading in public schools had "limited, if not dubious value"; and second, such practices might operate "with coercive effect on the objectors." Nevertheless, he was also willing to assert that the "general grounds and broad propositions" argued by the Court "are properly the cause of some concern," although he did not agree with those who believed the Court hostile to religion or an advocate of "godlessness."[51]

After the Kauper report was released, President Fry and the board and staff expected the Commission on Church and State to proceed with the formulation of a statement for the July convention. The commission balked at this task in February of 1964 and argued that its study report was sufficient and that what the church needed was a general study program more than a discrete statement on such a complex issue. The commission also took into account the nature of a convention:

> The kind of objective study of the meaning and implications of these [Supreme Court] decisions required today could be frustrated rather than furthered by asking the convention to take a stand on questions on which the delegates were neither adequately prepared nor ready to agree.[52]

Fry was still insistent on a policy statement. He had already been approached to testify before the House Committee on the Judiciary in response to the "Becker Amendment" proposed to the U.S. Constitution to reverse the effects of the Supreme Court rulings. Fry had agreed only to having his statement, as adopted by the Executive Council, read into the proceedings with a description of its context.[53] At his request, staff member Cornelsen was assigned to prepare an "interpretive memorandum" based largely on Kauper's report to accompany the Council's statement for presentation to the convention.[54]

The memorandum adopted in conjunction with Fry's statement was also penned in the more politicized atmosphere of an election year and seeming strong support for an amendment to the Constitution. (See Appendix, "Prayer and Bible Reading in the Public Schools.") Consequently, it was somewhat less empathetic toward those fearful of the changes brought by the Court's decisions, and it was explicitly opposed to the use

58

of an amendment. It argues that such an amendment would be "only a piece-meal" way of dealing with the issue; that it could raise new problems of interpretation with unsuspected results touching on religious liberty; and that it would promote sectarian practices "impinging upon freedom of conscience and belief and creating divisiveness in the community." Charles Bergstrom, former member of the board and currently director of the Lutheran Council's Washington Office for Governmental Affairs, claims that he has used this statement more regularly than any other in presenting the position of the church to national and state governments.[55]

Joseph Rinderknecht, one who had provoked study of this issue in the first place in 1962, flagged even more fundamental matters in a resolution adopted in 1964 requesting the study of "the extent to which the statements contained in the Lutheran Confessions as to the relation of church and state are relevant at this time" and a study "of the circumstances under which the corporate church may speak directly to the state rather than . . . to its congregations and its people for their information and appropriate action."[56] His questions recognized that the Lutheran church was itself in watershed times. Rinderknecht's resolution confirmed an agenda in the making for the next biennium and established him as one of the most thoughtful critics of the board's work.

NOTES

1. The National Council of Churches, the National Catholic Welfare Conference, and the Synagogue Council of America jointly sponsored the event.

2. This overview draws on the masterful account of Allen J. Matusow, *The Unraveling of America: A History of Liberalism in the 1960s* (New York: Harper & Row, 1984).

3. *Social Statements of the ULCA*, 8-43; Svendsbye, "Developing Social Responsibility among Lutherans," 413-26.

4. "Social Pronouncements of Augustana," 16-18.

5. Board of Social Ministry Minutes, 23–25 April 1963, 14; Agenda, 8; 23–24 July 1962, "Constitution of the Board of Social Ministry of the Lutheran Church of America," Article IV, Section 4. Hereafter these minutes, now located in the ELCA Archives, shall be cited as BSM Minutes.

6. BSM Minutes, 23–25 April 1963, 8.

7. J. William Youngdahl, telephone interview with author, 11 February 1987. The Executive Council had ruled out an official delegation because it was not in conformity with "evangelical and representative" principles governing interchurch relations. Executive Council Minutes, 27–29 August 1962, 97-98. See Matthew Ahmann, ed., *Race: Challenge to Religion, Original Essays and An*

Appeal to the Conscience from the National Conference on Religion and Race (Chicago: Henry Regnery, 1963), vii-x.

8. Matusow, *The Unraveling of America*, 87.

9. Haas, interview with author, 17 February 1987.

10. Jensen, interview with author, 7 May 1986.

11. BSM Minutes, 19–21 November 1963, 25.

12. Haas, interview with author, 17 February 1987; Richard Niebanck, interview with author, New York City, 24 July 1985.

13. BSM Minutes, 25–27 February 1964, 16-19.

14. Luther D. Reed, *The Lutheran Liturgy*, rev. ed. (Philadelphia: Fortress Press, 1947), 308-9.

15. Ellis, interview with author, 17 April 1986.

16. Betty Amstutz, interview with author, Camp Hill, Pa., 4 March 1986.

17. William Lazareth, telephone interview with author, 11 September 1986.

18. *Life in Community*, vol. 2 of *Christian Social Responsibility*, 23.

19. Ibid., 37.

20. Ibid., 74.

21. Amstutz, interview with author, 4 March 1986.

22. Lazareth, interview with author, 4 April 1986.

23. Joseph Sittler, interview with author, Chicago, 11 September 1985.

24. Robert H. Fischer, ed., *Franklin Clark Fry: Palette for a Portrait*, Supplementary Number of *The Lutheran Quarterly* 24 (1972): 57.

25. Ibid., 160.

26. See BSM Minutes, 25–27 February 1963, 12-19, for a comparison of the text of the statement as proposed and as revised.

27. Ibid., 16.

28. Lazareth, telephone interview with author, 11 September 1986.

29. I am indebted to historian Charles Tilly for this phrase.

30. LCA, *Minutes . . . 1964*, 654-55.

31. Ibid., 661, 663-65.

32. George Forell and Philip Johnson had their negative votes recorded. LCA, *Minutes . . . 1964*, 577.

33. For some, the offense was in the proposed draft. UPI news service printed the text of the draft and on July 6 the *Savannah* (Georgia) *Evening Press* printed the text under a headline referring to "blasphemy." CBS television reportedly also mentioned the language of the proposal. (Correspondence of Franklin Clark Fry, race relations file, July 1964, ELCA Archives.)

34. LCA, *Minutes . . . 1964*, 666-67.

35. Ibid., 677.

36. Richard Niebanck, interview with author, New York City, 24 July 1985; Cedric Tilberg, interview with author, Gettysburg, Pa., 12 March 1987.

37. BSM Minutes, 25–27 February 1964, 5-6.

38. Haas, interview with author, 17 February 1987.

39. BSM Minutes, 25–27 February 1964, 12; Agenda, 6-7.

40. ULCA, *Minutes . . . 1956*, 1157, 1188, as quoted in *Social Statements of the ULCA*, 86-87.

41. *A Study on Marriage and Family Life,* 2d ed. (BSM/LCA, 1964), passim.

42. The thirteen statements appear in LCA, *Minutes . . . 1964,* 494-96.

43. Ibid., 629-30.

44. LCA, *Minutes . . . 1962,* 128-29.

45. Ibid., 251. To recall the American context, the phrase *under God* had been added to the Pledge of Allegiance only a decade earlier.

46. Franklin Clark Fry to William M. Lightsey, Franklin Clark Fry Papers, Box 33, file "Supreme Court Prayer Decision," ELCA Archives.

47. Executive Council Minutes, 27–29 August 1962, 48-49.

48. Executive Council Minutes, 28–29 June 1963, 611f.

49. *Church and State: A Lutheran Perspective* (BSM/LCA, 1964) was approved by the board for publication in its Christian Social Responsibility series.

50. Staff of BSM, "The Supreme Court on Prayer and Bible Reading in the Public Schools," Study Report, 1 (July 1963): 3.

51. Ibid., 7-8.

52. BSM Minutes, 25–27 February 1964, 12; Exhibit G, 1.

53. Fry to Emmanuel Cellers, 20 April 1964, Fry Papers, Box 33, ELCA Archives. In the wake of the Supreme Court decision in June of 1963 and in an election year, some 140 legislators had introduced bills proposing amendments to the Constitution's First Amendment. In the effort to unify the diversity, Congressman Frank Becker of New York, a Roman Catholic, had become the spokesperson for the drafting committee. The amendment went beyond the specific prohibitions in public schools to insure the constitutionality of prayer or other references to "God or a Supreme Being" in any governmental or public school, institution or place. Robert E. Van Deusen, National Lutheran Council, "Washington Memorandum," 18 April 1964.

54. See Fry to Thomas Busich, 26 June 1964, Fry Papers, Box 33, ELCA Archives.

55. Charles Bergstrom, telephone interview with author, 24 June 1987.

56. LCA, *Minutes . . . 1964,* 2–9 July 1964, 498-99.

4

THE BOARD OF
SOCIAL MINISTRY IN CHARGE,
1965–1966

By the mid-sixties, the national mood favoring social reform reached its peak. John Kennedy had stoked America's perfectionism with urgent rhetoric. The civil rights movement had also introduced white America to the "squalid underside of American life." The poverty of most American Blacks confronted the white majority with the reality of deprivation, even though it had always been in their own midst as well. At the same time, an affluent economy fed optimism about the possibilities for social change. Without disclosing any strategy, President Lyndon B. Johnson declared "unconditional war on poverty" in his State of the Union address on January 8, 1964.

During the next four years the boundaries and fault lines in the age's liberalism were exposed. The March on Selma, Alabama, in support of voting rights in the spring of 1965 marked what has been called the "valedictory" of the Southern movement. Johnson worked for enforcement of civil rights legislation and broke the back of Jim Crow. When the action moved North, his political allies became divided, and he lacked support to pursue enforcement. What had been brief riots in the summer of 1964 turned into ground war in the Watts section of Los Angeles in 1965. At the same time, Johnson had launched his own ground war in Vietnam at the prompting of General Westmoreland. The hopes of an era began to unravel.[1]

Against this backdrop, the staff and members of the Board of Social Ministry found themselves, by constitutional mandate, stage center in the LCA: "The object of this board shall be to inquire into the nature and proper obedience of the church ministry within the structures of social life."[2] In 1964 at the LCA convention, the board had exercised its prerogative by proposing the creation of a Coordinating Committee on Race

Relations made up of representatives from all denominational offices to monitor and plan efforts in behalf of racial justice.[3]

As the board reckoned with its responsibilities, its structures seemed too restrictive.[4] The division of its work between departments of social missions and social action had become irrelevant when, in Haas's words, "everything in the portfolio of the board's responsibilities has been clamoring for attention at the same time." Instead, Haas proposed to LCA's Executive Council on behalf of the board the more "dynamic and flexible categories of 'issues' and 'operations.'" Standard also in the National Council of Churches, the three "issues" areas—civil and international affairs, intergroup relations and economic affairs, and social welfare—now required three "secretaries" to oversee the study of issues, the formulation of positions, and the convening of conferences. Specialists in "operations" would attend to "the life of the church in consultations, materials, conferences, interpretations, etc."[5] Thus, the board's work was realigned.

SOCIAL MINISTRY:
BIBLICAL AND THEOLOGICAL PERSPECTIVES

For Haas, finding the right form of organization belonged to his larger concern to discern and articulate a *Lutheran* character for social ministry, one that would motivate the church to become more active. He had been both chronicler and director of the ULCA's efforts to this end. Increasingly since the days of the New Deal, the definition of Lutheran social responsibility had come to encompass not only works of charity but also social reform, often defined along the axis favored by the liberal wings of the nation's two political parties. And so, the question of how to persuade Lutherans had political as well as theological overtones.

Under Haas's guidance and with the encouragement of Fry, the board's executive committee had tackled this issue at its first meeting in 1962 and assigned William Lazareth to draft a position statement on social ministry.[6] After a first discussion in November of that year, the board poked at the subject until April of 1965. Between April and the following February, the board modified and adopted Lazareth's draft and then reported it to the 1966 convention as "a guide to its [the board's] present theological understanding of its work."[7] Subsequently, the statement was published and widely circulated as *Social Ministry: Biblical and Theological Perspectives*.

Despite the momentum leading to this statement, uncertainty had dogged the board's early deliberations. At its April meeting in 1965 Joseph

63

Sittler had pleaded for an eschatological perspective that emphasized the world as God's "theatre" of activity and the "demands" of "an historical obedience" from the people of God. He had also criticized the church for reflecting rather than confronting in its organized centralization the very "totalization" that leads to "depersonalization." Moreover, the local congregation, "far from being a center of servanthood, is a reinforcer of national-cultural triumphalism."[8] Sittler's stinging critique carried in it the barbs of a generation, typified by Gibson Winter's appraisal *The Suburban Captivity of the Churches.*[9]

Haas said he appreciated Sittler's "jostling": "As BSM staff, we are somewhat 'trapped' in certain mental and emotional fixities." Haas pondered whether the "vertical ('God-relationship') and horizontal ('neighbor-relationship') dichotomy, like the two-kingdoms theory, has left social ministry as a kind of afterthought" [in ecclesiastical organization] and puzzled over "how much of the board's resources should be invested in the basic task of theological re-education in order to correct such a false bifurcation."[10] William Lazareth, on a trip abroad, was not present for this discussion.

A small committee, chaired by Lazareth, was then appointed to develop a statement "in contemporary theological and sociological terms, of the social character of Christian faith and obedience" and a second statement for President Fry on "the question of the appropriateness of present church structures to the reality of church and world."[11]

Lazareth himself responded to the first part of the assignment with a theological statement built on his effort of a decade to argue that God's dual reign through law and gospel provided a sufficient motivation for Christian social responsibility and enabled Christians, in the words of the final document, "both privately and corporately, as citizens and as churchmen, to join hands with all men of good will in working together for the common good of humanity."[12] His argument is largely prefigured in an essay which he wrote in 1960 for the ULCA and which was reissued by the board in 1965 as *A Theology of Politics.*[13]

Section I of the social ministry statement, "Servant Lord," argues from Scripture's testimony that the very perfection of "Jesus' proclamation and demonstration of the sacrificial love of God" accuses sinners "of contempt for God" when they fail to serve those created in God's image, "the poor, the hungry, the imprisoned and oppressed" and calls "a vital social ministry" "integral to the mission of Christ's church because it is integral to the mission of Christ himself."[14]

Section II, "The Servant Church," describes God's Word as a "weapon" against traditional Lutheran quietism and contemporary activism. Quietism occurs "whenever Christians forget that a major part of the church's ministry is inescapably *social* in service to the needy world of God the Creator." Activism is characterized in one part of the document as unmindful that the "the church's engagement in society is inherently a *ministry* of love and justice empowered by God the Sanctifier" and, elsewhere, as salvation by self-justification.[15]

The crux of his argument claims the interpenetration of the two realms and the complementary dual uses of law and gospel:

> It is through the continual interaction of the law and the gospel that the Triune God rules the two realms of creation and redemption. As Creator and Judge, God employs the law to perform two crucial functions. Its theological task is to judge the self-righteousness of sinful men in the realm of redemption. Its ethical task is to prompt the civil-righteousness of rational men in the realm of creation. As Redeemer and Sanctifier, God is at the same time employing the gospel to perform two other indispensable functions. Its theological task is to reckon the righteousness of Christ to faithful men in the realm of redemption. Its ethical task is to empower the Christian righteousness of loving men in the realm of creation.[16]

Lazareth is at pains to clarify this "Reformation doctrine" because of its "past and present misuse" as a justification for the "evasion of Christian social responsibility." Because God is Lord of creation and redemption, there is no dividing of life into "sacred" and "secular" realms. Christians live simultaneously in both realms and are judged in terms of God's rule in each. In particular, he stresses the rule of God through "reason and justice":

> This means that reasonable men, even apart from faith in Christ, are capable of a high degree of social justice in the building of a peaceful and humane society. It is wholly unevangelical to deny that God has written his law on the hearts of all men created in his image. Moreover, the moral zeal of a humanitarian, however motivated, often exceeds that of an apathetic Christian. Especially in our kind of pluralistic society, the church's social ministry will often take the form of working together for human justice under the law with other civic minded groups, both voluntary and governmental.[17]

In this passage the statement counters an American Protestant ethic, common even among Lutherans, that required a "Christianizing" of the social order before social problems could be solved. Partnership with non-Christian humanists is not only possible but necessary in God's world. Nevertheless, while successfully bridging the divisions between Christian and non-Christian, the statement begs two other issues that remain problematic throughout the history of the denomination's statement making. First, how does one discern God's law through reason from other human predispositions? Second, what constitutes the common

65

good, or "a peaceful and humane society"? By neither flagging these as issues nor suggesting self-critical tests, *Social Ministry: Biblical and Theological Perspectives* allows for their resolution in reigning social psychologies and political ideologies.

Lazareth then states, without elaboration, the need for both a personal and a corporate Christian witness. The personal witness of "Christian neighbors, workers and citizens" is the "primary" way through which "Christ's Servant Lordship becomes operative in contemporary society." Luther's doctrine of vocation becomes explicit here.

Contrary to the initial proposal of the board, Lazareth builds no case for a corporate response by the church. He simply notes that "in an age of corporate decision-making, the public witness of official representatives of the church can be particularly effective in expressing and reinforcing the ethical judgments of the Christian community."[18] In the next biennium, George Forell's work on religious liberty would supply some of the missing argument.

During committee and staff discussions of the draft, some of the "categories"—presumably the two kingdoms—were questioned. Lazareth argued that his purpose was not to break new ground, but rather to answer opponents of social ministry on their own biblical and confessional terms. When Sittler, despite his opposition to the approach, graciously expressed appreciation for Lazareth's efforts and moved the question for the statement's adoption, Lazareth answered that "he hoped this was the best expression of 'where the Lutheran church has been' and that he hoped we would move . . . to more adequate expressions in the future."[19]

Sittler quietly resigned from the board in early 1967. In a recent interview he said, "Our different points of view were not reconcilable and to continue ambiguity would retard decision-making."[20]

Under Haas's conscientious leadership, the Board of Social Ministry clarified procedures for the authorization of board publications. Haas was always careful to batten down the hatches. After ten years of directing first the ULCA's Board of Social Missions and then the LCA's Board of Social Ministry, both under the presidency of Franklin Clark Fry, he would resign in August of 1966 to accept the deanship of Wagner College. In November of 1965 the board adopted the schema proposed by the staff for a hierarchy of materials starting with "policy statements" whose subject and content were "authorized" by convention or the Executive Council. The board authorized policy guides, manuscripts for the Christian Social Responsibility series, other "guides and standards," and "staff study reports." Otherwise, the staff simply reported to the board its publication of such items as the research and study reports of others and its communications with synods.[21]

As the board prepared its agenda for the 1966 convention, it took under advisement that President Fry considered "three major policy statements" from all sources to be the upper limit for responsible convention action. Statements were anticipated on the doctrine of the ministry and on the nature and mission of the congregation. Nevertheless, the board sensed the church's need for social policy and had begun to work on many fronts: church and state; poverty; sex, marriage, and the family; and the liberties of religious minorities. There had also been a call for a statement on community organization and the board itself hoped for ones on world order and social welfare.[22]

As they pondered topics, board members also questioned the degree of specificity. Staff reported receiving letters and telegrams asking " 'the board's position' on issues like Viet Nam, Mississippi Freedom Democratic Party, 14b of Taft-Hartley Law, and Medicare." Such requests characterized the age and indicated that the LCA would not be immune to the pressures for a corporate approach to policy making affecting other mainline churches.[23]

From its earliest days, as in the ULCA, the LCA's Board of Social Ministry favored the use of study materials for specific crises and the use of social statements for establishing general principles.[24] The board was also concerned to allow more time for the review of statements prior to convention action. Open to the idea of conducting convention hearings, members nevertheless favored consultations with synodical social ministry committees prior to the writing of a final draft.[25]

"CHURCH AND STATE:
A LUTHERAN PERSPECTIVE"

At the 1964 convention, when Joseph Rinderknecht proposed studies of the Augsburg Confession's position on church and state issues and of the conditions under which the church might speak to the state, he, a political conservative, had tapped into a conversation within the liberal-leaning board and staff. Nevertheless, the first part of his question entertained the radical theological possibility, counter to the emerging viewpoint championed by Lazareth—that Reformation theology of church and state was *not* a resource.[26]

The board decided not to respond to Rinderknecht's resolutions directly, but rather to demonstrate that his concerns were being met by work already in progress. In the years ahead, the board's leadership did not look foward to directives from the convention floor. In Haas's words, "It can cost thousands of dollars to respond to a resolution and then

67

when the board reports back, the interest is gone."[27] In its report to the 1966 convention, the board stated that the resolution informed especially the theological statement on social ministry and the proposed statement on church–state relations.[28]

The report also states that the two statements proceed "on the assumption that the confessional stance of the Lutheran Church is valid for the contemporary age, and that it provides adequate theological grounding for the church to speak directly to civil authority."[29] The Commission on Church and State Relations in a Pluralistic Society had made this commitment early and the board had followed suit. Moreover, individuals otherwise leery of the Reformation doctrine of the two kingdoms found it a useful perspective on the role of church and state. Rufus Cornelsen, who served as staff for the commission in the early 1960s, spoke for others when he called Lazareth's theological work "most significant on church and state" and "very creative."[30]

Because the board had been active in the discussion of church–state issues since its inception, the formulation of a statement came easily.[31] The Commission on Church and State played a central role. Established as an inter-Lutheran body in the ULCA on the principle that experts ought to be convened in the preparation of social statements, the commission came into the LCA ready to stake out a position. In 1963 they had completed *Church and State: A Lutheran Perspective*, and also reviewed Paul Kauper's essay on the "Supreme Court and Prayer and Bible Reading in the Public Schools."

Church and State would provide the basis and name for the social statement adopted three years later. Part I, "The Challenge of Pluralism," delineated the historical and contemporary character of church/state relations. After "A Brief Retrospect," the study analyzed contemporary religious pluralism and its constitutional aspects. Part II, "An Evangelical Response," considered the biblical witness and the Reformation's understanding of God's work as creator and redeemer. The final chapter, "Ethical Guidelines," written by Lazareth,[32] lays out a specifically Lutheran interpretation of church, state, and the Christian's role in each.

Because the Bible proclaims that God is sovereign over all of human life, there can be no such thing as "absolute" separation of church and state:

> By clearly distinguishing God's law of creation from his gospel of redemption, the Reformers found a way by which church and state could interact without being united and yet remain distinct without being divorced.

Lazareth claims that though it is not redemptive, the secular realm "is still a sacred reality of God's creation" and provides the " 'masks' through which God graciously preserves the world from its sinful self-destruction." To emphasize the point, he notes that "the state cannot be too secular (civil) from the Christian point of view!"

Lazareth proceeds to call for theological clarity and to use the catch phrase that would become the denominational trademark for analysis of the church/state relation:

> We shall defend both the institutional separation and the functional inter-action of church and state in the United States and Canada. This position is determined by our fidelity to the Christian view of history. We believe that Jesus Christ has inaugurated but not yet consummated the kingly rule of God in the midst of the secular kingdoms of this world. During the present age, both the church and the state are divinely commissioned to play their distinct but related roles in God's preservation and salvation of mankind.[33]

The commission's work was timely for the LCA delegation of thirty-two attending the National Council of Churches' Study Conference on Church and State in February of 1964.[34] The board sent advance copies of the commission's study and Kauper's analysis on school prayer to all conference delegates, and also hosted a gathering with Lutheran delegates and observers from The American Lutheran Church and the Lutheran Church–Missouri Synod.[35] Commission member George Forell had prepared one of the six study papers for the conference. Harold Haas, vice chair of the conference, moderated the plenary sessions.[36]

Agreement within the Lutheran delegation on a common language and an aggressive presentation enabled them to curb the language of strict separation favored by other Protestants. In fact, the general findings of the conference were published under the title "Separation and Interaction of Church and State."[37]

Dean Kelley recalls the influence of the Lutherans and suggests that they may have had more of a rhetorical than an actual victory, since he does not believe the general findings played "a very salient role in the NCC." He judges the formula of "separation" and "interaction" to be a "typically churchy assertion where a benign hope is expressed that you can have the advantages of separation without the problems of interaction."[38] Forell wonders whether the conference was "asleep" when they adopted that language and recalls that the real rub in the Lutherans' position came with the "claim that you can be righteous without being Christian."[39]

After the conference, Lutherans continued discussions among themselves. Fifty representatives from the three major Lutheran denominations attended the Consultation on Church and State Relations in Minneapolis.[40] Following the consultation, the Board of Social Ministry was more conscious of disagreements among the Lutheran bodies, especially on the church's use of federal poverty funds and on public funding for nonpublic schools.[41] LCA leaders had come to favor the NCC's restrictions on any government funding of parochial schools and therefore faced conflict with the Missouri Synod which was, next to the Roman Catholics, the denomination with the largest school system.[42] Moreover, the Commission on Church and State, which had begun to study the provocative issues of religion and education, had undergone changes in membership, including the loss of Rufus Cornelsen, the experienced staff member who left in January of 1965 to work for the National Council of Churches.[43] In April of 1965, at the staff's recommendation, the board voted to dismiss its own inter-Lutheran commission and to look to the emerging Lutheran Council in the USA to sponsor such a study group.

At the same meeting the board weighed options on a social statement on church and state for the next convention. The staff proposed one approach by drafting a nine-page document entitled "Issues Involving Church-State Relations." The draft responded to the increasing number of inquiries addressed to them on a great variety of issues. Another option, the course preferred by the board, was to state the theological principles governing church/state relations and avoid specific recommendations in a time of legal and social flux.

The board had been advised by a subcommittee of the need for "a core theological stance approved by the church" and a "wide-ranging" study document with the status of "a Christian Social Responsibility booklet" to cover specific issues.[44] At its preconvention meeting in 1966, the board voted to recommend the adoption of a two-and-one-half-page statement—in essence, a précis of the last chapter of *Church and State: A Lutheran Perspective.* Lazareth oversaw this distillation and also moved the adoption of the statement by section on the afternoon of June 23 at the Kansas City convention.[45]

At the convention fourteen motions to amend were made; six, for the most part stylistic, were adopted. Edgar Carlson added to the church's responsibility when he proposed for the section on functional interaction that the church should not only hold the state accountable to God's sovereign law but should also help "the state to understand" that law. The convention agreed. Robert E. Van Deusen of the National Lutheran Council's Washington office proposed that the church should pray in behalf of the state "and its officials." The convention concurred.[46] By its action, the convention adopted Lazareth's interpretation of the Reformation doctrine of God's dual reign as "policy" on matters of church and state. (See Appendix, "Church and State, a Lutheran Perspective.")

This framework would shape most subsequent denominational and inter-Lutheran commentary on public affairs.

"CAPITAL PUNISHMENT"

The same convention, in the statement "Capital Punishment," declared its opposition to the death penalty, while also affirming the state's right to bear the sword. This approach can be foreseen in "Church and State": "A government is accountable to God for the way in which it uses, abuses or neglects to use its powerful civil 'sword.' " The board assumed that the church ought to take a stand on this issue. The first paragraph of the adopted position describes a contemporary climate of intense debate in the U.S. and Canada "accompanied by the actual abolition of capital punishment in ten states and two dependencies of the United States, qualified abolition in three states, and in six states the cessation in the use of the death penalty since 1955."

Both the ULCA and the Augustana Synod had prepared statements advocating abolition of the death penalty, although the 1960 convention of the ULCA had rejected one after a delegate read a letter of objection from J. Edgar Hoover, who argued that capital punishment remains a deterrent to crime.[47]

The new statement originated with the board's October meeting in 1965. After reviewing a summary of contemporary research in sociology, criminology, and theology supplied by a special committee from the Ohio Synod, the board requested the staff to prepare a statement and to consult with experts to update the background ULCA study on capital punishment and synodical social ministry committees to determine the adequacy of the statements previously prepared by Augustana and the ULCA. Mr. Victor Evjen, assistant chief of probation, Federal Probation System, and member of Church of the Reformation in Washington, D.C., had already submitted suggested revisions on the study.[48] Rev. Clifton L. Monk of the Canadian Lutheran Council later provided parallel updating on Canada.[49]

Richard Niebanck, who drafted the new statement, reported that respondents to the survey on the older statements were especially concerned that the LCA should call for reform of "the total system of correction and law enforcement." Some asked specifically for "a basic revision of the penal code and judicial process." Many argued that a church statement advocating the end of a death penalty also ought "to appeal to the church constituency for the support of law enforcement," including cooperation in giving testimony.

Niebanck reported no clear winner between the Augustana and ULCA statements but explained why his draft followed "somewhat" the ULCA approach. First, he argued for treating matters of civil justice "under the rubric of 'civil righteousness' and not 'redemption.'" The Augustana Statement, passed in 1957, began with three contrary assertions:

a. We recognize the Spirit of Jesus Christ, revealed in the Scriptures, as regulative for conduct in all matters;
b. We recognize the right and the duty of society to defend and protect itself against criminals;
c. We believe that the Christian's attitude toward an offender of the law should be redemptive even in the administration of justice.

Niebanck asserted that a call for an end to capital punishment must "be balanced by a clear recognition of the state's inherent right to take life in the exercise of its proper functions."[50] The defeated ULCA statement had taken such a position, while also reasoning that recognition of the state's right to take life "does not imply a mandate to exercise it."[51]

Niebanck's draft for the LCA statement proceeded from a summary on the status of capital punishment in the various states and Canada, and an overview of the growing concern over the penal justice system and for "persons who, because of ethnic or economic status, are seriously hampered in defending themselves in criminal proceedings." Then he provided three considerations necessary for making "a responsible judgment" on capital punishment: first, the state's right to take life; second, the question of equality before the law and human rights—including the new argument that this punishment ends "the possibility of restoring the convicted person to effective and productive citizenship"; and third, the "impossibility of demonstrating the deterrent value of capital punishment." The statement closes with the church's call to abolish capital punishment and to urge "citizens everywhere" to improve "our total system of criminal justice" and the continued development of "a massive assault on those social conditions which breed hostility toward society and disrespect for law."[52]

The board, in its review of Niebanck's work, was largely satisfied. The final draft recommended to the convention includes further clarifications in the initial overview of the United States and Canada and a sharpening of language in the closing set of guidelines. The LCA is explicitly made the speaker in urging the abolition of the death penalty. There was one further emendation which Niebanck later came to view as flawed. The argument from "the invalidity of deterrence" was amplified with evidence to demonstrate "no pronounced difference in the rate of murders and other crimes of violence between states in the United States which impose capital punishment and those bordering on them which do not."[53] Niebanck now finds such evidence nothing more than correlations which cannot prove causation.[54]

In Kansas City the statement was treated summarily, no doubt in large part because it was the very last major item of business at the convention's final session. (See Appendix, "Capital Punishment.") Delegates were in no mood to amend it and only three minor editorial changes among a total of fourteen suggestions were adopted. Delegates defeated any attempt to alter the substance. George Whittecar proposed adding a section called "The Gospel Witness" to assert that, because God is a God of both love and justice, those who administer justice "seek always to temper justice with love." Such an addition would have undercut the argument's framework of civil righteousness in which the case for mercy depended primarily on the fact that a disproportionate number of those convicted to death were poor and Black. Rinderknecht would have preferred, although his motion was defeated, to have the statement entitled "Improvement of Criminal Justice."[55] In 1972 at its convention in Dallas, the LCA would address that concern.

"POVERTY"

The convention took a more active approach when presented on the previous night with the proposed statement on poverty. Ten of the fourteen motions to amend the statement were accepted, and all ten sharpened the language or broadened the church's duty while also emphasizing the government's primary role in the elimination of poverty and the establishment of social justice. Clearly the majority of the convention's delegates shared in the enthusiasm for President Johnson's Great Society. They even defeated an amendment offered by Mr. Carl T. Swenson of the Wisconsin–Upper Michigan Synod "to look to other avenues than governmental programs as additional sources for help for those in need," including "enlisting talent from private industry."[56]

No one ever questioned that the LCA should have a statement on poverty in 1966, or that it should be called by that name. The political and religious ethos familiar to LCA leaders drew them into the national discussion on poverty's causes and remedies. Herluf Jensen, who had become the board's secretary for intergroup relations and economic affairs and was principle writer of the statement and the background study, recalls that he must have heard dozens of speeches in which the same analysis of the cycle of poverty was given and the minimum level of income required was discussed. He remembers both an openness and an optimism, since the government was putting in such a massive effort. This was the era of "grand schemes." "The Marshall Plan had worked in Europe, why not here?" He was present at the opening of the federal government's Office of Economic Opportunity in 1964 and recollects the huge number of small projects and the constant "barrage of materials" he studied to keep up with developments in the field.[57]

Johnson's War on Poverty fed a national conversation about the poor. An underlying tenet held that poverty was a matter of relative, not absolute, deprivation. All classes had been increasing in income during this century, while the bottom 20 percent of American families never caught up. If the cause of poverty was lack of income, then the proposed solution was income redistribution. The radical potential of this analysis was always present, but not permissible within a war that was to be fought without political casualties.

Johnson himself needed political capital from the war's momentum, and, therefore, untried programs that were haphazard in conception were launched prematurely on a massive scale. At their best, these programs dispensed needed services, notably through community health clinics, Head Start, and legal services. They also tended to provide the greatest financial aid to the middle-class professionals who administered them and to increase fragmentation and bureaucratic rivalry at all levels of government. The most radical approach, the Community Action Program, which called for the "maximum feasible participation" by residents and had the potential to redistribute decision-making power in local communities, would be domesticated rapidly as established local interests took charge.[58]

But such results could not have been foreseen in the heyday of the war's launching. Ironically, by the fall of 1965 when the church leaders were in the midst of committing their members to antipoverty ideals, the shadow of the Vietnam conflict had already fallen across the federal budget, and government bureaucrats responsible for antipoverty programs were reckoning with the administration's pullback on the domestic front.

The National Council of Churches served as an important center of the conversation about the poor among the mainline Protestant churches and provided their national staffs with resources and training. The LCA's Board of Social Ministry in turn disseminated such information throughout the church. For example, in April of 1965, at the same meeting where the board first reviewed the draft of its social statement, it also voted to provide synodical social action committees with the NCC's "Action Objectives for the Program of the Churches Toward the Elimination of Poverty."[59] By the fall, the board published its own study report, "The War on Poverty: An Analysis of the Economic Opportunity Act," based on the work of Robert E. Van Deusen. This essay made specific suggestions about church participation in such programs as Community Action, VISTA, Job Corps, Neighborhood Youth Corps, Work-Study and adaptations for the rural poor.

Jensen's initial draft of the social statement mirrored the day's social analysis. For his theological framework, he drew from Henry Clark's newly published book *The Christian Case Against Poverty*. The argument works by analogy from words of the prophets and of Jesus directed at the people of Israel and to the disciples. The book prescribes a prophetic role for the church in the American nation: "Motivated by the love of God in Christ, the church has this double commission: to serve human need and to testify prophetically for justice in the ordering of society and the distribution of its resources." The possibility that the American nation may not be the analogue of people of Israel is not considered. Jensen does not build a case from the civil righteousness of two kingdoms theology, although the recommended affirmations assume a "functional interaction" between church and state.

Theology was not the issue in the debate Jensen's work provoked within the board. Jensen proposed that the LCA affirm that "in an age of affluence, justice demands that every member of society be guaranteed—as a matter of right—that minimum standard of living upon which he can develop himself in accordance with his capacities."[60] Because the board could not reach consensus on guaranteed income, and staff members Jensen and Henry Whiting offered no revisions, the board appointed its own committee, with members Emil Weltz, Charles Bergstrom, Howard Gustafson, and H. Harrison Jenkins to work out differences.[61]

Jensen produced for the committee a background document which laid out the sources of his thinking and was later published as "The Church's Concern for Poverty," a "staff background study." Ten pages of the study rehearse Henry Clark's review of the treatment of poverty in the Old and New Testaments and the early church. Jensen then summarizes contemporary projections on the "population explosion" and the increasing shortage of employment ("structural unemployment") brought about by the "cybernetic revolution." Next, he lays out the statistics on poverty and interpretations of the American economy's increasing reliance on the artificial stimulation of consumer demand for expansion. He summarizes solutions proposed by such varied political commentators as Gabriel Kolko (*Wealth and Poverty in America*), Robert Theobald (*The Guaranteed Income*), and Milton Friedman (negative income tax) and quotes the 1964 report of the President's own Council of Economic Advisers that "the conquest of poverty is well within our power:

> About $11 billion would bring all poor families up to the $3000 income level we have taken to be the minimum for a decent life. The majority of the nation could simply tax themselves enough to provide the necessary income supplements to their less fortunate citizens.[62]

Ultimately the committee worked out a compromise.[63] Niebanck had a hand in revising Jensen's draft to include changes proposed by board members. The document is true to the substance of Jensen's proposals, but includes more explanation and nuance. For example, Jensen's sentence "Today's situation presents vastly new dimensions of justice and confronts serving love with opportunities hitherto undreamed of" is given a context. It is preceded by the statement: "The possibilities for good inherent in God's new gifts to mankind in technology will not be realized without changes in some attitudes and in some economic arrangements." Jensen's sentence is followed by a clause that allows for uncertainty and disagreement: "Realizing that no conclusive word can yet be spoken about new forms of social and economic order, or even of proper attitudes underlying them, the Lutheran Church in America sets forth the following ethical judgments." The statement's last paragraph also allows the possibility of Christians disagreeing on public policy, although "commitment to the struggle" [against poverty] is not "an open question."

A second significant change occurs in the discussion of employment. Jensen's proposal on guaranteed income is now embedded in a commentary on employment. On the one hand, where nations are wealthy, their national economies should "provide every able-bodied adult with the opportunity for meaningful employment" sufficient to procure the minimal necessities. On the other hand, where "a full employment economy is not possible or not desirable, or where personal or physical inadequacies exist," such countries should move "as readily as possible to assure to every person income adequate to secure the minimal standards of living."[64]

When the delegates considered this draft in Kansas City, they did not for the most part argue substance, but rather refined language. The significant substantive suggestion, which the convention adopted, came from D. Willard Zahn of Temple University, delegate from the Eastern Pennsylvania Synod. Zahn proposed that the LCA affirm not only that the government bears the responsibility to enact "innovative programs to counteract the causes of economic deprivation" but also that "any agencies"—presumably including those owned by the churches—shoulder the same obligation.[65]

76

"Poverty" was the denomination's fledgling effort in economic analysis. It offered no new word among the reform-minded of the day, but approved greater cooperation between public and voluntary agencies in attacking the roots of poverty. In effect, the statement reflected an emerging consensus on the future role of Lutheran social welfare agencies. It also staked out territory that would be more carefully surveyed in the thoroughgoing statement "Economic Justice" in 1980.

"VIETNAM"

The convention did not follow all of the board's recommendations. It rejected one statement and adopted another that had not been reviewed or even proposed by the board. The recommended statement on Religious Liberty, renamed the "Resolution on Religious Minorities," was referred back to the board for further work.[66] (See pp. 91ff.)

At the convention's opening session, the secretary's report on memorials indicated strong interest in a position statement on Vietnam. Three synods—New England, Ohio, and Minnesota—had presented memorials calling for convention action on the subject. Niebanck, who felt strongly that the church ought to speak on this issue, brought to Kansas City a draft of one he had written. His action was entirely unofficial, and he did not inform Harold Haas of his intentions until the convention.[67] Only the Minnesota Synod had proposed a text, that of a recent policy statement by the General Board of the National Council of Churches.[68]

By the summer of 1966 some LCA members who had been engaged in discussions of public policy since the early sixties were ready to press for action on a matter of questionable foreign policy. They reflected a national mood of perplexity and anxiety that had been increasing throughout 1965 as the war escalated. President Johnson had inherited Kennedy's approval of increasingly expensive and active military engagement in Vietnam. By December of 1964 the United States had sent a total of 15,000 military advisers and $500 million in aid. By August of 1965, Johnson, at the urging of the Pentagon, had maneuvered support for the Tonkin Gulf resolution, giving him extraordinary power to act in Southeast Asia in the face of increasing military activity by the Vietcong and North Vietnamese Army. Yet only in late winter of 1965, after his inauguration, did he authorize bombing raids on North Vietnam. By year's end, two hundred thousand American troops were present; by the end of 1966 the figure would stand at four hundred thousand.[69]

In early 1966 J. William Fulbright, as chairman of the Senate Foreign Relations Committee, hosted nationally televised hearings on war policy.

The hearings had the effect of legitimizing dissent. Intense discussion emerged nationwide, and Fulbright and others increasingly spoke out in opposition to U.S. policy. Meanwhile, American planes continued to bomb North Vietnam, while so-called "pacification" programs to promote economic, social, and political projects in South Vietnam had become subordinate to the fighting.[70]

Discussion of the issue had been regularly on the agenda of meetings sponsored by the National Council of Churches in 1965. Delegates to its sixth national Study Conference on World Order—with twenty-five assembled from the LCA by the Board of Social Ministry—in St. Louis in October had made policy suggestions to the United States for a negotiated settlement to the conflict.[71] The National Council's General Board had incorporated many of these in its policy statement of December 3, 1965, which acknowledged "sincere differences among us" on the war and its possible solutions, and pressed for increased efforts toward negotiations. The broad outlines of such an approach were directed somewhat ambiguously to the whole nation. The statement also advocated dialogue between Asian and U.S. Christians in cooperation with the East Asia Christian Conference."[72]

At the LCA convention, on Friday, June 25, the Committee on Resolutions presented Niebanck's statement anonymously for the consideration of the convention.[73] Action was postponed until the last evening of the convention on Tuesday, June 28, and came after passage of the statement on poverty. Unlike the National Council's statement, this proposal was directed unambiguously to the church, that is, to the LCA and its members. After listing as facts six troubling aspects of the escalating warfare, the statement rejects indifference among Christians, since "all men, regardless of nationality, politics, or ideology, are equally the object of God's judgment and loving kindness in Jesus Christ." The statement also asserts that Christians cannot accept the simplistic solutions of either extended war or the unilateral withdrawal of U.S. troops.

Most of the discussion on the floor of the convention centered around Niebanck's sixth fact: the troublesome "current struggle of dissident non-Communist elements in the South Vietnamese population to secure representative government." Delegates disagreed among themselves over this characterization, particularly over the use of the term *non-Communist*, and offered twelve amendments before settling for the compromise of vague language. The approved substitute motion spoke of "the turmoil and frustration among the people of South Vietnam in seeking to establish representative self-government."

As delegates struggled over this section late that night, they reflected a national debate over the continued usefulness of a monolithic understanding of communism, one legacy of the Cold War. The only substantive change in the statement boldly expressed this disagreement. Pastor Gordon C. Lund of the Virginia Synod proposed a fifth danger in the list of views to be avoided when Christians studied the issue: to "ignore or underestimate international Communism's declared purposes of aggression, conquest and destruction of freedom."[74] Niebanck recalls the sorrow he felt when the convention adopted this "Cold War amendment." He found it a serious flaw in a statement that he thought was "irenic and capacious enough" to support a range of viewpoints. Today, he suspects that its inclusion enabled the majority of delegates to support the statement.[75]

On June 29, the day after the LCA convention adopted its statement on Vietnam, American aircraft were bombing oil depots near Hanoi and Haiphong. The war would go on. By the next convention, more people had become resolute in their judgments about Vietnam, and the board's recommended statement on selective conscientious objection would attract much of the convention's energy.

The sixties were testing the young church body in ways unanticipated by its founders. With so many issues of public policy under scrutiny, church members felt constrained to make church policy. The LCA had become a forum for the political issues troubling its members. A younger voice within the board's staff had grown more prominent in these discussions. Richard Niebanck, staff assistant on research and program, had proven himself in the formulation of the statements "Capital Punishment" and "Vietnam" and in the revisions on "Poverty." As a seminarian at Philadelphia he had been a member of Lazareth's first class in systematic theology and social ethics and had gone on for a year of graduate work at the University of Chicago (1957–58). He had joined the staff in 1963 after five years in the pastorate at Christ Church on East Nineteenth Street in Manhattan. Niebanck's reflections on church and society would continue to shape the church's social statements for two decades more.

NOTES

1. Matusow, *The Unraveling of America*, 120-27, 153-216.
2. BSM Minutes, "Constitution of the Board of Social Ministry of the LCA," 23–24 July 1962, 8.
3. LCA, *Minutes . . . 1964*, 677.
4. BSM Minutes, 17–19 November 1964, Exhibit G, 1-2.

5. Memorandum prepared by Haas for Executive Council meeting, 29–30 January 1965, quoted in BSM Executive Committee Minutes, 26 January 1965, 6-7.

6. BSM Executive Committee Minutes, 19 September 1962, 2.

7. LCA, *Minutes . . . 1966*, 498-502.

8. BSM Minutes, 20–22 April 1965, Exhibit W, 1, 3.

9. Gibson Winter, *The Suburban Captivity of the Churches* (Garden City, N.Y.: Doubleday & Co., 1961).

10. BSM Minutes, 20–22 April 1965, Exhibit W, 4.

11. Ibid., 1, 7.

12. BSM Minutes, 15–17 February 1966, 11.

13. BSM Minutes, 17–19 November 1964, 23; Agenda, 12, notes Lazareth's willingness to revise the piece and his judgment that although "some of the material in the pamphlet also appears in the final section of 'Church and State: A Lutheran Perspective,' . . . duplication may be a beneficial reinforcement." Lazareth had worked out his position in his doctoral dissertation, published as *Luther on the Christian Home* (Philadelphia: Muhlenberg Press, 1960).

14. [William H. Lazareth], *Social Ministry: Biblical and Theological Perspectives* (BSM, LCA, 1976), 7-8.

15. Ibid., 8-9.

16. Ibid.

17. Ibid., 10.

18. Ibid., 11; BSM Minutes, 5–7 October 1965, Exhibit P-2, 1.

19. BSM Minutes, 15–17 February 1966, 11.

20. Sittler, interview with author, 11 September 1985.

21. BSM Minutes, 17–19 November 1964, 11-14.

22. BSM Minutes, 20–22 April 1965, 16; Agenda, 4-5.

24. See, for example, report from Committee on Civil and International Affairs, BSM Minutes, 5–7 October 1965, 16; Agenda, 7-8.

25. BSM Minutes, 20–22 April 1965, Exhibit F, 2.

26. Joseph Rinderknecht (interview with author, Toledo, Ohio, 27 May 1986) indicated that he was sympathetic to fellow Ohioan Karl Hertz's long-standing criticism of the two kingdoms theory.

27. Haas, interview with author, 17 February 1987.

28. LCA, *Minutes . . . 1966*, 21–29 June 1966, 514-15; BSM Minutes, 5–6 October 1965, 14-15.

29. LCA, *Minutes . . . 1966*, 514.

30. Cornelsen, interview with author, 21 February 1986.

31. Haas, interview with author, 6 September 1985.

32. BSM Minutes, 23–25 April 1963, Exhibit H, 1.

33. Ibid., 35-36.

34. The total number of Lutherans accounted for nearly one-sixth of the 303 delegates in attendance. NCC, "Report of the National Study Conference on Church and State held at Columbus, Ohio, 4–7 February 1964" (NCC, New York, 1964, Mimeographed), 1.

35. BSM Minutes, 19–21 November 1963; Agenda, 26; BSM Minutes, 25–27 February 1964, 6-8.

36. "Report of the National Study Conference on Church and State," 1; Dean Kelley, interview with author, New York, 11 April 1986.

37. "Separation and Interaction of Church and State," *A Journal of Church and State* 6 (Winter 1964):147-53.

38. Kelley, interview with author, 11 April 1986.

39. George Forell, telephone interview with author, 13 April 1987.

40. BSM Minutes, 20–22 April 1965, Exhibit G, 1.

41. BSM Executive Committee Minutes, 26 January 1965, 3.

42. In the Spring of 1965, the staff circularized the BSM, synod presidents and social ministry committees, the LCA Cabinet of Executives, and seminary and college libraries with a packet of pronouncements on the subject from the LCA, the NLC, the ALC, and the NCC. BSM Minutes, 20–22 April 1965, 17-18; Agenda, 7-8.

43. BSM Minutes, 17–19 November 1964, Exhibit J.

44. BSM Minutes, 5–7 October 1965, 14; Exhibit J, 1-3.

45. LCA, *Minutes . . . 1966*, 451-53.

46. Ibid.

47. ULCA, *Minutes . . . 1960*, 1110-1111. Rev. Edward K. Rogers of the Pittsburgh Synod read the letter and then moved that action on the statement be postponed until the next convention. After rejecting his motion, delegates defeated the motion to adopt the statement, 238 pro, 248 contra.

48. BSM Minutes, 5–7 October 1965, 16-17; Exhibit L.

49. See BSM, "Capital Punishment," Study Report, No. 5, April 1966.

50. Ibid., "Civil and International Affairs," Exhibit A, 1-3.

51. ULCA, *Minutes . . . 1960*, 800-801.

52. BSM Minutes, 15–17 February 1966, Civil and International Affairs, Exhibit A, 5-6.

53. BSM Minutes, 15–17 February 1966, 59-60.

54. Richard Niebanck, telephone interview with author, 15 July 1987.

55. LCA, *Minutes . . . 1966,* 821-22.

56. Ibid., 808-9.

57. Herluf Jensen, telephone interview with author, 13 February 1987.

58. See Matusow, *The Unraveling of America*, 97-127, 217-71.

59. BSM Minutes, 20–22 April 1965, 18.

60. BSM Minutes, 20–22 April 1965, Exhibit S, 1; BSM Minutes, 5–7 October 1965; Agenda, 10.

61. BSM Minutes, 5–7 October 1965, 17.

62. Herluf Jensen, "The Church's Concern for Poverty" (A Background Study), BSM, LCA, Mimeographed, 1966, 22.

63. Two versions of the statement appear in the minutes of the February 15–17, 1966, meeting. See "Intergroup Relations and Economic Affairs," Exhibit A, 21-23 and Exhibit A-1, 1-2.

64. BSM Minutes, 15–17 February 1966, 42-44.

65. LCA, *Minutes . . . 1966*, 808-11.

66. LCA, *Minutes . . . 1966*, 613. This distinction between "statement" and "resolution" had been developing throughout LCA's early years and echoed the NCC's division between comprehensive policy on the one hand, and reactions governed by that policy to specific circumstances, on the other.

67. Niebanck, telephone interview with author, 15 July 1987.

68. LCA, *Minutes . . . 1966*, 57, 58, 616, 620.

69. Stanley Karnow, *Vietnam: A History* (New York: The Viking Press, 1983), 679-81.

70. Ibid., 486.

71. BSM Minutes, 15–17 February 1966, 65-68.

72. "A Policy Statement of the National Council of the Churches of Christ in the U.S.A. on Vietnam," adopted by the General Board, 3 December 1965.

73. LCA, *Minutes . . . 1966*, 620. The text of the proposed statement can only be found as an addendum appended to p. 621 in the official set of minutes kept in the ELCA Archives.

74. Ibid., 812-13.

75. Niebanck, telephone interview with author, 15 July 1987.

5

CONTINUING EFFORTS, 1967–1968

Franklin Clark Fry dictated his report to the LCA's 1968 convention from his hospital bed one week before his death. He prefaced his commentary with a description of the times:

> It would be a cliché to say that we live in . . . a time of gestation of a vastly different era that is in the process of being born. Many are exhilarated,— others so panicky that they are ready to throw the rigging overboard; all of us are at least perplexed and to a degree insecure.[1]

Two years of horrific riots, assassination, and carnage in Vietnam had polarized the nation. Fry died of cancer on June 6, the same day that bullet wounds inflicted by Sirhan Sirhan claimed Robert F. Kennedy's life. In one of his last official acts, Fry attended the funeral of Martin Luther King, Jr., slain by a rifle shot on April 4.

During that violent spring of 1968 President Johnson lost further credibility as his policies failed and protest mounted. Inflation plagued the economy. After King's death rioting Blacks once again scorched urban ghettos. Black self-styled revolutionaries railed against American political values, including integration. Poor people denounced the Great Society. January's Tet Offensive belied all prior claims of American military success in Vietnam, while draft resistance captured the imagination of the young and old who joined forces in the new left.

On March 31, Johnson threw election politics into disarray by withdrawing from the presidential race and depriving Democrats and Republicans alike of a scapegoat for the nation's ills. Only now in retrospect can we understand that his rout belonged to a larger saga, the unruly retreat of the American electorate from the liberalism dominant since 1960. Richard Nixon moved in to capitalize on the mood with the campaign rhetoric of "law and order."[2] The Democratic party's Chicago convention in late August was the setting for an ugly parody of the nation's divisions as antiwar demonstrators faced the fury of Mayor Daley's police force.

The seismic shift forecast by Franklin Clark Fry was occurring along lines other than he had predicted. Many Lutherans, along with other middle-class Americans who had cut their political eyeteeth on the activism of the sixties, would now have to work to recover their bearings. With the loss of a widespread liberal consensus, neither the Good nor the possible good could remain unexamined assumptions for would-be prophets.

The three social statements presented by the Board of Social Ministry to the Atlanta convention reflected in varying degrees the social upheaval. "Conscientious Objection," the most topical, attracted the most controversy. "The Church and Social Welfare" and "Religious Liberty in the United States," with longer histories and fewer symbolic issues, provoked less debate.

All were developed under a new committee structure, itself evidence of a growing desire to regulate the formulation of statements more closely. As staff and board jockeyed for a new understanding of their roles during the biennium preceding the convention, they chose contemporary organizational methods. By relying increasingly on the professional staff and establishing more rules for procedure, they advanced the bureaucratization of social ministry at the national level. The outcome would be greater centralization of the board's work in the salaried staff and increasing use of the social statements as expressions of policy.

Begun under Harold Haas, these changes became formalized under Carl E. Thomas, the new executive secretary. Haas left his position as executive director in August of 1966. In October, the board, in consultation with President Fry, elected Carl E. Thomas to the position. Thomas would serve until 1972, when the board's functions would be absorbed by the Division for Mission in North America. Thomas, who had joined the staff in 1963 as secretary of agencies and institutions, came to the attention of the LCA leadership for his skillful resolution of the financial crisis at the Florida Lutheran Retirement Center.[3] He was a graduate of Hamma Divinity School, with ten years of ministry at the Oesterlen Home in Springfield, Ohio, and a master's degree in social work from Ohio State University.[4]

In his first report to the board in February of 1967, he stated that the experiment with organizing the board's work in "issues" and "operations" had proven to be "an artificial dichotomy," since the church always needed to be guided in its response to issues. He would center the board's work around three "priorities": program and leadership, study in Christian social concerns, and social services.[5] After staff positions and committees had been realigned, he also oversaw the creation of *ad hoc* committees to help the Committee on Social Concerns monitor the drafting of social statements.[6]

In 1968 Senator Philip A. Hart's request that the LCA testify in favor of abolishing the federal death penalty precipitated further development in the notion of policy. The board adopted a staff proposal to limit testimony strictly to "matters to which the Lutheran Church in America has spoken officially through either its Biennial Convention or its Executive Council." Moreover, such testimony had to include the disclaimer that the board did not speak for the members, congregations, and constituent synods of the LCA, but only for the church in convention or the Executive Council. Either the board or its executive committee had to authorize the appearance of its representative before a government agency. No steps toward such testimony were to be initiated "without prior approval of the executive secretary with the concurrence of the president of the board and in consultation with the president of the church," who was also to receive the content of such testimony in writing prior to any testimony.[7] There were to be no loose cannons on the ark.

The Atlanta convention held in late June of 1968 was designed to harness the political concerns of delegates in behalf of church unity and the urban poor. Atlanta had been chosen as the convention site to strengthen relations with those in the southern synods who felt most pressed by the passage in 1964 of the race relations statement. Two guest speakers addressed the convention as part of the board's report: Honorable Herbert T. Jenkins, chief of the Atlanta Department of Police and a member of President Johnson's Advisory Committee on Civil Disorders, and the Rev. Martin Luther King, Sr., pastor of Atlanta's Ebenezer Baptist Church.[8]

The LCA's Board of American Missions proposed the adoption of a special churchwide appeal, later entitled ACT, for $8 million in emergency funds for riot-torn communities. The Board of Social Ministry recommended to the synods its own program focus on "Justice and Social Change—the Urban Crisis" for the next biennium.[9] The convention voted to adopt a different version of the special appeal, proposed by William Ellis of the Executive Council, and also the program focus of the Board of Social Ministry.[10] Delegates also adopted a resolution from the floor to urge Congress to pass strong gun control legislation and to instruct the Board of Social Ministry to prepare study materials for congregations "on gun control, violence and law enforcement."[11]

85

"CONSCIENTIOUS OBJECTION"

President Fry's printed convention report anticipated the gathering's most contentious issue—the proposed statement on conscientious objection. He argued that "life itself" had foisted this issue on the church and offered as proof that "every other church assembly that has been held within the past year has found itself confronted with the same demand to declare itself."[12]

In early October of 1967, Richard Niebanck had argued in a written brief to the board's newly constituted *ad hoc* Committee on Peace and Justice for a statement on selective conscientious objection.[13] At its core, his position depended on Lutheran theology. The absence of any distinctively Lutheran statement on the subject left the church in the "curious position" of providing no guidance for those who stood within the tradition of Augustine and Luther, while supporting "those who, at least in the matter of war, deviate from it" with "convictions of an essentially Anabaptist or Tolstoyan character" in opposition to all wars.[14] The Executive Council's statement of conscientious objection, adopted in 1964 to accommodate LCA members seeking this status, provided only for the mechanics of recording such a position with the church and for their pastoral support.[15]

The committee had already received the advice of Rufus Cornelsen, Philip A. Johnson, and O. Frederick Nolde that the church should move with exceeding caution on the matter of war and that perhaps a statement on world community ought to take precedence.[16] Introducing a sense of urgency, Niebanck noted an ever-increasing number of inquiries from LCA conscientious objectors.[17] Furthermore, during the previous August the council of the Lutheran Student Association of America had adopted a statement based on Article 16 of the Augsburg Confession in support of *selective* conscientious objection.[18] When the Eastern Pennsylvania Synod in convention requested the Executive Council to study the same issue for the guidance of the church, President Fry expected the board to take action.[19]

Although Niebanck had spent the previous summer of 1967 preparing drafts of a background study and statement, along with his brief to the *ad hoc* committee, nevertheless in the absence of both Niebanck and a committee quorum at the October board meeting, the board was unable to assess his work. Instead, the board directed the staff to proceed with the formulation of a draft statement and supporting study document.[20]

Coincidentally, October of 1967 proved to be the most dramatic month in the draft resistance movement. On October 12, *The New York Review* published a "Call to Resist Illegitimate Authority," signed by 121 of America's leading intellectuals. "Stop the Draft Week," scheduled later in the month, included the storming of the Pentagon by antiwar activists.[21] The times would make it hard for advocates of the LCA's statement to dissociate its carefully nuanced reasoning from the bombastic, antiauthoritarianism of the more radical antiwar activists.

In February of 1968 the board approved Niebanck's manuscript *Conscience, War, and the Selective Objector* for the Christian Social Responsibility series.[22] In it he provided a "theology of conscience," a reappraisal of the "just war" theory and the rights of conscience under civil authority, and a discussion of the political, legal, and ecclesial aspects of selective objection. The forty-six-page essay, completed without benefit of consultation, was the only coherent religious argument of its kind when it was released and soon became the board's best-selling study.

In the book, Niebanck claims that Lutheran ethics does not consist in applying immutable truths to particular cases since sin and history change circumstances continually. The just war tradition represents historical experience, not changeless law. Can war be justified in the particular instance? What is needed in an age of "international power politics" is a kind of Niebuhrian political realism that seeks to retain the connection between ethics and politics because human beings can learn from experience and act "to discover and execute approximations of justice." Selective conscientious objectors are among those who link politics, ethics, and religion in their questioning of "crisis management" of the war in Vietnam with its unclear goals and tactics. They "are not moral purists indulging in the luxury of self-purgation." What distinguishes them from "some other protestors" is "the practical and therefore the political character of their urgency."[23]

The board did not adopt the Niebanck's study without suggesting a modification. There were times, such as during the heat of battle, when, for the sake of a military unit's security, the Lutheran balance between the individual's duty to obey conscience and the rights of civil and military authority ought to shift toward obedience.[24]

While his study report met with board approval, the statement he abstracted from it provoked a three-hour discussion before its passage by the twenty-one-member board. Three members asked that their votes be recorded: Philip A. R. Anttila, negative; H. Harrison Jenkins and Ray W. Westergren, in abstention. Anttila, a parish pastor originally from the Suomi Synod, requested permission to file a minority report in both the minutes of the board and to the convention. Board president Charles

Bergstrom ruled to admit the report in the minutes, but not to forward it to the convention.[25]

While Lazareth, who chaired the Committee on Peace and Justice, supported the statement, he also helped Anttila frame his minority report.[26] Anttila's concerns centered around the delusions of conscience and the impossibility of judging motives. He believed that "while the church is called to provide a supportive ministry of the conscientious objector, it is not called to encourage conscientious objection as such, as this statement tends to do." He then suggested as an alternative statement the elimination of all references to objection to particular wars in the statement.[27]

At the convention, George Forell stood in for Lazareth at the last minute as the theologian representing the board's position. Board member Harold Lohr, who had been an infantry officer in combat during World War II, presided and gave the history and logic of the statement. Lohr recalls that the correspondence the board received on the statement prior to the convention had been "overwhelmingly negative."[28] Forell recalls the intense debate which stretched over three sessions. He judges that delegates shifted from four-fifths in opposition to four-fifths in support and thereby made the denomination the first nonpacifist church to endorse selective conscientious objection.[29] (See Appendix, "Conscientious Objection.")

Forell used the Augsburg Confession as his primary tool to teach the reasoning that underlay the statement. He remembers his efforts with deep satisfaction: "In those days, an LCA convention could develop a corporate identity; it could argue, learn and change its mind."[30] Niebanck attributes the statement's passage to Forell's "wit and charisma," but also recalls the support of Martin Heinecken and Edmund A. Steimle, noted preaching professor at Union Seminary in New York, who described the statement as "theology with its overalls on."[31] Board member Robert Herhold, a pastor from California and former student of Joseph Sittler, believes that the logic of the two-realms argument had less to do with its passage than the atmosphere of respect for conscience created by Martin Luther King's witness.[32]

Convention minutes demonstrate that church leaders were deeply divided on the issue. At the statement's first session on Tuesday evening, June 25, the opposition lined up at the microphones immediately. Within the first moments there were motions to keep the convention from recommending the study report until action on the statement had been completed, to "commend" the statement for study and discussion rather than "adopt" it as "official policy," and to substitute part of the ULCA's 1940 statement on conscientious objection. Notice was also given that the entire text of the ULCA's "Statement on the Rights and Duties of the Christian Citizen in Emergencies of War" would be offered should the substitute motion fail.[33] Delegates rejected the first two motions, and then time ran out.

On the following afternoon, the statement was treated as "a special order" starting at 3 P.M. Beginning after a dinner break, the third session did not end until 9:45 that evening. The first proposed substitute was withdrawn, and Joseph Rinderknecht offered instead the ULCA statement.[34] The effect of Rinderknecht's motion was to make conscientious objection a minor consideration of individual rights based on the scriptural principle of the "supreme moral responsibility of the individual conscience" in a statement which emphasized the "duty to render loyal support and service to the nation whose protection and benefits" the Christian citizen enjoys.[35]

The remainder of the session was spent amending both the original and the substitute. Reuben T. Swanson, president of the Nebraska Synod, moved to delete all references to selective conscientious objection. His motion was declared out of order since it "would negate the entire intent of the statement" and a negative vote would accomplish the same result.[36] Former board president Alfred Stone succeeded in adding the phrase *while rejecting conscientious objection as ethically normative* to the sentence "Lutheran teaching . . . requires that ethical decisions in political matters be made in the context of the competing claims of peace, justice, and freedom." When the time for amendments came to an end, Forell presented the board's case and the motion to substitute was defeated. A pattern had become clear: most of the speakers in behalf of the statement were members of the clergy; most opponents belonged to the laity.[37]

Only one amendment to the board's proposed statement was adopted in the evening session, the addition of a phrase by A. Roy Anderson: "and until such time as these exemptions are so provided, persons who conscientiously object to a particular war are reminded that they must be willing to accept applicable civil or criminal penalties for their action."[38] In a division of the house, 426 had voted for the statement, 146 against, and 7 had abstained. Of the sixty-four delegates who requested that their negative votes be recorded, nearly two-thirds were lay members. Future officers James R. Crumley, Jr., and Swanson were among the named dissenters.[39] The nation's polarization was mirrored in the convention's divided house and left the church with the dilemma of keeping faith with principles and with the people.

89

"RELIGIOUS LIBERTY IN
THE UNITED STATES"

Religious liberty had again become an issue during the 1960s. The church body's membership in the National Council of Churches made LCA leaders familiar, even as their ULCA and Augustana predecessors had been, with the efforts of the council's Department of Religious Liberty. Pastors George Harkins and Paul Empie served as vice-chair and chair of that department at various times during those years and oversaw the work of its executive, Dean M. Kelley.[40] NCC leaders were pressing the right of the Amish to exemption from compulsory education.

At the National Council's Study Conference on Church and State in 1964, George Forell, who would have the major influence on the LCA's statement, supplied the working paper on religious liberty. When he specified the roots of religious liberty in civil liberty rather than in Christian freedom, he attracted criticism from other Protestants who did not value such distinctions and were not prepared for his positive, Lutheran treatment of the state's role.[41] He differentiated between freedom from the "bondage of the will" in sin, death, and the demonic forces and "religious liberty," a relatively new emphasis historically on the "right of the human race and of each person to worship or not to worship God or the gods."[42] His seminal article was published later that year in *The Lutheran Quarterly*.[43]

Forell's framework would shape the LCA's statement on religious liberty, although at first the board took a less theological and more topical approach. In 1964 the Minnesota Synod asked the church "to register its deep concern through proper channels of our government regarding the religious harassment of the Hebrew people in Russia and other areas." Clarence C. Stoughton, president of Wittenberg College, offered a substitute motion which was adopted—that the memorial be referred to the Board of Social Ministry with the request "that a statement on relations between Christians and Jews in present-day society be prepared for submission to the next convention if possible."[44]

At the board's request, the staff had drafted a "Resolution on Harassment of Jewish People" in the spring of 1965 for recommendation.[45] When reactions to the proposed statement were solicited in late 1965 from members of synodical social ministry committees,[46] at least half the responses indicated dissatisfaction over its vagueness.[47]

At its preconvention meeting in 1966, the board abandoned the original resolution for a two-paragraph statement. The first paragraph noted the church's awareness of "instances of discrimination, harassment, and persecution of religious groups in many nations." It specifically mentioned the Minnesota Synod's concern by name, but also the liberty of the Amish in the United States, Protestants in Spain, and Christians in Eastern Europe. The second paragraph generalized the church's concern for "the right of all religious groups to the free expression of their faith, including especially free assembly, the practice of ritual, and the propagation of the faith" and called upon church members and "our representatives" in government "to be sensitive to the needs and rights of religious groups in our nations, and to do all that is possible to secure the religious liberty of all men."[48]

The statement, again labeled "a resolution" at the convention in Kansas City, was nevertheless rejected.[49] Delegates agreed with two professors at state universities who voiced their disgruntlement with its limited scope. George Forell moved to refer the resolution back to the board and Charles Y. Glock moved to instruct the board to provide the 1968 convention with "a comprehensive position statement on Religious Liberty, supported by a study report." Glock, lay delegate from the Pacific Southwest Synod and a professor at the University of California, Berkeley, had recently written with Rodney Stark the book *Christian Beliefs and Anti-Semitism*, a sociological study.[50] Glock's motion also stipulated that the study should provide a theological framework and give attention to "the liberties of persons who elect not to be religious."[51]

Following the convention, the board proceeded to reformulate the statement and sponsored an "exploratory consultation" in December of 1966 with theologian Carl Braaten, sociologist Charles Glock, law professor Paul Kauper, and philosopher Romaine Gardner. The consultants and staff agreed that a statement ought to articulate "a theological understanding of the foundation and character of religious liberty" and focus upon the individual's religious rights "while, in a general way, stating the nature of corporate religious expression."[52] The consultation proposed three study papers on religious liberty from the theological, legal, and sociological viewpoints. Kauper volunteered to cover the legal issues.[53] Glock located and agreed to supervise a Lutheran graduate student at the Graduate Theological Union, Dwight Oberholtzer, to write on religious liberty and religious intolerance from a "socio-historical" perspective.[54] Braaten was working in other areas, and so the staff approached Forell.

After a second consultation in which the authors, along with Glock and staff members Thomas and Tilberg, had reviewed the three manuscripts, the board adopted them for publication in the Christian Social Responsibility series.[55] Tilberg served as editor of the new volume *Religious Liberty*, and began to draft a statement and to solicit responses

91

before bringing a version to the board's preconvention meeting in February of 1968.[56]

As in the case of the other two statements presented at the Atlanta convention, the background study was crucial. Forell's essay warrants particular attention because of its influence on the convention statement. The architecture of his argument remains the same as in his papers for the NCC and for *The Lutheran Quarterly*.[57]

After distinguishing between Christian freedom and religious liberty, Forell uses the remainder of his argument to demonstrate how much they have to do with each other for the Christian and for the church in the preservation of all civil liberties. The Christian, freed by Christ, can foreswear idolatries of religion, politics, economics, nation, or race and therefore may recognize the impact of such idolatries on the civil liberties of others. Even though religious liberty is not dependent on Christian freedom, because the Christian knows that "all civil liberties are rooted in the fact that man is created by God for fellowship with Him," respect for religious liberty is "not only a demand of civil justice but a necessary implication of the Christian faith."[58]

Forell is at pains to present a view of religious freedom that is consistent and can help the church guard itself from ideologically motivated intolerance. The church has "no ideological concern" over the nature of civil community, but only "a practical concern with its functioning." The very absence of ideological political commitment necessarily means that the church prefers "open societies" in which "there is room for politically uncommitted people whose ultimate concern is not the state or even society" and in which there are other checks and balances to correct excess.[59] In the only major addition for this publication, the study calls the church to exercise its religious liberty by serving as a forum for the discussion of controversial issues surrounding "due process of law." The church should provide "an umbrella of faith under which people who disagree profoundly on matters of public policy can debate the issues and perhaps reconcile their differences."[60]

By the time of the board's preconvention meeting, the staff had circulated early drafts of the proposed statement to "some 700" people, including board members, other LCA denominational executives, synod presidents, staff and members of synodical social action committees, executives of social service agencies and "a select group of other competent persons inside and outside the LCA." The final changes made by the board sharpened the imprint of Forell's theological analysis and limited the scope of the statement to the United States, since Canada had no explicitly stated bill of rights.[61]

Tilberg recalls President Fry's avid interest in the topic and his scrupulous attention to its language.[62] Fry noted in his comments to the convention "the pitfalls" inherent in any assertion of the "equal right to adore or ignore God" or in giving "paramount value" to human freedom rather than to God's claims. Fry accepted "the key to the riddle" found in the emphases on "the non-coerciveness of God" and on "natural law which goes rather further than I, at least, have been accustomed to go."[63]

Fry's remarks did not fuel any convention debate. In fact, of the three amendments proposed from the floor, only one touched on the substance of the case. William H. Baumer, lay delegate from Upper New York Synod, moved a substitute sentence on the limits to religious liberty, which was adopted: "Nothing less than a serious and immediately threatened *violation of other basic human rights* [rather than, *breach of the peace*] should warrant restrictions on religious liberty."[64] When the convention adopted "Religious Liberty," the church had gained both a platform from which to support those whose religious rights were jeopardized and an account of its own obligations in the free exercise of religion.[65] (See Appendix, "Religious Liberty in the United States.")

"THE CHURCH AND SOCIAL WELFARE"

The easy passage of "The Church and Social Welfare," one of the last items on the agenda of the Atlanta convention, masked its significance. In an age when government involvement had increased dramatically, the statement articulated the meaning of "institutional separation" and "functional interaction" for Lutheran social service institutions, the largest system of American church-related agencies outside of Catholic Charities.

Little wonder that Dean Kelley and others in the National Council of Churches had difficulty appreciating the Lutheran position. Most other Protestants had less at stake either theologically or institutionally. For Lutherans, respect for the God-given role of the state made such cooperation theologically possible. The institutional legacy of inner missions put Lutherans in the position of having to decide on a case-by-case basis the appropriate kind of cooperation.

A revolution in welfare had been occurring since the years of the New Deal as the federal government began providing the needy with various forms of social insurance and service. Government initiatives along with the growth and diversity of urban populations, challenged church bodies and other associations in the so-called "voluntary" sector to redefine their role in social welfare. Lutherans, under the leadership of Clarence E. Krumbholz and Henry Whiting of the National Lutheran Council's Division of Welfare, and Henry Wind of the Missouri Synod, had been at work since World War II reforming the institutional approach to social welfare adopted during the inner mission movement for a "social services" orientation.

The LCA's statement was the distillation of a conversation begun in the last years of the ULCA, when Harold Haas had pressed its Executive Board to authorize a study commission on "Christian Service."[66] In 1959 the board appointed theologians, sociologists, and agency executives to an inter-Lutheran Commission to Study the Role of the Church in Social Welfare.[67]

Four years after its first meeting, the commission completed *The Church in Social Welfare*, published by the LCA's Board of Social Ministry in the Christian Social Responsibility series.[68] The study was designed for a specific audience—leaders of synods and of Lutheran institutions and agencies. These bodies were newly charged under the LCA Constitution with developing lines of oversight and accountability through the regional synods. Haas recalls expressions of appreciation at a time when these new connections were not yet comfortable; although Harold Reisch, former staff member for the board's "special ministries," recollects that the real excitement and debate occurred not after the study's release but within the commission itself.[69]

The study is divided into two parts: perspectives and judgments on social welfare. The theological grounding for social welfare is central in both and reflects Haas' own concern. He was among those influenced by Anders Nygren of the Church of Sweden who spoke at the Lutheran World Conference on Social Responsibility held at Wittenberg College in 1957 prior to the Minneapolis assembly of the Lutheran World Federation. This gathering, convened by Henry Whiting, considered the church's role in the welfare state. Nygren argued that prior to redeveloping its social services, the church needed "a theology of serving," of "the diakonia." Service does not simply go hand in hand with faith, but "has its place at the core of the gospel" because Christ was the suffering servant who gave himself for all."[70]

Haas, who drafted the section on "judgments," reiterated the theme in *The Church and Social Welfare* when he wrote that "Christian service is one form of the witness of the church to the salvation and newness of life available by God's grace in Jesus Christ. This *diakonia* is always inextricably involved in and with the other forms of witness, namely *leitourgia* (worship) and *kerygma* (proclamation)."[71]

94

After summarizing the theological orientation presented earlier by Martin Heinecken, Haas located social welfare within the broader category of "diakonic service in contemporary society." Social welfare includes "the response of Christian persons to their vocation; the social ministry of the congregation; special ministries to handicapped, disadvantaged or isolated persons in our society; specialized service agencies and institutions; and participation by Christians, both individually and corporately, in the formulation of social policy."

He expressed the commission's consensus on a number of policy guidelines. Most important, the commission opted for close interaction among public, church-related, and voluntary sectors of social welfare. They understood public welfare as the government's "basic mechanism" for meeting needs that it ought "in justice" to meet. Public financing can fund services in all kinds of welfare agencies; precise needs can only be determined "through public discussion and debate." Such interaction leaves Lutherans "in tension" with the other two sectors, a "constructive" tension if all "recognize and maintain respect for the unique motivations and contributions of one another."[72]

Haas also warned that "there is little diaconic reality" if church-related agencies have no "ecclesiastical visibility" and provide only those "relatively light, easily reimbursed needs" and ignore the hard problems for which there is no funding. His caveat is based on the challenge faced by the church at a time when the 190 agencies and institutions related to its synods spent $40 million, of which only $5 million had come from church sources, and when the proportion of church financing was expected to decline further.[73]

At the convention President Fry commented that the statement "The Church and Social Welfare" built upon three prior ones: "Race Relations," "Church and State: A Lutheran Perspective," and "Poverty."[74] His allusion helps to explain some differences in tone and substance between the study of 1964 and the statement of 1968. By 1968 not only was there a greater sense of social crisis, but poverty programs inaugurated a new wave of government involvement in social welfare. In addition, the denomination's leadership was more solidly aligned with the social reform movement and more committed to bringing along the rest of the church.

Despite or perhaps because of the four years of discussion compressed into the background study, board and staff members had difficulty deciding how much to include in a statement. Numerous drafts were developed between April of 1965 and February of 1968, when the board adopted the statement for recommendation to the convention.[75] Recollections of participants indicate no significant disagreement on content.[76]

95

The draft defines the changes that have occurred in social welfare, lists basic considerations for the church's response, affirms certain directions, and concludes with a theological interpretation of social welfare.

The statement emphasizes the church's potential for studied, creative, and flexible responses to contemporary needs, and urges the church to strive to correct welfare policies in any sectors which "threaten the rights and dignity of those who require aid" and to involve those who are served "in determining the services and the manner in which they are administered."[77]

In its conclusion, the statement takes greater theological risks than the study had. Drawing on Nygren's approach, it speaks of "the indelible mark of servanthood" that Jesus Christ gave "to his people" along with "the mission to identify with all who are disadvantaged and suffer hurt." This approach is not without its own snares, since it uses Jesus' life as ethical model and makes the pursuit of the common good dependent on redemption. The proposed statement demonstrated that the board, wanting the church and its agencies to be more activist, remained anxious about a motivating force.

In convention, one of the "basic considerations" drew the most debate by rekindling the issue of a guaranteed annual income first raised in the 1966 statement on "Poverty." The proposed version left the matter ambiguous by first stating that "justice requires that the state promote the general welfare" and then asserting that "income adequate to maintain a decent and healthful standard of living, education, health services, and a wholesome living environment" was among the means to be provided. After considerable discussion, representatives of the board, under questioning, indicated that this item "was not intended to speak to that issue" and were willing for the ambiguous reference to income to be deleted.[78]

Dr. Martin Heinecken successfully proposed striking the infinitive phrase *to cooperate with others of like concern* in a sentence that dealt entirely with the motivation of Christians for working to resolve social problems. A. Earl Mgebroff, M.D., of the Texas-Louisiana Synod succeeded with his proposal to add an affirmation: "This church reaffirms its belief that social welfare services carried on through the church either in its individual or corporate expression are a joyous and selfless response of love growing out of faith in Christ."[79] Following this addition, the statement passed. (See Appendix, "The Church and Social Welfare.")

The statement's and the commission's agonizing effort to theologize the motivation for social ministry contains an irony. At the very time when "institutional interaction" with the state through programs and funding had become characteristic of Lutheran social welfare, church policy emphasized almost exclusively the activating power of the gospel. Thus, more than a hint of inner missions theology lingered at the time when inner missions institutions themselves were judged inadequate. The framework of both civil righteousness and faith-active-in-love, so prominent in the other two social statements presented in Atlanta, was more muted in "The Church and Social Welfare."

The Atlanta convention was the last to consider more than two social statements. In the future, conventions would act upon fewer and longer statements as the board and staff extended its understanding of Lutheranism's "evangelical ethic" to broader issues. Conventions in turn would begin to assign the denomination's staff more items for study and comment, if not for policy formulation.

The tide was turning. Richard Niebank, who was elected secretary of social concerns in 1967, recalls that in its early years the board felt responsible to awaken the church to social responsibility. In the seventies, church members began to push the board into a wider range of issues, and many expected a more activist stance.[80] If the sixties had been the age of bureaucratizing social ministry, the seventies brought more participatory democracy. By the 1980s, interest-group pluralism would become the reigning model.

NOTES

1. LCA, *Minutes . . . 1968*, 37.

2. Matusow, *The Unraveling of America*, 376-404.

3. Carl Thomas (telephone interview with author, 14 August 1987) recalls that there were no precedents in the new church to handle the indebtedness of the Florida Lutheran Retirement Center in Deland. Unincorporated and originally under the wing of the Augustana Synod's New England Conference, the home threatened its new parent body, the Florida Synod, with bankruptcy. For the solution see LCA, *Minutes . . . 1968*, 214.

4. Thomas, telephone interview with author, 14 August 1987.

5. BSM Minutes, 21–23 February, 5-10.

6. BSM Executive Committee Minutes, 3 October 1967, 10-14; BSM Minutes, 3–5 October 1967, 9-16.

7. BSM Minutes, 3–5 October 1967, 13; 14–17 February 1968, 54-58, and Program Agenda, 1.

8. LCA, *Minutes . . . 1968*, 639-40.

9. Ibid., 600, 630-31.

10. Ibid., 362-63.

11. Ibid., 772.

12. Ibid., 40.

13. This lively group included former staff and now board member Rufus Cornelsen, Frank P. Zeidler, Rudolph Featherstone, and Robert Herhold.

14. BSM Minutes, 3–5 October 1967, "Peace and Justice," Exhibit A.

15. LCA, *Minutes . . . 1964*, 145, quoted from Executive Council Minutes, January 1964, 766. See also BSM Minutes, 19–21 November 1963, 31-32 and Exhibit R, 1.

16. BSM Minutes, 21–23 February 1967, 68-69, "Civil and International Affairs," Exhibit A, 1-3.

17. E.g., BSM Minutes, 4–6 October 1966, 29. Staff suggested that the board provide the service of compiling a directory of Lutheran health and welfare agencies which complied with regulations governing the employment of conscientious objectors in alternate service.

18. BSM Minutes, 3–5 October 1967, "Peace and Justice," Exhibit A, 1.

19. LCA, *Minutes . . . 1968*, "Report of the Executive Council," 356. Niebanck, interview with author, 24 July 1985, and telephone interview with author, 24 August 1987; Carl Thomas, telephone interview with author, 31 August 1987.

20. BSM Minutes, 3–7 October 1967, 111; 14–17 February 1968, "Report of the Ad Hoc Committee on Peace and Justice," 59. Niebanck had to leave the meeting because of a death in his family.

21. Matusow, *The Unraveling of America*, 328-30, 387-88.

22. BSM Minutes, 14–17 February 1968, 59; Richard Niebanck, *Conscience, War, and the Selective Objector* (BSM/LCA, 1968; revised, DMNA/LCA, 1972).

23. Ibid., 16-18, 21-27, passim.

24. Ibid., 36-38, and Niebanck, telephone interview with author, 24 August 1987. The war veteran cited is Herluf Jensen.

25. BSM Minutes, 14–17 February 1968, 60-62.

26. Niebanck, telephone interview with author, 24 August 1987.

27. BSM Minutes, 14–17 February 1968, 63-64.

28. Harold Lohr, telephone interview with author, 3 September 1987.

29. The Lutheran Church–Missouri Synod adopted its statement on the subject at its convention in July of 1969; The American Lutheran Church took such action in convention in October of 1970. See *Conscience, War, and the Selective Objector*, 2d ed., 57-61.

30. Forell, telephone interview, with author, 13 April 1987.

31. Richard Niebanck, telephone interview with author, 24 July 1987.

32. Robert Herhold, telephone interview with author, 5 September 1987.

33. LCA, *Minutes . . . 1968*, 739-50.

34. See ULCA, *Minutes . . . 1940*, 138, 557.

35. "We must obey God rather than men" (Acts 5:29, RSV) LCA, *Minutes . . . 1968*, 756-57.

36. Ibid., 757.

37. Ibid., 757-60.

38. Ibid., 761.

39. Ibid., 760-62. Bishop Crumley (interview with C. von Dehsen, New York, 1 September 1987) recalls that he voted against the statement because it allowed for an individual decision against a particular war.

40. Dean Kelley, interview with author, 4 April 1986.

41. "Preparatory Papers for the National Study Conference on Church and State: Columbus, Ohio, 4–7 February 1964" (NCC, New York, 1964, Mimeographed), 23.

42. Ibid., 16.

43. George Forell, "Religious Liberty," *The Lutheran Quarterly* 16 (November 1964):327-42.

44. LCA, *Minutes . . . 1964*, 332, 547.

45. BSM Minutes, 20–22 April 1965; Agenda, 19-20. See also LCA Executive Council Minutes, 25–26 June 1965, 420, quoted in BSM Minutes, 5–7 October 1965, Exhibit C, 7-8.

46. BSM Minutes, 5–7 October 1965, 17; Agenda, 10-11.

47. The board received a dozen-and-a-half-letters in response. Eight favored the statement; four opposed it; and another half-dozen made suggestions for its alteration. BSM Minutes, 15–17 February 1966, 44-45.

48. Ibid., 45-46.

49. LCA, *Minutes . . . 1966*, 532-33, 613.

50. Charles Y. Glock and Rodney Stark, *Christian Beliefs and Anti-Semitism* (New York: Harper & Row, 1966).

51. LCA, *Minutes . . . 1966*, 613.

52. BSM Minutes, 21–23 February 1967, "Civil and International Affairs," Exhibit D, 1.

53. BSM Minutes, 3–5 October 1967, "Religious Liberty," Exhibit F, 1.

54. Charles Glock, telephone interview with author, 19 June 1987.

55. BSM Minutes, 3–5 October 1967, 110-11, and "Religious Liberty," Exhibits A–F.

56. Cedric Tilberg, ed., *Religious Liberty* (BSM/LCA, 1968).

57. See ibid., 19-22. Most changes occur in the final section, "Religious Liberty as a Common Concern of Church and State." An opening paragraph delineating the uses of the terms *state* and *power* in the New Testament is omitted, while three paragraphs on the corporate role of the church in society are added.

58. Ibid., 5, 15.

59. Ibid., 12-13.

60. Ibid., 19-20.

61. BSM Minutes, 14–17 February 1968, "Religious Liberty," Exhibits A and B; LCA, *Minutes . . . 1968*, "Report of the President," 39.

62. Tilberg, interview with author, 12 March 1987.

63. LCA, *Minutes . . . 1968*, 40.

64. Ibid., 750. The minutes mistakenly call this sentence an addition rather than a substitution. See p. 634 for the original.

65. Ibid., 750.

66. President Fry did not lend his support to the proposal at first because he found its language vague. BSM Minutes, 23–26 April 1958, 47-48; Harold Haas, telephone interview with author, 26 July 1987; ULCA Executive Board Minutes, 30 June–1 July 1958, 1008-9.

67. Minutes of the Commission to Study the Role of the Church in Social Welfare, March 4–5, 1960; BSM Minutes, 26–28 April 1960, 42-43. The members were E. Theodore Bachmann, Reuben Baetz, Cordelia Cox, Martin Heinecken, Karl Hertz, Arthur Hillman, William J. Villaume, and George Whetstone. Harold Haas and Harold Reisch served as staff; Lawrence Holt, president of the Board of Social Missions of the Augustana Synod, and Henry Whiting of the National Lutheran Council were present as observers.

68. *The Church in Social Welfare: An Exploratory Study of the Role of the Lutheran Church in America in Social Welfare* (Commission on the Role of the Church in Social Welfare, BSM/LCA, 1964).

69. Haas, telephone interview with author, 26 July 1987; Harold Reisch, telephone interview with author, 27 July 1987.

70. The Contexts Within Which the Church Develops Responsible Service," *Report of the Lutheran World Conference on Social Responsibility, August 7–10, 1957, Springfield, Ohio* (Sponsored by Commission on Inner Missions, Lutheran Welfare Federation; arranged by Division of Welfare, National Lutheran Council), 45-46.

71. *The Church in Social Welfare*, 61. The commission wrestled with whether *diakonia* was one of the church's "marks," a technical term from Luther's theology denoting the gospel bearing characteristics of the church, or whether it was an "essential function." Martin Heinecken, the theologian consultant, opted for the latter. Ibid., 37-38.

72. Ibid., 65, 67-68.

73. Ibid., 73-76, 70.

74. LCA, *Minutes . . . 1968*, 38.

75. BSM Minutes, 5–7 October 1965, Agenda, 14-15; BSM Minutes, 15–17 February 1966, 71-72, "Social Welfare," Exhibit A, 1-4; BSM Minutes, 4–6 October 1966, 62-63; BSM Minutes, 21–23 February 1967, 110, "Social Welfare," Exhibit A, 1-9; BSM Minutes, 3–5 October 1967, 108, "Social Welfare," Agenda, 1, Exhibits A and B; BSM Minutes, 14–17 February 1968, 91-94.

76. Telephone interviews conducted by the author with James Raun (23 July 1987), Harold Reisch (27 July 1987), Carl Thomas (27 July, 14 August 1987). Richard Niebanck (interview with author, 24 July 1985) saw the statement as evolving from "Church and State."

77. Reisch, telephone interview with author, 27 July 1987.

78. LCA, *Minutes . . . 1968*, 631, 465, 767-68.

79. Ibid., 768.

80. Niebanck, interview with author, 24 July 1985.

6

POWER TO THE PEOPLE,
1969–1970

Each of the two social statements presented to the Minneapolis convention in 1970 had come late and with a history. Both "Sex, Marriage, and
Family" and "World Community" had been intended for the 1968 convention.[1] Each stood in the tradition of basic theological and social commentary established in the United Lutheran Church in America and had
a direct antecedent. The Lutheran Church in America had already adopted the ULCA's 1956 statement "Marriage and Family" in 1964, antici-
pating an updated version. The ULCA's statement on nuclear war, adopted
in 1960, had established a perspective on international affairs drawn from
Lutheran theology.

Despite such precedent, the 1970 convention was anything but business as usual. Its atmosphere was charged with the excitement of change
and confrontation surrounding a number of episodes. "With a resounding
voice vote" the convention approved the ordination of women when it
struck the word *man* and inserted the word *person* in the constitutional
bylaw that defined "a minister of the church."[2] Delegates adopted a
resolution calling for prayer, fasting, repentance, and political action "in
concert with other men of good will" in the wake of continuing warfare
in Vietnam and Cambodia, the Mylai massacre, and the deaths of four
student protestors at Kent State University.[3] The first "Youth Convo"
included strains of the rebellious youth culture, by now well developed
in American society. The American Indian Movement sent a delegation
in full native dress. Dennis Banks read a seven-point challenge to the
churches which asked delegates "to issue a decree or proclamation for-
bidding construction of any further churches until all social injustices
which have been committed against the Indians are corrected."[4]

The 1970 convention seemed to mark a change in the tide. Convention
delegates, synods, and outside interest groups were competing more

101

openly with the national staff to set the denomination's agenda. And at the very time when the movement for social reform within the nation was slowing, its momentum was increasing within the church. In one of the most direct indications of this shift, the number of resolutions submitted by synods reached an all-time high when seventy were proposed, of which more than one-third called for action or study on social issues.[5]

President Franklin Clark Fry had fretted in 1968 that the 1970 convention would be "overburdened" but "lively and interesting" because of the incomplete but authorized studies on confirmation, on the ministry, on sex, marriage, and family, and on the church-related colleges. In his presidential report in Minneapolis, Robert Marshall warned that "not every enthusiasm of the various segments of the delegation, and not every headline that sways our 'global village' can dominate the convention's attention."[6] To ease the press of issues and in response to convention action in 1968, the Executive Council introduced hearings to allow delegates "studied consideration" of social statements and recommendations from special studies.[7] Thus, on the evening of June 26, hearings were held simultaneously on "World Community" and "Sex, Marriage, and Family" and on proposals from the studies on ministry, confirmation, and theological education.

"WORLD COMMUNITY: ETHICAL IMPERATIVES IN AGE OF INTERDEPENDENCE"

The formulation of "World Community" launched the LCA's corporate discussion of international affairs and is premised on a theme which Richard Niebanck had articulated in the study *Selective Conscientious Objection*. Lutherans by theological heritage could balance their recognition "of the factors of power and might with an assertion about the capacity of men and nations for law-abiding conduct."[8]

Niebanck, who would draft both "World Community" and its background study, originally urged the Board of Social Ministry to abandon its plans for a general statement on world order in favor of one that dealt with specific issues. Because Lutherans viewed political issues under "the rubric of creation and preservation, not redemption," they could get beyond the abstraction of the Manichean arguments employed by the Right or the Left in favor of "careful analysis of a particular set of issues." One case study suggested itself—the uses of American military power, especially in Latin America, where the Central Intelligence Agency's efforts to topple Salvadore Allende's government in Chile had become known.[9]

Niebanck, along with the rest of the staff, would have been privy to discussions conducted under the National Council of Churches' Priority Program for Peace.[10]

A few months later, Niebanck and others had grown more sober about rendering credible judgments on specific issues in the form and within the biennial calendar of a social statement. Instead, the staff proposed that the study of military power should proceed and inform a statement, but that the statement should speak from the Lutheran tradition with its "readily available elements" for defining "sovereignty/law/world order" and such other nonjuridical elements as "arms control and disarmament, economic development, and the significance of popular revolutionary movements."[11]

During the following spring and summer, the staff developed a statement on world community and contracted for four background booklets for the Christian Social Responsibility series. Frank Zeidler, who chaired the Committee on Peace and Justice, wrote *Armament or Disarmament?*, reviewing the politics and technology of the arms race, suggesting ethical guidelines, and calling the church to minister to all whose vocations are linked to armaments.[12]

The board also drew on the expertise and commitments of two young students. Christopher Herman, at Yale law school, wrote *International Law & Institutions: Some Current Problems,* in which he noted the "infant condition" of international law and flaws in the charter of the United Nations that weakened its capacity to settle international disputes. Brian Hull, another graduate student, wrote *International Development: Challenge to Christians.* Niebanck's *World Community* summed up the series and provided the basis for positions taken in the statement.[13]

Once the manuscripts were completed and the statement drafted, Niebanck hosted a series of consultations at a Lutheran school or social agency in Milwaukee, Berkeley, Ottawa, Chicago, and Springfield, Ohio. He recalls the "sage advice" of Charles Cooper, who taught Old Testament at Pacific Lutheran Theological Seminary, not to confuse temporal peace within the world order with eschatological peace, a distinction that Niebanck found increasingly useful in his theological approach to political analysis.[14] Leaders in Lutheran and interchurch agencies of world mission and service also commented on the statement before it was finalized by the board in February of 1970 for recommendation to the convention.[15]

"World Community" is a broad statement which delineates the interconnectedness of modern life on this globe and, therefore, its shared perils and opportunities. (See Appendix, "World Community.") Delegates responded with animated interest at the convention hearing, but offered few changes during the one session on the afternoon of June 30 in which the statement was considered and adopted.[16] They did, however, amend the "enabling" resolution which called for denomination-wide *preparation* for study and action to call for the action of distributing the statement "to each national government of the world, to the United Nations, and to the churches of each nation."[17]

The statement ends with an articulation of its "fundamental premise" that a church body, "as a corporate entity within a given nation," "has the God-given responsibility of generating support for national policies which contribute to the building of a world community." In the study booklet, Niebanck develops this principle more fully. He asserts that the church is responsible not only to "awaken" its members to the concerns of peace and justice which lie at the heart of their Christian vocation but also to speak directly to the makers of national policy—not in behalf of a "Christian" policy or for the conversion of politicians but as partners with others committed to helping the state define its own interest in broad terms that are consonant with standards of human justice.[18]

In the statement, the existence of a world neighborhood is predicated on the advances in the technologies of communication, transportation, and weaponry to the point that "the actions of any nation or interest can lead to instantaneous and irreversible consequences for all." Such a neighborhood is one of shared vulnerability and opportunity. Christians have an added biblical perspective of humanity's "natural oneness in Adam," including stewardship over the earth and humanity's "eschatological oneness in Christ." The statement proceeds to discuss five topics of concern within such a global context: global civil order, human rights, "the international public domain," security and war prevention, and the development of peoples.[19]

The section "Security and War Prevention" attracted the most discussion at the convention and was the most thoroughly amended. Delegates voted to charge "all nations," and not only their home countries of Canada and the United States, with the need for arms reduction. The lengthiest amendment came from Fred Melton, a delegate to the youth convocation. It was introduced by convention delegate Pauline Redmond, lay delegate from the Michigan Synod. With this amendment, the section treating the role of civil power was lengthened by five sentences to underscore the needs of the oppressed under "existing power relationships," to condemn the loss of "freedom given to all men" and to note that "the history of free people reflects a tradition of liberation."[20]

104

In the treatment of developing nations, the statement calls for more ethical politics and for church involvement. It asks Christians of the affluent nations to expand their commitment in overseas missions to include proclaiming "the obligations of the wealthy and the rights of the poor." The churches of the developed countries are also called upon to aid those in new nations to acquire the "political skills" necessary to "challenge their governments and people toward a higher level of well-being."

As amended, the statement stops short of describing the Christian church as symbolizing "the essense of world community." Dean Krister Stendahl of the Harvard Divinity School, delegate from the New England Synod, convinced the convention to eliminate such language and emphasize instead the "duties of organized churches" to promote opportunities for dialogue among peoples trapped in conflict and divided along political and ideological lines.[21] The statement ends on a note of urgency, with the denomination committing itself to "redoubled effort in the building of world community."

As the proceedings came to a close, Joseph Rinderknecht offered an amendment to strike the description of the statement as "official policy" and to substitute the phrase "an expression of concern." He felt that delegates did not have the expertise to make such binding judgments. They were elected "because they are faithful workers in congregations, not skilled in world affairs." Moreover, too many were new to convention procedures, and time was too short to air all of the issues. Therefore he judged the process "a bit dishonest."[22] His motion failed.[23]

With this policy position, the Lutheran Church in America entered the discussion among mainline Protestants on international affairs. What distinguished its position were two commitments that would become more developed in the statements on ecology (1972), human rights (1978), economic justice (1980), and peace (1984). First, "World Community" restates the classic Christian doctrine that political authority requires "the component of force" to maintain peace, and, second, it maintains the distinction between humanity's "natural oneness in Adam" and "eschatological oneness in Christ." The full meaning of such commitments held in tandem had yet to be explored.

"SEX, MARRIAGE, AND FAMILY"

The two social statements among the church's total of nineteen to provoke the most heated controversy were "Peace and Politics" of 1984 and "Sex, Marriage, and Family" of 1970. The disagreements surrounding their formulation and passage continue to dominate memory. The 1970 statement tested the developing theological perspective called "the evangelical ethic" and tried all the processes of formulation and review. To this day, participants and close observers judge the results with mixed responses.

From the outset, the major stumbling blocks were theological. Those who joined the deliberations were agreed that the church needed a fresh approach to the subject, and yet they took six years to reach accord on a theological viewpoint. Their own difficulties not only foreshadowed the struggle to achieve passage of the statement in convention but also foreshortened the opportunity church members would have to study the report before voting on it. The entire episode represents one instance of a battle raging within Christian ethics and popularized by Joseph Fletcher's book *Situation Ethics* over the weight to be assigned to the personal and cultural context.[24]

Board leaders launched three distinct forays in 1964, 1966, and 1968 before there was sufficient consensus for a report. Pivotal for each of these initiatives was the question of how to interpret the traditional Lutheran view of the family as an "order" within creation. Ultimately, the board would propose materials which reinterpreted the concept along relational lines, while loosely maintaining its contours. Carl Braaten's work, commissioned early in the deliberations, offered a fresh statement of the traditional approach and thus served as a center of debate during each of the three initiatives.

The first effort followed the 1964 convention.[25] Three consultants were asked to produce working papers following a general consultation held in September. These papers, completed the following years and discussed at a consultation in February of 1966, expressed the basic tensions that would dog the whole effort. Gerald K. Johnson, director of the Division of Pastoral Services of Lutheran Social Services, Illinois, and later president of the Illinois Synod, covered "Pastoral Counseling and Troubled Marriages" and described the gap between what theologians claimed and what the "helping disciplines" offered as "pragmatic solutions." Floyd Martinson, professor of sociology at Gustavus Adolphus College, had noted in the consultation that "many church people are discovering that 'breaking the rules' is not as bad as the church had said it would be and that 'keeping' them is not as satisfying." He had called the specifics of the ULCA's statement "dogmatic and legalistic, thus contradicting its own avowed evangelical basis."[26] His paper "A Sociological Perspective" described the family's loss of dominance as a socializing agent.[27]

With his paper "Sex, Family & Marriage," Carl E. Braaten of the Lutheran School of Theology at Chicago divided the group between those who favored what was labeled his "ontological-normative" method and those who preferred a more "situationalist" approach "born of a concern that the ethicist take with utter seriousness the questions of contemporary man before offering answers to them."[28] His draft, later duplicated for private distribution, places human sexuality within God's scheme of creation and of redemption. Sexual differentiation of male and female is creation in the image of a God who is love. "Sexuality is the means God built into man and woman to drive them towards each other" and "the human analogy for the love of God," made manifest in the incarnation and resurrection of Jesus of Nazareth.[29]

Marriage, as an "order of creation" or as "a secular reality" is "as much a part of God's intention for man and woman as for the lilies to grow in the field or the birds to fly in the air." Because married partners are accountable to the living God, marriage is no "mere contract between two persons who just happen to be in love."[30]

Braaten understands the tradition to rule out venereal experiences prior to and outside of marriage because "sex is an inseverable dimension of the totality of the love which can attain its consummate fulfillment in marriage alone."[31] He holds for an "organic conception of marriage" because of the disagreement among theologians on its "efficient cause." With warnings about the dilution of engagement's meaning in contemporary society, he nevertheless rejects "a legalistic view" of premarital intercourse that places it on the same moral plane as "the promiscuous sexual relations of two persons who have made no irrevocable decisions for each other."[32]

He states that the Christian church "must clearly teach that basically there are no grounds for divorce which can excuse it or atone for its sin and guilt." The church must consider divorce as "an emergency measure, a rescue operation" after a marriage has been shattered beyond repair. Since the gospel is "not for the guiltless and sinless," it cannot "reverse history and deal with a person as if God's judgment did not stand against his guilt." Instead, ministers of the gospel should not assume that there be an innocent party in a divorce, "but help persons realize their share of the guilt, to repent, to be reconciled and renewed by the power of grace." In remarriage the church should expect the couple to profess "their present readiness to enter a new marriage in the awareness of God's infinite mercy to make all things new, in spite of their sin and guilt."[33]

The consultation proved inconclusive, and the board made plans to produce two more papers, one "from the perspective of depth psychology" and also "a paper utilizing a different theological approach."[34] Thus began a search which both Martinson and Braaten characterized similarly in recent interviews. Martinson claims:

> We went through a lot of theologians until we found the kind we wanted. We were looking for a theologian who could develop a love-based, relational evangelical ethic over against code morality.[35]

Braaten recalls that "they didn't think they could use my paper. They felt it was out of phase. They were looking around for a theology to negotiate their differences" and believed "that the church should not say things that do not work out in counseling." He held that the Lutheran tradition of pastoral care (*Seelsorge*) and absolution could handle the gap between behavior and norms.[36]

As a result of the stalemate, the board sought permission from the Executive Council to establish a Commission on Marriage.[37] This second initiative consumed the months of 1967 and revealed both the continuing difficulties and the developing approach that would shape the final study. The commission would be responsible to develop a publishable study; the board, the social statement. Both were to have a "positive" thrust, "give real guidance to the church," and "not be pre-committed to certain systems of behavior and then proceed to defend them."[38]

Six of the commission's ten members were ordained: Haas, Johnson, William E. Lesher, Obed B. Lundeen, Franklin E. Sherman, Lee E. Snook. They were known for their work in social ethics, pastoral counseling, or in campus or parish ministry. The four lay members came from diverse fields: Kenneth Eckert, physician; Avis Johnson, urban social worker; Dorothy Jaeger-Lee, psychiatrist; and Floyd Martinson, sociologist. Philosophy professor Romaine Gardner was hired as writer of the report.[39]

Haas wanted commission members to view their work within the broad context of contemporary discussion. The 1961 North American Conference on Family Life, sponsored by the National Council of Churches in Green Lake, Wisconsin, had been pivotal for raising the same concerns now faced by the commission.[40] By the end of the first meeting, the commission agreed that they did not want to start "with conclusions and then [seek] facts to support them." They held that "the study would communicate best with modern man if it dealt with the issues in the areas of sex, marriage, and family in terms of interpersonal relationships— among human persons and between human persons and a personal God." They judged that the basic question, Who am I? had more meaning in contemporary culture than, What is God's will for me?[41]

Midstream during the second meeting, the agenda was changed to give the group an opportunity for "a frank, off-the-record, sharing of opinion about the crucial issue of extra-marital sexual intercourse." The group divided between those who argued "on the basis of probable consequences" and "those who believe that there are ethical absolutes." Commission members then pondered the "reality of the Law" and fretted about how to address teenagers without "the absolute yes and no."[42]

By the third meeting in June of 1967 the commission was debating Braaten's original paper, which polarized the group. Franklin Sherman described Braaten's work as representative of the "general consensus among Lutheran theologians." Arguing against the findings of anthropology and psychology, Braaten claimed that Christians seek a different authority: "Christians are ultimately persuaded by the fact that the New Testament picture of marital love as a parable of Christ's love for his church presupposes monogamy."[43]

The fourth meeting in September was to be the time of consensus, but Romaine Gardner's written report of the commission's deliberations and Sherman's review of the theological issues served only to underscore the differences among its members.[44] By October the board had established its own committee on marriage to review the commission's work and to develop a statement. The committee judged that the commission would not complete its work in time for the 1968 convention.[45] A December consultation with theologians also failed to advance the project.[46]

The third major effort to produce a report began during the 1968 church convention when eight members of the commission met as a "subcommittee" to determine "next steps." Haas agreed to draft a document that would "speak to society as well as the church."[47] The board's Committee on Marriage, chaired by William Lazareth, began to prepare for writing a statement.[48]

After a hiatus of sixteen months, the commission assembled for its fifth meeting in February of 1969 to discuss Haas's paper.[49] The outline he created would hold. The first section on the "impact of changing culture" he had derived from Martinson's research. The second on Christian ethical decision making came from a paper by Dr. Charles W. Kegley of Wagner College, where Haas was dean. The third, on biblical and theological perspectives, condensed Braaten's original paper. The final section raised several cases of urgent ethical problems.

At this meeting, after four years of wrangling, the commission members present broke with Braaten's approach. The summary of the proceedings noted:

> Although they could accept much of the substance of the paper, they could not accept its authoritarian framework. They felt that answers seem to come

109

before questions are asked. Perhaps, as one member suggested, our tradition is so eroded that we simply can no longer make a statement of this kind.

Resigned to "the apparent lack of theological consensus" within the commission and among theologians of the denomination, the body agreed that "whatever the approach, a basic view of man should emerge as clearly as possible." The commission determined to proceed with a report, probably to be the work of several authors, and aimed to complete their work in October of 1969.[50] The commission met twice more to complete its report prior to the board's October meeting.

Martinson marveled recently that the group ever reached consensus on the study and that no minority report was filed. The commission, he felt, was always aware that the church was "conservative" and had never taken a "non-legalistic" approach to these issues. He pondered whether true agreement had been reached.[51] In fact, Sherman had absented himself and resigned from this final stage. In a recent interview, he indicated his frustration: "I was impatient with the pace of the work and unhappy with some of the directions taken." He feared that the "LCA was about to position itself right smack in the middle of the Zeitgeist."[52] Sherman anticipated the response a number of the church's theologians, including Forell and Heinecken, would have to the later statement.[53]

Cedric Tilberg served as editor of the commission's final report, *Sex, Marriage, and Family*. Its introduction, following Haas's outline, characterized the three parts as descriptive—"The Contemporary Cultural Context"; normative—"A Contemporary Theological Context"; and regulative—"Some Current Issues."

Martinson's work informed the first section, which emphasizes the shrinking role of the family to one of affection and nurturance from its earlier economic and political functions. The "separability" of sex, marriage, and family has become "characteristic of contemporary life," and the quest for a "new morality" is an effort to validate this shift. "Cultural relativity" is the cardinal issue facing Christians.[54]

For the second section, Tilberg worked from a lengthy draft supplied by consultant Martin Heinecken.[55] The section begins with an account of two shifts in theological perspectives. The first occurred after World War II and emphasized a positive view, Braaten's included, of human sexuality, marriage, and family as part of the structure of creation. Yet, "within the span of a single generation" the situation changed again, becoming more complex and requiring another ethic. The complexity derives from three competing viewpoints: those who advocate "extreme permissiveness on matters of sex"; those whose conservative reaction

110

would repeat "the old virtues and call for stricter laws and more discipline"; and those who judge that neither reaction "will serve present
needs."[56]

The rest of the section proposes an approach aimed for those seeking
a middle ground, particularly the young who "wish to break through the
facade of outer conformity and pretense to what has integrity." The study
proceeds to build its theological approach first on the assertion that the
church "is bound by a given revelation and by the mighty acts of God
in history centering in the Christ," and second on the need for continuous
restatement of dogmas and ethical principles. The study affirms the goodness of sexuality. Sin is "a basic mis-relation to God" that leads to an
"overestimation or underestimation of man's finite freedom." Because of
the pervasiveness of sexuality, such "mis-relation manifests itself in pe-
culiarly fearful ways."[57]

In its most pointed effort to chart a new course, the study builds on
its definition of marriage and family as "structures of God's created
order," by linking the Christian faith with the kind of personal relationship
in monogamous marriage: *From a theological perspective, a life-long,
covenanted union of one man and one woman, based on fidelity, is
indicative of the creator's intention for a cradle of community.*" Thus the
study stops short of Braaten's overt assertion that monogamy is "the
perfection of marriage" by placing the emphasis on the relationship, not
the form. In the covenantal approach, "it is the responsible, interpersonal
relation that matters, not primarily the legal contract."[58]

Thus, while marriage is a secular reality, Christians who enter it will
treat it as a covenant. Likewise, ethical decision making for the Christian
is dependent on "a mode of relationships between God and man, and
man and man, rather than from some ethical principles." Hence, pre- and
extra-marital sexual intercourse "more frequently are than not" "acts of
sin, done by a sinner, because they betray God's love in harming the
interpersonal relationship." Their sinfulness does not derive from their
having been performed "outside whatever the accepted rules for a 'legitimate' marriage may be in a given society." The study also calls for
particular attention to the revision of marriage and divorce laws "to make
them just and human."[59]

In its final section, the study provides guidelines, "the best insights
available from both the contemporary world and the church's biblical
and theological heritage" in four areas: human sexuality, marriage, questions related to conception and parenthood, and sex education. Only the
first two topics are integrated with previous argument. The sections on

contraception and abortion are not. For example, the decision for having a child makes no reference to the covenanted relationship of marriage as a God-given "cradle of community," but only to medical, numerical, financial, and ecological issues. And it is taken as self-evident "that every child has a right to be a wanted child, both as his birth is anticipated and as he is reared toward manhood or womanhood." [60] This final section illustrates the commission's difficulties in achieving consensus based on any single theological or philosophical approach. It also prefigures the continuing challenge in the church's future statements to relate the "normative" to the "regulative." The Board of Social Ministry greeted the commission's report at its October meeting in 1969 with an expression of "congratulations and commendation" and a vote authorizing its publication in the Christian Social Responsibility series. [61] The following February the board reviewed the statement prepared by Lazareth and Herhold and staff members Jensen, Thomas, and Tilberg for the Committee on Marriage. After five hours of unrecorded discussion, the statement was adopted for recommendation to the 1970 convention. [62]

Recollections of the convention hearing, held on the evening of Friday, June 26, remain vivid. The room, next largest to the convention hall itself, "was packed to the limit." [63] Lazareth presided and aimed, as he remembers, to make clear the statement's theological foundation, a positive expression of natural law in which sexuality is understood as grounded in God's image. Teenagers from the youth convocation responded positively to his teaching. [64] The main points of contention centered around the definition of marriage as a "covenant of fidelity." Following the hearing, the staff met to revise parts of the statement for submission to the convention.

On Monday afternoon, June 29, the statement was first presented for adoption. (See Appendix, "Sex, Marriage, and Family," for the final version.) Carl Thomas had to step in as presenter for Lazareth who had become ill, although the staff had tried first to find another theologian. [65] Lohr offered some substitute paragraphs to clarify the section on marriage in response to the hearings. Most of the discussion in this session and the two subsequent ones prior to approval centered on the statement's definition of marriage and distinctions made between it and marriage as a legal contract, particular cultural pattern, or physical union. At this first session only one amendment passed, the addition of the sentence: "The existence of a true covenant of fidelity outside marriage as a contract is extremely hard to identify." [66]

At the next session, a special order on Wednesday afternoon, July 1, board members and delegates continued to explicate the meaning of "a covenant of fidelity—a dynamic, life-long commitment of one man and one woman in a personal, sexual union." John Reumann of Philadelphia Seminary successfully proposed an amendment providing an alternative phrase for the biblical covenant language, "mutual commitment to life-long faithfulness." There was a motion, which lost, to postpone action on the entire statement until 1972 after regional forums had been held.[67]

Then W. Emerson Reck of Wittenberg College successfully proposed an amendment for the introduction to make explicit that the church did not condone "either pre-marital or extra-marital sexual intercourse."[68] Harold LaVander, governor of Minnesota and lay delegate, had also expressed similar views on the convention floor in the presence of television cameras covering his campaign for re-election.[69] President Marshall allowed delegates to give written notice of their opposition and twenty delegates submitted their names to the secretary.[70]

On the morning of July 2, the session in which the entire statement was approved, Reck, perhaps by way of compromise, moved the substance of his amendment from the statement's introduction to its "regulative section." Delegates approved this change. Thomas expressed the board's displeasure with the amendment, but preference, nevertheless, for its new location.[71] Recalling this amendment, former board and commission members judged that its inclusion may have insured the passage of a statement that otherwise allowed more ambiguity than delegates found acceptable.

Three other issues were the subject of more limited discussion. The section on interracial marriage was honed into a more positive declaration of such marriage as "a witness to the oneness of humanity under the one God."[72] The section on homosexuality was lengthened to include mention of the inconclusive evidence from scientific research on its causes. The descriptive language was also altered. "Deviation" was changed to "departure."[73]

The third issue, abortion, attracted but little attention in 1970, when abortion was yet outlawed in many states and before the Supreme Court's decision on *Roe* v. *Wade* in 1973. The church was confronted with the question of how to advise "a woman or couple" deciding whether to seek an abortion in another state or country. The statement called for "an evangelical ethic" as the source of a responsible decision for abortion and then listed a series of situational considerations. The statement did not make clear whether the considerations themselves answered the criteria of "an evangelical ethic."

Few delegates addressed this section. Reck called for recommitting this section to the Board of Social Ministry. The motion lost as did another motion to delete the entire section.[74] Delegates did not foresee the potential for abuse once the right to abortion became the law of the land. Lazareth said in a recent interview that the statement's "terseness" on the issue of abortion "was an error" and had been subject to misinterpretation.[75] By the 1978 convention, three synods submitted memorials calling for a more thoroughgoing stance on abortion.[76] Robert Marshall recalls the effort to avoid doing what had never been done before, namely, amending a social statement.[77] Instead, the Committee on Memorials took the lead from his presidential report and asserted that "Sex, Marriage, and Family" provided basic principles on abortion based on theological grounds and socio-ethical considerations. Specific decisions are to be dealt with in counseling situations. The committee then quoted two sections of the statement, one to oppose specifically "abortion on demand," and the second, "use of abortion as an alternative form of contraception." Reference was also made to a study book written by Franklin Sherman, *The Problem of Abortion After the Supreme Court Decision*. Together, these items were called a "convention minute" and transmitted to the Nebraska, Central Pennsylvania, and Wisconsin-Upper Michigan Synods in response to their memorials.[78] (See Appendix, "1978 LCA Convention Minute on the Subject of Abortion.")

In 1982 the convention requested the Division for Mission in North America to study the issue further. The division's Management Committee reported to the convention in 1984 that it was unable "to arrive at an agreed upon recommendation because of the divergent views held across the church."[79] The committee had in fact rejected the draft of a convention resolution proposed by the staff of the department for Church in Society in October of 1983. It had also voted to distribute again a copy of the 1970 social statement along with the 1978 "Clarifying Minute."[80]

In 1984 the division released a collection of four "theological and ethical perspectives" under the title *Abortion and the Christian Conscience*. Paul Nelson, who edited the papers, noted that the division preferred to represent the variety of theological and ethical perspectives in the church rather than "try to find a single individual who would be prepared to advance 'a lowest common denominator' view of abortion."[81] The division promised the 1984 convention to continue its study, as requested again by the Wisconsin-Upper Michigan Synod.[82]

The deadlock of the abortion debate demonstrated the limits to policy making in the denomination. Not until 1984 were procedures proposed for changing a social statement. At the same time, the insulation of the process leading to both the report and the statement would be rejected later in Marshall's administration in favor of "constituency" reviews.

"Sex, Marriage, and Family" had raised issues for policy formation that far exceeded even its volatile content.

NOTES

1. BSM Minutes, 20–22 April 1965, 16.
2. LCA, *Minutes . . . 1970*, 539, 433.
3. LCA, *Minutes . . . 1970*, 661-62.
4. Ibid., 591. See p. 645 for the resolution adopted which proposed an inter-Lutheran approach toward meeting challenges expressed by the Indians. Carl Thomas (interview with author, Columbus, Ohio, 2 May 1987) recalls negotiating with the AIM delegation and the creation of a special order of business to hear their protest on the convention floor.
5. Twenty-six memorials had been submitted in 1966 and only nineteen in 1968, about a third of which in each case dealt with social concerns. LCA, *Minutes . . . 1966*, 54-65; *1968, 53-58.*
6. LCA, *Minutes . . . 1970*, 41.
7. LCA Executive Council Minutes, 16–17 October 1969; LCA, *Minutes . . . 1970*, 389-90.
8. Richard Niebanck, *World Community: Challenge & Opportunity* (BSM/LCA, 1970), ii. Niebanck, who would draft the statement and the primary background study on world order, pursued graduate work in political science at the New School for Social Research to prepare himself for these tasks.
9. Peter N. Carroll, *It Seemed Like Nothing Happened: The Tragedy and Promise of America in the 1970s* (New York: Holt, Rinehart & Winston, 1982), 75-79.
10. BSM Minutes, 4–6 October 1966, 25-27.
11. The *ad hoc* Committee on Peace and Justice convened in Toronto in January of 1969 to make plans with members Frank Zeidler, Rufus Cornelsen, and Aarne Siirala, along with Niebanck and Lee Wesley from the staff, and consultants M. Darrol Bryant, a graduate of Harvard Divinity School, Gerhard Elston, of the National Council of Churches' Department of International Affairs, and Rev. Albert Ahlstrom. BSM Minutes, 25–27 February 1969, "Peace and Justice," Exhibit A, 1-2.
12. Zeidler, who had been mayor of Milwaukee from 1948 to 1960, remained prominent in political, municipal, and church circles as a consultant on resource management and international affairs. Frank Zeidler, interview with author, Milwaukee, 1 August 1986.
13. All four were authorized for publication in the Christian Social Responsibility series. BSM Minutes, 25–27 February 1970, 116. Niebanck recommended the four along with O. Frederick Nolde's *The Church and World Affairs* and M. Darrol Bryant's *A World Broken by Unshared Bread* in a memorandum to "Persons Interested in World Community," 29 April 1970 (BSM files, LCA, ELCA Archives).
14. BSM Minutes, 1–3 October 1969, 85-86; Richard Niebanck, telephone interview with author, 31 August 1987.

15. BSM Minutes, 25–27 February 1970, 115-16.

16. Niebanck, interview with author, 24 July 1985; LCA, *Minutes . . . 1970*, 559-65.

17. LCA, *Minutes . . . 1970*, 565.

18. Niebanck, *World Community*, 5-6.

19. In the discussion of global civil order, the United Nations is treated as a special instance of a "transnational" institution. Niebanck wonders that no one caught him in this misnomer at the time, since the U.N. is technically "international," that is, made up of the delegations of nations, not internationally minded interest groups. Telephone interview with author, 31 August 1987.

20. LCA, *Minutes . . . 1970*, 560-61.

21. Ibid., 561.

22. Joseph Rinderknecht, telephone interview with author, 21 September 1987.

23. Ibid. Rinderknecht's and another similar motion were the only failed motions recorded for this session. From 1970 the convention minutes no longer consistently provide an account of failed motions. Another change in record keeping had already occurred with the founding of the LCA when the previous pattern in the ULCA of providing a log of discussion was abandoned. The fact that minutes document fully the reports of the various denominational offices but not of convention proceedings is another evidence of increasing bureaucratization.

24. Joseph Fletcher, *Situation Ethics* (Philadelphia: Westminster Press, 1966).

25. BSM Minutes, 25–27 February 1964, 9; 17–19 November 1964, 24.

26. BSM Minutes, 17–19 November 1964, Exhibit P, 3-8.

27. BSM Minutes, 15–17 February 1966, "Social Welfare," Exhibit B, 4.

28. Ibid.

29. Carl E. Braaten, Lutheran School of Theology at Chicago, "Sex, Family & Marriage," 3-5, passim.

30. Ibid., 15-16, passim.

31. Ibid., 27.

32. Ibid., 28, 29.

33. Ibid., 30-34, passim.

34. BSM Minutes, 15–17 February 1966, 75.

35. Floyd Martinson, telephone interview with author, 4 September 1987.

36. Carl Braaten, telephone interview with author, 5 August 1987.

37. BSM Minutes, 4–6 October 1966, 63-64.

38. BSM Minutes, 21–23 February 1967, Social Welfare, Exhibit C, 1-5.

39. "Summary," Third Meeting of the Commission on Marriage, 22–23 June 1967, BSM Minutes, 3–5 October 1967, "Marriage," Exhibit C, 1.

40. "Summary," First Meeting of the Commission on Marriage, 9–10 February 1967, BSM Minutes, 3–5 October 1967, "Marriage," Exhibit A, 3-4.

41. Ibid.

42. "Summary," Second Meeting of the Commission on Marriage, 13–14 April 1967, BSM Minutes, 3–5 October 1967, "Marriage," Exhibit B, 6.

43. Braaten quoted in "Summary," Third Meeting of the Commission on Marriage, 22–23 June 1967, BSM Minutes, 3–5 October 1967, "Marriage," Exhibit C, 3.

44. "Summary," Fourth Meeting of the Commission on Marriage, 14–15 September 1967, BSM Minutes, 3–5 October 1967, "Marriage," Exhibit D, 1-5.

45. BSM Minutes, 3–5 October 1967, 109. Committee members included Gerhard Lenski, chair, Reuben Baetz, Charles Bergstrom, Avis Johnson, and Paul Orso.

46. BSM Minutes, 14–17 February 1968, 90.

47. BSM Minutes, 3–5 October 1968, 124-25.

48. BSM Minutes, 25–27 February 1969, "Marriage," Agenda, 1.

49. Four of its sixteen members, including Sherman, were absent. "Summary," Fifth Meeting of the Commission on Marriage, 24–25 January 1969, BSM Minutes, 25–27 February 1969, "Marriage," Exhibit A.

50. Ibid., 7, 2.

51. Martinson, telephone interview with author, 4 September 1987.

52. Franklin Sherman, telephone interview with author, 5 August 1987.

53. Martin Heinecken said with "reluctance" that he did not think this statement was one of the LCA's "best." He felt there was a "weasel" about it because in the reaction to a narrow conservatism, there was no clear understanding that monogamy was "the intention" of God's creation. Heinecken, telephone interview with author, 29 July 1987. After Lazareth became ill at the 1970 convention, Forell recalls being asked to participate in the panel on the convention podium defending the proposed social statement. He was "not comfortable" with it and would not take that role. Forell, telephone interview with author, 13 April 1987.

54. Cedric Tilberg, ed., *Sex, Marriage, and Family: A Contemporary Christian Perspective* (Commission on Marriage, BSM/LCA, 1970), 23, 30-31.

55. Harold Haas also worked on reducing this material. Haas, interview with author, 17 February 1987.

56. *Sex, Marriage, and Family*, 35.

57. Ibid., 39.

58. Ibid., 41-45.

59. Ibid., 54-55, 59-61.

60. Ibid., 76.

61. BSM Minutes, 25–27 February 1969.

62. BSM Minutes, 25–27 February 1970, 49-55. Harold Lohr, telephone interview with author, 3 September 1987; Herhold, telephone interview with author, 5 September 1987.

63. No documentation on the hearings was discovered; however, Tilberg (interview with author, 12 March 1987) and Niebanck (interview with author, 24 July 1985) described it similarly.

64. William Lazareth, telephone interview with author, 15 September 1987.

65. Carl Thomas, interview with author, 2 May 1987; Tilberg (interview with author, 12 March 1987) said that both Edgar Carlson and George Forell refused to serve in Lazareth's stead.

66. LCA, *Minutes . . . 1970*, 488.

67. Ibid., 614-15.

68. Ibid.

69. Niebanck, interview with author, 24 July 1985; Tilberg, interview with author, 12 March 1987; Lazareth, telephone interview with author, 15 September 1987.

70. LCA, *Minutes . . . 1970*, 615-16.

71. Ibid., 653. Lazareth (telephone interview with author, 15 September 1987) recalls telephone deliberations in his hospital room when this amendment was proposed and his judgment that it was acceptable if interpreted in the spirit of the statement's definition of marriage as "covenant of fidelity."

72. LCA, *Minutes . . . 1970*, 654.

73. Ibid., 616. Memorials to later conventions led to the establishment of a study commission on homosexuality in 1983 and the report *The Study of Issues Concerning Homosexuality* (DMNA/LCA, 1986) submitted to the Executive Council for circulation in the church.

74. Ibid., 654-55.

75. Lazareth, telephone interview with author, 15 September 1987.

76. LCA, *Minutes . . . 1978*, 51, 59, 60.

77. Robert Marshall, telephone interview with author, 30 September 1987.

78. LCA, *Minutes . . . 1978*, 28, 110-11.

79. LCA, *Minutes . . . 1984*, 392.

80. DMNA Management Committee Minutes, 27–29 October 1983, P, Collateral Paper, "Proposed Convention Resolution on Abortion and Christian Conscience"; ibid., 2–4 June 1984, 11.

81. Paul T. Nelson, ed., *Abortion and the Christian Conscience* (DMNA/LCA, 1984), 2. Essays are by Hans O. Tiefel, Joy M. K. Bussert, Jann Esther Boyd Fullenwieder, and Martha Ellen Stortz.

82. LCA, *Minutes . . . 1984*, 392, 48.

7

CHANGING WAYS, 1971–1977

The 1970 convention had marked the beginning of an era of reassessment within the eight-year-old denomination. Neither its financing nor its board structure was meeting expectations. President Robert Marshall first attacked these problems by initiating a system of management by objective, a method borrowed from private industry. His administration also set in motion the Commission on Function and Structure to study the organization and to propose reorganization to the 1972 convention in Dallas.[1]

After the 1970 convention staff and members of the Board of Social Ministry came to feel that procedures and traditions dating to the late 1950s faced an uncertain future. Records of their meetings convey concern to protect the independence of social ministry which they had known under a separately incorporated board. Church members were also restless. At the 1970 convention, Walter R. Harrison, superintendent-pastor of the Lutheran Home in Germantown, Pennsylvania, spoke for others when he called for study of the means used to develop statements and suggested greater participation by members and synods.[2]

Social statements played a less prominent role at the 1972 convention not only because they were eclipsed by the agenda of reorganization but also because the parlance of social reform had grown more familiar. Increasingly, synod conventions called for statements and studies in tandem with their own efforts. Under such prodding, the 1970 convention had shaped the directions for two social statements presented in 1972: "The Human Crisis in Ecology" and "In Pursuit of Justice and Dignity: Society, the Offender, and Systems of Correction." Neither would generate the intensity of debate that had surrounded the adoption of statements at the two preceding conventions.

Seven synods had approached the 1970 convention with memorials on environmental issues. The Board of Social Ministry was assigned the task of mounting "a massive effort to explicate and implement" in two years a set of affirmations about "man and his use of the environment as well as his involvement in the world's population crisis." The board was to educate the church "for the development of personal and corporate responsibility" and to report its "ongoing study" to pastors and congregations.[3] At the same convention the Metropolitan New York Synod raised the issue of criminal justice by memorializing the denomination to oppose "preventive detention" and its incorporation in legal or court systems at either the federal or state levels where "deliberate imprisonment without conviction" would result. The same resolution urged the Board of Social Ministry "to study possible further actions on the subject."[4]

The two social statements would be the last adopted by the church until 1978. In the intervening years, the new Division for Mission in North America would be preoccupied with a reexamination of the ways and means of formulating social policy and with the meaning of pluralism in church and society.

"IN PURSUIT OF JUSTICE AND DIGNITY: SOCIETY, THE OFFENDER, AND SYSTEMS OF CORRECTION"

At its October meeting in 1970, the board mandated a study of reform in the correctional systems of the United States and Canada. The presence of Myrl Alexander on the board provided in-house expertise. Alexander, who had been elected to the board in 1967, was completing twenty-three years with the U.S. Bureau of Prisons, the last six as its director. Raised in the Church of the Brethren, he had chosen a career in prison work out of his religious convictions. He entered the Lutheran church after his marriage in the mid-1930s, while he was working at the federal prison in Lewisburg, Pennsylvania. Deeply committed to reform, he shared the view of the critics of criminal justice systems; he belonged to the American Correctional Association and was on record for his opposition to capital punishment.[5]

Alexander's guidance would bring both scope and practicality to the board's effort. This project was never designed simply as a general study on the subject or as background for church advocacy work. From the outset it aimed to provide support and information to a very specific population, namely, Lutherans working in the fields of law enforcement, the courts, and prisons.

The board pursued its pattern of study with a consultation of nine experts whom Alexander had helped to convene. Staff and board participants came away from the December gathering aware that they could not study the correctional system without also considering "pre-trial procedures, the court systems, and post-release supervision." They drew the line at including crime prevention in their projected study and established three purposes for their work: to awaken church members to the need for reform; to provide information about productive types of social action to effect reform; and to prepare to promote social policy changes at the level of the national governments of the United States and Canada.

The consultation also outlined the structure for a study which would include an account of the criminal justice systems in the United States and Canada, a theological perspective which demonstrated "the systems' incompatibility with implications of a Christian doctrine of man," and a proposal for the church's role in the reform movement. The board adopted proposals from the consultation and appointed an *ad hoc* committee to oversee the development of a statement and a study.[6] Further impetus came from the Texas-Louisiana Synod, which had memorialized the denomination in June of 1971 to develop a national program of education and action "for the purpose of promoting and sustaining a fairly-dispensed justice for all peoples, in the context of supporting law, order and justice."[7]

Public awareness would grow dramatically even as the board tackled the issue. Although the civil rights movement had been drawing attention to the inequities of criminal justice since its earliest days, nevertheless, not until the jailing of such militants as the Black Panthers did prison populations themselves become politicized.

Racially segregated Soledad Prison in California attracted attention in the early seventies for authorities' violence toward angry Black inmates. When George Jackson, author of *Soledad Brother*, was killed at San Quentin in August of 1971, sympathizers at Attica, the maximum security prison in upstate New York, staged a silent protest which triggered greater repressiveness on the part of their anxious wardens. A week later convicts seized control. Four days after that, Governor Nelson Rockefeller abandoned negotiations and directed that the facility be retaken by force. The subsequent deaths of thirty-three prisoners and ten of their hostages, all killed by police bullets, riveted attention on the need for prison reform.[8]

By October of 1971, the first meeting of the board after the tragedy at Attica, Alexander could report that his committee had adopted a prospectus for the background study. He himself had provided staff member

Frank Gunn with materials to write the descriptive section. George Forell was drafting the theological perspective, and Karl Hertz of Hamma Divinity School was at work on the church's role in reform. Through the *Ministers' Information Service*, a newletter supplied by the denomination, the committee had gathered names of Lutherans involved in all aspects of criminal justice and hoped to stimulate discussion and give encouragement to these individuals.[9] The board authorized the committee to proceed with the formulation of a social statement. Richard Niebanck, the principal drafter, was aided by Gunn.[10]

Authors, staff, and committee members worked hard during January and February of 1972 to satisfy criticisms of initial drafts of the background study. A revised version was discussed at length during a small consultation in Washington, D.C., with Alexander, Victor Evjen, who was assistant chief of probation for the U.S. Courts and a member of Washington, D.C.'s Reformation Lutheran Church, and Robert E. Van Deusen, who directed the Public Affairs of the Lutheran Council in the USA. The first two-thirds of the social statement was also reviewed and then mailed to some hundred others "representing a broad spectrum of interests and expertise in relevant areas."[11]

At its March meeting, the board authorized the study for publication in the Christian Social Responsibility series, called for its distribution to convention delegates, and approved the statement "In Pursuit of Justice and Dignity: Society, the Offender, and Systems of Correction" for recommendation to the convention. The committee also reported plans for a three-part popular study on criminal justice in the Board of Parish Education's "Impact" series with a focus on the work that could be done by the church and its members in helping ex-offenders relate to the social order.[12]

At the convention, delegates readily passed the statement. After a hearing on Sunday afternoon, July 2, and subsequent minor revisions by the staff, the convention adopted it, at George Forell's recommendation, the following evening. Alexander had been able to secure the services of Judge A. Leon Higginbotham, Jr., of the U.S. District Court, Philadelphia, an Episcopal layman, as a speaker prior to the convention vote. Higginbotham called for commitment to combat racism and to improve criminal justice. Alexander recalls that what might have been controversial had already been handled in the hearings.[13] So few changes were made on the floor that the minutes for the day do not include the statement as passed. Instead, the recommended statement in the board's report was edited to include all changes.[14]

The statement, like the background study, is structured in descriptive, theological and regulative sections, the last in two parts: "policy goals" and "strategies for the church." The denomination's opposition to capital punishment is recalled. The conclusion to the statement highlights its governing assumptions:

> Only when the offender is dealt with as a member of the community who must return to it will there be any real hope for a criminal justice system that is both just and effective.

The statement emphasizes the social sources of crime and of criminality, "in part reminders of the failure of society to establish justice for all its members." The removal and punishment of criminals is then in the long run, "neither prudent nor just." (See Appendix, "In Pursuit of Justice and Dignity: Society, the Offender, and Systems of Correction," Conclusion.)

The statement arrives at these conclusions based on a reading of the history of criminal justice provided in the background study. The removal of the criminal from society became a widespread practice in the nineteenth century; it was to some degree based on Christian understandings of repentance (hence "penitentiary") and has aggravated a tendency to view such persons as "worse sinners" in the eyes of God. Since "evangelical faith" defines sin as "broken relationships between man and God, and man and his neighbor," all are sinners and in need of constant forgiveness. Hence the church's task in criminal justice "is not one of vengeance or retribution but in the treatment of offenders as fellow human beings, assisting them to build viable relationships."[15]

The statement argues for the distinction between crime and sin and between "socialization" and redemption. Absolutizing the difference between the "criminal" and the "law-abiding" is in itself evidence of radical estrangement from God and evidence that the system which defines crime "is itself capable of criminality." The treatment of Jesus Christ as "a political/religious criminal" or of those who "champion a larger measure of social justice" reminds Christians not to "diabolize persons whom society has declared to be outside the law."

Moreover, since criminal justice institutions are civil institutions, their proper work is to attend to "the socialization of offenders into the society in such a way as to preserve both the dignity of the offender and the safety of the general community." Such an effort is not to be confused with the redemption of sinners—God's task. Furthermore, such institutions must be monitored and held accountable, but ought not be made "scapegoats" for larger problems or expected to improve without adequate allocations of public funds.

123

In a recent interview, Alexander noted that concern for reform in the American public has ebbed largely because of frustration over drug-related crimes. His point suggests one theological point which may have been underplayed in the early seventies—the particular shape which alienation from God may take in the offender. The nearly airtight distinction which the statement makes between crime and sin leaves no room for consideration of the historical forms which sin takes in the lives of individuals in community. The idolatry of drugs, for example, is an all-consuming, progressively physiological passion in which self-destruction leads to the destruction of others. To acknowledge the power of a particular evil would not require "diabolizing" the evildoer.

"THE HUMAN CRISIS IN ECOLOGY"

Following the 1970 convention, the board created a fifteen-member "Consultation on the Human Crisis in Ecology."[16] William Lazareth recalls that it was named to highlight the point on which the church could offer expertise, namely, a theological understanding of human beings in relation to the created order.[17] Yet the theological approach became the point of collegial debate. Ultimately, these differences were masked in the background study and statement and only became public in the book published by Fortress Press in its "Confrontation" series, *Ecological Renewal.*

This issue again brought to the surface the long-standing difference between Lazareth, member of the board's *ad hoc* Committee on Human Crisis in Ecology, charged with overseeing the development of the study and statement, and Joseph Sittler, a member of the consultation. Consultation member H. Paul Santmire, a theologian and college chaplain at Wellesley, shared Sittler's interest in a cosmological interpretation.

Paul Lutz, a biologist at the University of North Carolina, board member and chairperson of the consultation, recalls his impressions of the debate that occurred at the time when the study document and statement were reviewed by board members, probably in the late winter of 1972. Sittler and Santmire held "that nature in and of itself has value and that the goodness of creation ought to be preserved whether or not it was used by man." He perceived Lazareth as maintaining that nature indeed was creation, but in no way had the same value as humanity since redemption occurred only for the sake of people.[18]

Lutz had been elected to the board in 1970 because of his expertise in ecology. In 1969 his presentation on developments in biology for the Lutheran Council in the USA had attracted attention. He was touched by the opportunity to serve his denomination and recalls his work, particularly on ecological issues, as an experience that enabled him "to see a connection between my life as a scientist and my faith."[19]

The consultation began its work in the spring of 1971 with members voicing their varied perspectives on the problem. Lutz recalls that everyone "had their own soapbox speech to make." Santmire remembers his concern to get beyond a nature ethic which did not take account of the inherent political and economic questions. Concern for baby seals in Newfoundland ought not override awareness of low-birth-weight babies of the inner cities.[20] After polling synods to find out what they were doing on the issue and discovering that some were indeed deeply involved and there was broad awareness, the consultation noted that few had given the issue "high priority."[21] They determined to produce not only a study document but also a companion piece to describe "components for strategy and action at regional and local levels."[22]

After two further meetings consultation members working with the staff had produced a background study: Lutz supplied the opening essay by describing biological interdependence in "An Ecological World"; Santmire wrote two chapters, "Toward an Ecological Theology" and "The World as Community"; staff members Franklin Jensen and Cedric Tilberg wove together information gathered by the consultation in "The Community in Crisis" and "Imperatives of Survival"; Sittler wrote the epilogue "The New Creation." The board approved the document *The Human Crisis in Ecology*, edited by Tilberg and Jensen, for publication in the Christian Social Responsibility series at its preconvention meeting in March. It also adopted the social statement by the same name, drafted by Tilberg, and recommended, after five hours of debate, by the *ad hoc* committee.[23]

The statement is in essence a précis of the background study. It warns that ecological balance, necessary for survival, is deeply threatened by "exponential growth" in "production and consumption, sales and profits, population and power." The costs of pollution, depletion, and population pressures are recognizable not only in the environment, but also in social injustice within and among nations. (See Appendix, "The Human Crisis in Ecology.")

Root causes of the crisis are characterized in theological terms: it is not natural forces "but human arrogance and rebellion against God, what the Christian faith calls sin." Humanity's "self-serving" orientation leads to forsaking a "relational" understanding of creation. Ignorance also plays a part, as does the tendency "to perceive the nonhuman world not as possessing God-given integrity of its own."

The statement, therefore, calls above all for a reorientation in values which "give[s] priority to quality of life rather than to quantity of things, characterized by responsibility in human community and enlightened care of the earth and its resources." Here the church can play a crucial role, all the while recognizing the "ambiguity of decision-making."

Befitting such an emphasis on beliefs, the first and longest of nine "imperatives for action" is a "reaffirmation of the biblical doctrine of creation." The study declared as a basic assumption that there was "no cosmic fall," that nature is essentially what God intended it to be, and that the crisis is not one of nature but of humanity.[24] The proposed statement claims that "in one sense man is part of the vast ecosystem" and that "in another sense man is unique in creation" in "his capacity to rebel against God, alienate himself from his neighbor, and deal selfishly with the rest of creation." The statement then emphasizes the call to "responsible stewardship of the earth and all living things" to "work for the fulfillment of all creation and for justice in the human community."

The sharpness of these distinctions was modified quickly on the floor of the convention by Krister Stendahl, who called for omitting the language of two views of man (and also all references to "man" and "he," using rather "person" and "human being") and inserting instead, after the description of the human role in the ecosystem, "*only when this is remembered dare we speak of whatever uniqueness human beings may have,* uniqueness . . . to respond to God in faith."[25] The convention moved to adopt the statement after only brief discussion on Sunday evening, July 2. Stewart L. Udall, former U.S. Secretary of the Interior, had introduced the issue with an address on the ecological crisis.[26]

Notably, the statement does not draw upon the study book's emphasis on the "new creation," an eschatological vision which motivates Christians and is "kept vibrant by a holy judgment in an endlessly sounding counterpoint between the heavenly city that God's will causes us to envision—and the city of our present habitation."[27] That is Sittler's language and also the spirit behind Santmire's "ecological theology."

Only in the introduction to the book *Ecological Renewal*, by Lutz and Santmire, does the debate that had been swirling at the edges of the commission's work come to the fore. There Lazareth, as editor, calls into question Santmire's "eclectic synthesis" on the uniqueness of the human in history and human "solidarity" with nature. Lazareth's alternative is based, he says, "on a more radical view of man's sin and God's grace" and therefore "a consistently sharper distinction (without actual separation!) [his parenthesis] between the creative and redemptive activity of God." He goes on to say that since nature does not fall into sin,

Why should Christians try to base the ethical case for ecological renewal on God's redemptive activity through a cosmic Christology? Is the care of the earth not rather the rational responsibility of all men of good will, whatever their faith, whose living God is continually creating his good earth anew both through and among them?[28]

The board had also determined that the convention action would not be the last word. At their March meeting they had voted to prolong the life of the consultation "to advise the board concerning education and action strategy for dealing with the human crisis in ecology."[29] The consultation submitted a set of proposals for the new church structures which the board adopted in October of 1972.[30]

Lutz recalls Frank Zeidler of the board saying at the time that this was "the most revolutionary" statement yet passed by the church.[31] Indeed, given its scope in calling for a change in cultural values and life-styles, it echoed some of the most demanding proposals of the secular ecology movement. The theological division which the statement tried to straddle may have contributed to its later relative obscurity within the church. The church would find it difficult to maintain momentum after the national tide of reform had ebbed.

SOCIAL CRITERIA FOR
INVESTMENTS

The board also presented to the 1972 convention a report on the social responsibility facing Christians who invest in industrial and financial corporations. This document proposed guidelines and a study paper addressing individual church members, churchwide agencies, and related schools. The board recommended that the report be studied throughout the church and that proposals for following the criteria and exercising "investment responsibilities" be forwarded to the board. An amendment from the floor urged that the board continue to study the issue and provide "advice, counsel and assistance" as requested. The convention quickly adopted the amendment and the report following the board's presentation on Saturday evening, July 1. In so doing, foundations were established for future shareholder action by the binational church.[32]

The report cites four social statements—"Race Relations," "World Community," "Vietnam," and "Poverty"—along with the "Manifesto on the Nature and Mission of the Congregation" as the source for policy that ought to govern its institutional life. Six criteria are established as guidelines: fiduciary responsibility, social justice at home and abroad, the public good, the mutuality of nations, the witness of the community of faith, and ambiguity in the interplay among these criteria. Following the

127

guidelines, a variety of "strategies" are proposed as the appropriate means for goals which the Lutheran Church in America has declared as part of its mission through its social statements, namely, "raising the level of social justice, ending racism and poverty and establishing peace and world community." The list includes research, direct advocacy with corporate managers, public hearings and petitions, stockholder proposals and proxy votes, litigation, selective and special purpose investment, and lay conferences on life and work to bring these issues to the attention of individual investors.[33]

RESTRUCTURING DENOMINATIONAL
SOCIAL MINISTRY

Most board and staff members had approached the 1972 convention with a sense of dread. Myrl Alexander, who had been their liaison on the Commission on Function and Structure, experienced firsthand both the commission's optimism and the board's mood. He agreed at the time with the commission that the boards were operating too independently from the church's administration. At the same time, he feared that the new Division for Mission in North America would "dilute" the work of the board.[34]

At its last board meeting prior to the convention, the board took two actions as a hedge against the loss of independence. First, they sent Charles Bergstrom, Philip Anttila, William Lazareth, Emil Weltz, Frank Zeidler, and Carl Thomas as representatives from the board to meet with President Marshall "to discuss the role of social ministry in the future structure." Second, they set the founding of a "Center for Ethics and Society" as a priority. Both efforts to maintain autonomy failed.

The delegation was unable to change the commission's proposal. Social ministry was to become one part of a division. Legally, this would be accomplished when the separately incorporated Board of Social Ministry merged with the denomination's corporation.[35] Consequently, the board members and supporters bent their efforts to a direct appeal to the delegates at the 1972 convention. There can be no doubt that the board's executive committee was in full support of this effort, since at its final meeting in December of 1972 it requested that the full transcript of this effort be made part of the board's own record.[36] The sources of anxiety included long-standing tensions with the well-financed Board of American Missions, which controlled the ACT fund established in the wake of riots in 1968 and thus was deeply involved in social action.

Paul Lutz presented the amendment to create a fifth division, "The Division of Church and Society," to formulate social statements for the consideration of conventions, to relate to social ministry projects, to sponsor faith and life institutes, and to promote education and action based on the church's statements and studies. Lutz argued that without a separate agency the church could not "effectively minister to the concerns of social justice." George Forell made an appeal in the language President Marshall had used on the "priestly and prophetic" tasks of the church: "If you put the prophetic under an agency which has precisely a priestly function, then the prophetic will be lost." Would an essentially programmatic division not mute the church's voice on social issues? Four other speakers, three of them current or former board members, also favored the motion.

The concerns of the motion's opponents reflected the origins of the plan to restructure. Wesley Fuerst of the commission argued that this division would provide for greater coordination of the sometimes overlapping work of the Board of Social Ministry and the Board of American Missions. Moreover, he did not see "that the prophetic voice is muted in any way by being lined up with avenues for service and for effective implementation." Melvin Hansen, also of the commission, noted that departments within divisions would handle specific "objectives." Five other delegates also expressed opposition.

The amendment failed, and the chair refused the request for a division of the house. Delegates did not lend their support to a subsequent appeal.[37] With its demise in sight, the full board spent its final meeting in October of 1972 in review and planning for the transition. Lazareth summarized the board's work and gave a listing of all statements and studies along with a review of the various formats. He articulated the board's view that "study and action belong together as integral parts of the church's witness to the world" and that responses to urgent problems "must not be divorced from the discipline of rooting these activities in the church's understanding of itself and its theological heritage."[38] Reflections of other board members were later reprinted in the publication *Social Frontiers for Mission* and "offered with the prayer that the full mission and ministry of the church may thereby be strengthened and deepened."[39]

The board also reviewed plans for a Center for Ethics and Society.[40] A consultation held the previous May judged that such a center would function best as a "para-structure," quasi-autonomous in relation to both the church and the academic community, but with the assignment of proposing "how the church can relate to the academic community and voluntary and private groups in the study of ethics and society."[41] This conception demonstrated both an immediate concern for autonomy and a long-range plan to create points of contact between the LCA's proponents of theological ethics and academicians in the emerging field of social ethics.

By December, the board's executive committee no longer held that a separate center would fit with the denomination's more centralized, "new managerial model." Moreover, it would compete with the new division's department on church and society's function and resources. Instead, they proposed that this center for research and networks of communication be developed within the department and have additional staff and resources. Perhaps, with the location of external funding, the center could develop "as a quasi-institutional setting."[42]

The new division and department got under way in January of 1973. President Marshall proposed Kenneth C. Senft as the executive director. Native to York County, Pennsylvania, Senft had previously served for two years as assistant executive secretary of the Board of American Missions and prior to that as secretary for church vocations on the Board of College Education. Active in the Christian student movement after World War II, he had been a leader in the Lutheran World Federation's program for the resettlement of European refugees, where he came to know volunteers Herluf Jensen and William Lazareth. Senft had also been a parish pastor in California.

Franklin Jensen, former president of the Board of Social Ministry from 1967 to 1968 and subsequently a staff member, was chosen to be the first director of the Department for Church and Society. He was joined by staff members Richard Niebanck and Cedric Tilberg. Later in 1973, Elizabeth A. Bettenhausen, who had completed her doctoral studies under George Forell at the University of Iowa, also joined the department. Gerhard Elston served briefly as the director of the short-lived Center for Ethics and Society. Senft recalls that the division's new management committee of twelve included numerous opponents of restructuring, among them Paul Lutz, Frank Zeidler, and George Forell.

At its first meeting in January of 1973, the Management Committee picked up a concern that had been delegated to the Board of Social Ministry—a review of the procedures leading to the formulation of social statements. Raised at the 1970 convention, this matter had surfaced repeatedly in the regional panels conducted by the Commission on Function and Structure.[43] The Executive Council had assigned the topic to the board, which convened a consultation in the fall of 1971.

Five issues emerged immediately in a retrospective on the Minneapolis convention: first, delegates, 60 percent of whom were attending their first national convention, had too much reading material to digest; second, the costs of producing the materials were excessive; third, the Minneapolis convention could not complete its business; fourth, the documents presented differed in style; and finally, the church had difficulty "speaking prophetically by means of a legislative process."[44] Although "Sex, Marriage, and Family" in particular came to mind, all of the studies requiring convention action had contributed to this negative experience.

In a paper written for the consultation, Tilberg raised questions that were bequeathed to the new management committee. Future responses included "constituency reviews" of statements and the 1977 book on social policy *By What Authority?*. Tilberg argued for a more disciplined procedure of study to insure that the church could address issues without succumbing to pressures for a less tempered and more immediate response. He also underscored the lack of clarity on the purpose and authority of the statements. Were they for teaching or for policy?[45]

Tilberg surveyed the possibilities for wider review of proposed statements in the church, beyond the board's standard procedure of submitting drafts to theologians and experts. While arguing that drafts should be reviewed by representative pastors, congregations, and synods, he also noted the drawbacks. Such a process would increase the time needed to develop a statement, perhaps by two years. And although he did not believe that the church body's theology should be subject to democratic decision making, he could also imagine a convention rejecting a statement containing heresy.

Tilberg had also flagged the perennial question of the origins of social statements. Already in 1963, when asked, the Executive Council had told the Conference of Synod Presidents that only the convention or the Executive Council was authorized to speak for the church on national or international matters. Synods could speak to their own members on issues arising in their own territories.[46] The Council had restated the policy even more strongly in 1971 when it recommended that synods address memorials to a national convention to test opinion.[47]

In 1973, the Management Committee identified four sources of study topics—national conventions, requests from synods to the division, the division's Management Committee, and the staff of Church and Society—while also reserving to itself the right to determine the appropriateness of any study proposed outside the convention.[48] Two years later, Franklin Jensen sought more clarification, adding the Executive Council and officers to the list.[49]

The Management Committee had inherited from the board political pressures from both synods and church members that had been on the increase since the late 1960s. The national events of the era, along with the prodding of the board in its early years, had yielded greater interest in social issues. More Lutherans of competing political and ethical viewpoints looked to the corporate structures of their denomination as a platform for their views. In effect, the church body had become something of a "mediating structure" for church people in national politics.[50] In January of 1973 the committee adopted the plan, "except in times of crisis," that the division work with the Division for Parish Services to "enable congregations, through study and feedback, to participate in the formulation of such statements."[51]

Several unsuccessful attempts were made to produce social statements for the 1974 and 1976 conventions. As early as the spring of 1973, President Marshall and others urged that a statement be prepared for the next convention, in part to demonstrate that the "prophetic function" remained integral to the LCA's mission. There was talk of a statement on national health care for 1974 and on the ethics of power for 1976.[52] Other issues absorbed focus and energy. By early 1975, the Management Committee had solidified a viewpoint which would govern the formulation of the last five statements: "Statements should be on basic subjects, espousing principles which are applicable in different times and places, rather than on every social issue that emerges."[53]

BY WHAT AUTHORITY?

Richard Niebanck was asked to produce a study paper on social statements for discussion in the Management Committee. Building on the previous work of Tilberg, Niebanck wrote "Social Statements—Their Purpose and Development" in 1974. The committee endorsed the paper[54] that would become the nub of the 1977 addition to the Christian Social Responsibility series, *By What Authority? The Making and Use of Social Statements.*[55]

In his introduction to *By What Authority?* Kenneth Senft describes the work as one denomination's effort "to state the conditions for that coherence, integrity, and authority which ought to characterize the way in which a Christian community addresses itself corporately to questions of a social nature."[56] Niebanck lays out first the theology behind the preferred "evangelical ethic," then the ecclesial authority by which the church body addresses society, and finally the ecclesiastical procedures for preparing, ratifying, and enacting social policy.

Niebanck's work both codifies and elaborates upon principles already set forth in such items as William Lazareth's 1960 *Theology of Politics,*

132

his 1966 *Social Ministry: Biblical and Theological Perspectives*, and the background study *Church and State—A Lutheran Perspective*. In the first two chapters Niebanck restates the theological foundations for social statements by citing one of Christianity's classic paradoxes and Lutheranism's emphasis: "The world is said to possess, at one and the same time, a legitimate or God-given worldliness and an illegitimate worldliness born of human rebellion against the Creator." Living in this world, the Christian affirms both the institutions and "offices" that contribute to peaceful and just human life and the use of reason, talent, and human institutions in God's service. Thus Christians can promote efforts for justice without requiring the conversion of their partners in the cause to Christianity. And Christians can boldly confess God's act of redemption in Jesus Christ, but at the same time modestly propose directions for action without equating them with God's will.[57]

Niebanck then proceeds to state the Bible's role in the development of ethical positions. Because the Bible witnesses to God's self-revelation and is the norm of faith for the Christian community, and because the Bible mediates the divine Word in human words conditioned by historical circumstances, it is "not to be treated as a repository of propositional knowledge about God or the world."[58]

Misuse of Scripture is only one pitfall in the formulation of social ethics. Niebanck describes several others. Law and gospel become confused when God's rule in temporal society is identified with love and grace rather than with power and lawful authority. The law has two uses. Its theological use is to lay sin bare, to uncover the hypocrisy of those people and institutions hiding their sin behind self-righteous compliance with the law. Its political use corresponds to the "legitimate worldliness" of creation:

> This law is well described as the form of God's will for a fallen world. It governs human relationships and warns against the destructive consequences of license. It provides a framework for order and predictability for human life.[59]

This law exists apart from the gospel. Christians can work with others in the pursuit of justice without "baptizing" either secular offices or their programs; moreover, society need not adopt the church's categories. Still, the church may help to determine the content of justice because of its "living tradition of the Law and the Prophets."[60]

In describing two other errors in ethical thinking, Niebanck elaborates upon the now familiar descriptive, normative, and regulative "operational steps" that govern ethical decision making. He notes that these may not be sequentially the same in each case, nor are they necessarily separable in practice.

The normative refers to the general ethical principle founded in God's activity in history: "God's passion for justice to the oppressed, his covenant-faithfulness with his chosen, and his self-giving love in Christ become for Christians the standard by which to judge human action." In another statement of the standard, Niebanck writes that "God's will is that persons in his image are, like him, to love."[61]

The descriptive covers all that it takes to state the case, including the analytic and synthetic functions "that must be done with modesty and circumspection as well as rigor" because of the hiddenness of human assumptions and value judgments. Experts in the behavioral and natural sciences, history, journalism, politics, and business, as well as the consumer and the victim must be consulted.[62] The regulative marks the intersection of normative and descriptive and "is the arena of goal-setting and legislation," and therefore of reality-testing and compromise. Here the tests of "proportionality" and of "double," or unintended, effects must be administered.

When the normative is derived from the descriptive, "the 'ought' from the 'is,' " deterministic social or economic ideologies become confused with Christian theology. When the regulative is derived simply from the normative, the historical situation is not adequately addressed. "Sentimentality" is the final error Niebanck discusses and refers to the wishful or even utopian thinking which allows people to "escape from the world of ambiguity and compromise."[63]

Niebanck wrote from his own history with the denomination's developing ethical posture in North America and with implicit criticisms of the courses chosen by other church bodies. The activism of the late 1960s had divided the member denominations of the National Council of Churches and exposed the shallow and ephemeral views of some. Niebanck's case for a pragmatic theological approach set the tone for the remaining years of the LCA. His work also helps to explain why, when no agreement could be reached on regulative admonitions, as in the case of abortion, no statement was possible.

Niebanck reviews the statements "Race Relations" and "Capital Punishment" to illustrate theological and operational criteria prior to describing the function of statements and the process for their development. Three purposes are given. First, social statements teach and thereby provide a conceptual framework within which church members and agencies can grapple with issues and choose appropriate action. Second, the statements provide authoritative policy for the regulation of denominational institutions and for addressing other social and political bodies. Finally, the statements represent the church body's public witness on specific issues and therefore contribute to the formation of the public conscience.[64]

On this point, a small paper on public advocacy by Lazareth is included as an appendix in which he distinguishes it from lobbying, proscribed by law for tax-exempt organizations. Other appendixes provide constitutional references, bylaws, and actions by the Executive Council which together make up the "policy of the Lutheran Church in America governing the issuance of statements, testimony and other policy communication on social issues." There are also "administrative procedures" set by the division in April of 1976 to govern official representation before government agencies which are parallel to those established under the Board of Social Ministry in the late 1960s. Arrangements are described for informing all the educational and social agencies under the division's purview of shareholder action.[65]

In the book's final chapter Niebanck describes the procedure for developing statements, saying that people within the community of faith must draw upon each other's expertise and perspective. During the pre-legislative process, drafts of social statements are developed in consultation with theological experts and other experts in relevant fields. Drafts are then shared widely with the denominational constituency for comment and review. The more general statements ought to have the maximum exposure in congregations. Those "of more limited application" may require a "less comprehensive strategy."[66]

The legislative stage follows next, when delegates to the biennial convention study background materials, attend hearings, debate modifications on the floor, and then act upon a social statement. In the post-legislative phase the appropriate denominational agencies develop the means to implement the statement, including educational programs for church members, and to inform the appropriate secular institutions of the denomination's action. There may also be specific actions through denominational agencies, synods, and congregations to effect decisions made in convention.[67]

EQUALITY AND JUSTICE FOR ALL

The bicentennial celebration of the United States inspired another effort at reassessment that paralleled the reconsideration of social statements. President Marshall created the Consulting Committee on the Bicentenary in January of 1973. Chaired by Sydney Ahlstrom, American

church historian at Yale, the committee of nineteen included representatives of historic Lutheran families, historians, and analysts of public
policy. The committee was structured to represent the church's ethnic
diversity, the laity and the clergy, and women and men. The committee
developed two tasks: first, to generate ideas on the theme for denominational agencies and synods; and second, to provide analyses of social
issues facing the nation in its third century for the 1976 convention.
There were also plans to develop a social statement raising critical issues
for the 1976 convention which would then be answered in a 1978 statement.[68]

The consulting committee divided into four study groups on "civil
religion; continuing revolution; racism/sexism/ethnicity/pluralism; and
global needs and resources."[69] Ultimately, these meetings and some of
the consultants contributed to chapters within the book *Equality and
Justice for All*. Consensus for this publication did not come easily. Former
staff members Richard Niebanck and Elizabeth Bettenhausen recall that
the work was time-consuming and laden with controversy.[70]

In October of 1975 Franklin Jensen stepped down as director of the
Department for Church and Society to work as a consultant in synod
program planning, especially on matters of social concern.[71] When William Lazareth was appointed the new director in January of 1976,[72] the
work of the consulting committee became wedded more closely to the
theological tradition appropriated by the former Board of Social Ministry.

Mirroring both the issues and the climate of the times, *Equality and
Justice for All* was designed to "raise the consciousness" of the church
to inequities exposed by the emerging feminist movement and evident in
continuing racism, and to injustices in the nation's conduct of international political and economic affairs. The book's case for continuing revolution also resonated with concerns elevated during the Watergate crisis,
in which the constitutional foundations of the federal government were
tested as the events of the break-in and cover-up were disclosed. After
the threat of impeachment, President Nixon's resignation in August of
1974, and the transfer of the office to Gerald R. Ford, study of the
excessive use of power captured interest. At the same time, the media
had come to highlight problems facing the developing nations of the Third
World and calls for "a new economic order."

The opening chapters of the book not only rehearse the doctrine of
the two realms under God's rule but also treat civil religion along the
lines established in the 1964 statement "Prayer and Bible Reading in the
Public Schools." The authors call for theological dissent from the use of

civil religion as a means to refurbish any sense of American destiny. Such a religion is idolatrous. The times required critical loyalty, not nation worship.[73]

In the analysis of racism and sexism, both the civil and the "baptismal" communities are called to greater efforts to correct inequities and to change perceptions. The church is called to address sexism by distinguishing among the "cultural strands" of its tradition "to clarify the difference between God's Law and human regulations and between the Law which binds us and the Gospel which liberates us."[74]

The assessment of the nation-state in international affairs builds on the themes of interdependence in "World Community," the statement adopted in 1970, although the tone is more pointed. The "energy crisis" and the "ill-considered and immoral intervention in Indochina" had forced a reexamination in foreign policy of the "concentration upon a narrowly military-political concept of interdependence." Insufficient attention to human need and economic demand in the Third World confronts the nation with pressures "that threaten to reduce its affluent lifestyles as well as its national economic strength and moral credibility."[75]

The section on continuing revolution calls for "an agenda for justice" to sustain "the great American experiment" and lists seven preconditions: freedom of information; a vibrant voluntary sector; pluralism of economic and social interests and powers; openness in the cultural mainstream to new ideas and groups; checks and balances in government; written law informed by "higher law" and an independent judiciary; a tradition of "loyal civil disobedience."[76] A thoughtful Canadian perspective in one chapter conveys some of the cultural differences in a denomination spread over two nations. The book ends with an appendix containing the "Universal Declaration of Human Rights" adopted by the United Nations in 1948.

The Division for Mission in North America shouldered responsibility for two other churchwide committees during this era. The Consulting Committee on Minority Group Interests, authorized by the 1972 convention, replaced the Consulting Committee on Race Relations.[77] Its purpose was to develop ways of involving more "minority persons" in the work of the denomination. The committee proposed a resolution to the 1974 convention calling for an "inventory" on race relations since the passage of the social statement "Race Relations." This inventory studied the demography of membership and leadership, legislative actions of the church body in convention and the Executive Council, budgets and financial allocations of the denominational offices, and the attitudes of denominational leaders.[78]

137

Summarizing findings at the 1976 convention, the committee criticized efforts to date, especially the failure of the national staff (predominantly Caucasian males) to address institutional racism. Recommended correctives included affirmative action goals and timetables, oversight to give practical effect to the statement "Race Relations," and a "resource bank" of "minority" persons belonging to the Lutheran Church in America. The committee also recommended that the division include a Department for Minority Group Interests with a representative as director. Massie L. Kennard held the post until his death in 1986.[79]

The second body was also authorized by the 1972 convention. The Consulting Committee on Women in Church and Society, chaired by Louise P. Shoemaker, a professor of social work at the University of Pennsylvania, brought three denomination-wide objectives to the 1976 convention: equalization of the number of men and women employed by the church, educational programs to promote justice and human fulfillment for both women and men, and efforts to build awareness of these concerns in both the church and society.[80] The issues of feminism were debated intensely within the committee. Unable to achieve consensus itself, the committee encouraged discussion within the church. In late 1987 it completed a set of studies entitled "Women and Men in the Body of Christ."[81] The committee also examined the use of language, particularly in the review of liturgy and hymnody for the preparation of the new *Lutheran Book of Worship*.[82]

The years between 1971 and 1977 established new structures of governance and principles of representation in the work of social ministry. The convention-elected Management Committee of the Division for Mission in North America oversaw the work of departments in church and society, higher education, and outreach, and considered the implications of policy in any one sector for all others. In the same years, appointments to study commissions and churchwide consulting committees came to hinge more pointedly upon the gender, ethnicity, and ordained or lay status of nominees, and not only upon their diverse viewpoints or relevant areas of expertise. In the same years, the theological and ecclesial authority of social statements were all elaborated. The ways and means that would shape statements developed during the remaining decade of the Lutheran Church in America were set.

NOTES

1. See Richard G. Hutcheson, Jr., *Wheel Within the Wheel: Confronting the Management Crisis of the Pluralistic Church* (Atlanta: John Knox Press, 1979)

for an account of a parallel struggle within the Presbyterian Church in the United States.

2. His resolution was referred to the Executive Council. LCA, *Minutes . . . 1970*, 647.

3. Ibid., 49-58. The synods of Minnesota, Pacific Northwest, New Jersey, Western Pennsylvania-West Virginia, Metropolitan New York, Central States, and Southeastern Pennsylvania all submitted related memorials.

4. Ibid., 48, 59-60, 661.

5. Myrl Alexander, telephone interview with author, 8 September 1987.

6. BSM Minutes, 24–26 February 1971, 81-82. The *ad hoc* committee, chaired by Myrl Alexander, included Avis R. Johnson, Philip A. R. Anttila and Howard L. Paulsen. BSM Minutes, 27–29 October 1971, Exhibit A, 5.

7. Cited in BSM Minutes, 22–24 March 1972, 102-3.

8. Carroll, *It Seemed Like Nothing Happened*, 52-53.

9. LCA, *Ministers' Information Service* (July-August 1971), SM-26-27.

10. BSM Minutes, 27–30 October 1971, 112-13.

11. BSM Minutes, 22–24 March 1972, 101-3.

12. Ibid.

13. Alexander, telephone interview with author, 8 September 1987; LCA, *Minutes . . . 1972*, 621.

14. LCA, *Minutes . . . 1972*, 581-85.

15. *Reform of the Criminal Justice Systems in the United States and Canada* (BSM/LCA, 1972), 34.

16. Consultation members included Joseph J. Baker (board member), John W. Berge, Barbara Chaffee, Giles C. Ekola, Paul E. Lutz, Robert K. Menzel, H. Paul Santmire, Joseph A. Sittler, Jr., Richard L. Weis, and W. David Zimmerman.

17. Lazareth, telephone interview with author, 15 September 1987.

18. Paul E. Lutz, telephone interview with author, 10 September 1987.

19. Ibid.

20. H. Paul Santmire, telephone interview with author, 10 September 1987.

21. BSM Minutes, 27–30 October 1971, 102.

22. LCA, *Ministers' Information Service* (September 1971), SM-29.

23. BSM Minutes, 22–24 March 1972, 25-31.

24. *The Human Crisis in Ecology* (BSM/LCA, 1972), 40-41.

25. LCA, *Minutes . . . 1972*, 610, 613 (as revised with nonmasculine language, italics mine).

26. Ibid., 610-15.

27. Ibid., 102.

28. Ecological Renewal (Philadelphia: Fortress Press, 1972), xv.

29. BSM Minutes, 22–24 March 1972, 24-25.

30. BSM Minutes, 25–28 October 1972, 122-27.

31. Lutz, telephone interview with author, 10 September 1987.

32. LCA, *Minutes . . . 1972*, 596-97.

33. Ibid., 591-96.

34. Alexander, telephone interview with author, 8 September 1987.

35. This occurred on January 1, 1973. Executive Committee, BSM Minutes, 25 October 1972.

36. Without this action, the only complete record would have been tape recordings of the convention stored in the ELCA Archives.

37. Executive Committee, BSM Minutes, 13 December 1972, 9-19.

38. BSM Minutes, 25–28 October 1972, 86-92.

39. *Social Frontiers for Mission* (BSM/LCA, 1972).

40. BSM Minutes, 22–24 March 1972, 63-64.

41. Ibid., 92-93.

42. Executive Committee, BSM Minutes, 13 December 1972, 19-21.

43. LCA Executive Council Minutes, 26–27 February 1971, 174, quoted in BSM Minutes, 27–29 October 1971, Exhibit D-1, 7.

44. "Consultation on Development of LCA Statements," Executive Committee, BSM Minutes, 26 October 1971, Exhibit C, 1-3. Three parish pastors, two bishops, an attorney, a college student, the author of the resolution, and representatives from the board and its staff were present.

45. Cedric Tilberg, "Process for Developing Social Statements"; summary appears in BSM Executive Committee Minutes, 26 October 1971, Exhibit C, 3-5.

46. LCA Executive Council Minutes, 25–26 January 1963, 388.

47. Ibid., 26 October 1971, 491-92.

48. DMNA Management Committee Minutes, 12–13 January 1973, 50.

49. Ibid., 18–20 September 1975, 481.

50. Peter L. Berger and Richard John Neuhaus developed this concept in *To Empower People: The Role of Mediating Structures in Public Policy* (Washington, D.C.: American Enterprise Institute for Public Policy Research, 1977).

51. DMNA Management Committee Minutes, 12–13 January 1973, 70.

52. Ibid., 5–7 April 1973, 47; 18–20 September 1978, 748.

53. Ibid., 23–25 January 1975, 208.

54. Ibid., 24–25 January 1974, 51.

55. "Social Statements: Their Purpose and Development" (1974). DMNA Management Committee Minutes, 11–12 February 1976; 13 April 1976. The committee authorized the paper's publication as *By What Authority?* (DMNA/LCA, 1977).

56. *By What Authority?*, ii.

57. Ibid., 7-10.

58. Ibid., 10.

59. Ibid., 15.

60. Ibid., 16.

61. Ibid., 18.

62. Ibid., 19.

63. Ibid., 20-21.

64. Ibid., 29-34.

65. Ibid., 40-65.

66. Ibid., 36-37.

67. Ibid., 37-39.

68. DMNA Management Committee Minutes, 18–20 September 1975, 500; Church and Society Minutes, 8–9 April 1974.

69. DMNA Management Committee Minutes, 18–20 September 1975, 500.

70. Elizabeth Bettenhausen, telephone interview with author, 16 July 1987; Church and Society Minutes, 18 August 1975.

71. DMNA Management Committee Minutes, 18–20 September 1975, 481.

72. Ibid., 22–23 January 1976, 593.

73. *Equality and Justice for All* (DMNA/LCA, 1976), 28.

74. Ibid., 56.

75. Ibid., 62.

76. Ibid., 82, 75.

77. LCA, *Minutes . . . 1972*, 631-32.

78. *An Inventory of the Lutheran Church in America: Race Relations* (DMNA/ LCA, 1976), 5-6.

79. LCA, *Minutes . . . 1976*, 478-81.

80. LCA, *Minutes . . . 1972*, 632; LCA, *Minutes . . . 1976*, 481, provides names of the 12 members and 7 staff members representing the churchwide agencies.

81. "Study of Women and Men in the Body of Christ, Sequence of Documents and Decisions," 31 pp. (Consulting Committee files).

82. *Lutheran Book of Worship* (Minneapolis: Augsburg Publishing House; Philadelphia: Board of Publication, LCA, 1978).

8

THE DIVISION'S
FIRST STATEMENTS,
1977–1980

When delegates gathered in Chicago for the 1978 convention, they were reminded of the ongoing controversy surrounding the Equal Rights Amendment. First passed by Congress in 1972 and quickly ratified by thirty-three states, the amendment was now caught in a bog of local politics and disagreements over its legal implications. The 1972 LCA convention had supported the amendment and called upon congregations and synods to work in its behalf at the state level.[1] In Chicago, 143 of the delegates took their seats under protest because Illinois was not among the ratifying states.[2] Later the convention would reaffirm the denomination's 1972 commitment.[3]

The women's movement, if it can even be characterized as a single strand, had been gaining momentum since the mid-1960s. The political wing, led by the National Organization for Women, had originally worked to end sexual discrimination in employment and to establish day-care centers to care for children of working mothers. Pressures from its growing membership led to an enlarged agenda, including liberalized abortion laws; programs to equalize educational opportunities; revision of laws covering marriage, divorce, and rape; and adoption of the Equal Rights Amendment.[4]

Behind the political pressures lay widespread but also varied unrest, particularly among white middle-class women who enjoyed a higher level of education and more affluence than their mothers had known. They had grown up in a culture that was probably more tradition-bound than that of their counterparts in the 1920s, and was likely the result of the social disruptions wrought by the Great Depression and World War II. Nevertheless, the ingredients of education, money, the isolation of suburbia, and the increased acceptance of birth control gave many women in this generation, along with their daughters, the opportunity to question social patterns. Beginning in the late seventies, a shrinking economy pushed even more of them into the workplace and heightened the revolution in middle-class mores. Intellectual explorations of women's experiences and outlooks accompanied social change.

Such pressures helped to open the issue of women's roles in American Christianity. This wave may have taken longer to reach Lutherans because of ethnic family patterns. Moreover, Lutherans had a distinctive set of concerns about women's ordination. Unlike some Protestant traditions in which the ordained ministry is a matter of practicality, Lutheran doctrine holds it to be a mediating agency for the imparting of faith through the gospel and sacraments. Thus the case could not be argued simply as a matter of equality within a profession. Lutherans were forced to reconsider biblical sources and theological traditions before either the American Lutheran Church or the Lutheran Church in America accepted the ordination of women in 1970.[5]

Although the denomination had considered contemporary issues surrounding sex, marriage, and family at the 1970 convention, there remained considerable disagreement. The adoption of a "clarifying minute" at the Chicago convention in opposition to abortion on demand and abortion as birth control[6] signaled the great discomfort that continued to plague the denomination as the secular ideology of the women's movement tested "the evangelical ethic" adopted as policy.

Delegates to the Chicago convention also faced a change in leadership, since Robert Marshall had announced that he would not stand for reelection. The procedure of ecclesiastical balloting produced seventy candidates on the first round, with H. George Anderson in the lead with 244 votes. Next in number were William H. Lazareth (48), Kenneth H. Sauer (38), Herbert W. Chilstrom (37), and James R. Crumley, Jr. (29). Anderson and Sauer withdrew. Lazareth, Chilstrom, and Crumley, in that order, survived for the fifth ballot, which eliminated Chilstrom and left Lazareth ahead. The final ballot elected James Crumley with 337 votes to Lazareth's 330.[7]

Six years had elapsed since a social statement had been proposed to the convention. The Division for Mission in North America now presented "Aging and the Older Adult" and "Human Rights: Doing Justice in God's World." The first originated with the work of the Consulting Committee on Aging, created in 1973. The second, while long a concern of the church, was a direct result of a mandate from the 1976 convention.

"AGING AND THE OLDER ADULT"

A "Convo on the Elderly" held in Pittsburgh in 1973 had proposed a churchwide consulting committee on aging at a time when the topic was gaining attention. With annual increases, the number of U.S. citizens over the age of sixty-five stood at four million. Aging in a youth-oriented culture raised issues with political ramifications, duly noted in a White House symposium in 1971.[8] In 1974, the Management Committee created a consulting committee, with Martin J. Heinecken, recently retired from the faculty at Mt. Airy, appointed to the chair.[9] A staff team from all churchwide agencies joined the effort, and Cedric Tilberg, who would draft the social statement, served as liaison for the Management Committee.

Two issues attracted consultants' interest from the outset. First, many of the elderly in nursing homes or other facilities resided in substandard conditions.[10] Work with the elderly through church-related social service agencies needed evaluation. Second, the retired elderly who were self-sufficient and in good health had too few opportunities to share their learning and experience in either the church or the society at large.

In 1974 Heinecken presented a paper to the committee in which he argued that the church does not have "a theology of aging"; instead there is one theology which speaks not only to the concerns of the elderly but also to other social issues. Heinecken argued that Word and Sacrament had primacy in the ministry to and for older adults and that the church should be encouraged to cooperate with others to provide services for which the whole human community shared responsibility. While the church should call attention to unmet needs in its prophetic mission, it had no special competency in caring for the elderly. Partnerships with those who had the expertise were necessary to promote justice for the entire community.

The Management Committee approved the paper for publication in April of 1975, and it appeared in 1976 along with a study guide prepared by Ralph R. Hellerich of the Division for Parish Services under the title *A Theological Basis for the Church's Ministry for Older Adults.*[11] At the same time, the Management Committee recommended the preparation of a statement on aging for the 1976 convention, but later that year decided to forward only Heinecken's paper to the convention and to wait with a statement until 1978.[12]

Tilberg was assigned to draft a statement. After several revisions were discussed in staff, he circulated a draft among congregations, individuals, government officials in related fields, and friends. While admitting that this method of review would not be considered "scientific," he recalls that he achieved his intention to collect comments from many who were interested in the issue or working in the field.[13]

Several changes resulted from this review. In the section entitled "Agenda for Action," a paragraph on families was added and the one on retirement policy was shortened to a statement of principle. Review in the Management Committee led to the addition of a discussion of public policy.[14] The consulting committee had no formal role in the evaluation of the statement.

Tilberg credits Lazareth with creating the statement's title and treats its significance in his later book *Revolution Underway*. Those who had reached their senior years were not alone in deserving attention. Aging was, after all, "a natural process" that characterized all human beings throughout their lives.[15]

Two hearings on the statement preceded its consideration by the convention on July 18, when Heinecken presented it for action. While most of the amendments were editorial in nature, several expanded the scope of recommendations in the section "Agenda for Action." The first, directed to synods, instructed them to advocate for adequate levels of reimbursement from the government for services provided by church-related agencies and institutions. Another called for the government to establish responsible fiscal policies that took into account the severe impact of inflation upon the elderly and that provided more efficient delivery of human services and more frugality in non-service expenses. A final amendment encouraged the provision of skilled care in institutions, including hospices, in ways that treated individuals with dignity and kept links to family and community intact. After adoption, Franklin Drewes Fry of the Management Committee moved the adoption of a resolution requiring the church to study its retirement policies, a concern of the staff since 1975.[16]

As adopted, the statement contains three major sections preceded by a prologue. The tone of the statement is set by its opening line: "Life is a gift of God, and aging is a natural part of living." The first major section, "Aging: Prejudice and Injustice," has as its premise that negative attitudes within society often place undue restrictions upon the elderly. The elderly are often forced into retirement, and thereby removed from responsible positions in church and society and "protected" from making "life-affecting" decisions. The church claims a deeper foundation for human dignity than either work or status.

This last assertion provides a bridge to the next section, "Theological Affirmations." Holding in tension traditional Lutheran theological formulations about creation and redemption, this part opens with the confession that human beings have dignity because they are created in the image of God and thereby receive "the capacity to relate to God in responsible freedom." Sinful rebellion against God leads human beings of all ages to act destructively toward each other.

A "Christian view of the aging process" derives perspective from Christ's death and resurrection which promises that "the sting of death" will be overcome with the resurrection of the body and that "forgiveness and new life are granted to the faithful in daily and eternal fellowship with God." Baptism leads to "vocation," namely, faithful service to others in love and justice fed by the gifts of the Holy Spirit. After identifying such gifts of the elderly as wisdom and experience, this section concludes by naming civil authority as one of God's foremost ways for dealing with the human condition and, therefore, with seeking justice for the elderly in society.

The final, and by far the longest, section of the statement is entitled "Agenda for Action." Here the rights and responsibilities of the elderly to participate in family, the church, and the community, as well as the responsibilities of the church to attend to the special needs of the elderly, are presented. So thorough is this "agenda" that many contend that, with the exception of "Race Relations" (1964), no other single social statement has had a more pervasive effect upon the institutional life of church.[17]

This statement did not introduce a new area of social policy so much as it reminded the church of its ministry to the aging and elderly, and suggested appropriate actions. Heinecken liked to say that the Consulting Committee on Aging was the church's "goosing committee."[18] Tilberg, in retrospect, believes that the last section in all of its specificity might better have been presented to the convention as a separate set of implementing resolutions.[19] Because the statement was rooted in the experience of an aging generation within the denomination, certitude about its validity encouraged the staff to bypass the new format for constituency review.

"HUMAN RIGHTS: DOING JUSTICE IN GOD'S WORLD"

Concurring with the Bicentenary Committee's emphasis on human rights, delegates to the 1976 convention mandated the development of a social statement. The Maryland Synod's memorial, stemming from a spring symposium held at Gettysburg Seminary's Lutheran House of Studies in Washington, D.C., initiated the action. One of the most influential speakers was the Rev. Helmut Frenz, exiled Lutheran Bishop of Chile and advocate of the human rights of political prisoners and refugees after the 1973 military coup.[20]

By 1976, "human rights" had already achieved a prominent place in social and political discourse. The issue had been highlighted in 1975 with the adoption of the Final Act of the Conference on Security and Cooperation in Europe, commonly known as the Helsinki Accords.[21] Human rights had also become the foundation for antidiscrimination agendas in America. In 1977 the Carter administration began to treat human rights as a major element in the development of foreign policy.

Evidence of further abuses contributed to support for a statement. Infringements were widely known to exist in Chile, the Soviet Union, and southern Africa. Lutherans were especially concerned about their coreligionists in Namibia. The United Nations pressed the issue in 1978 with the adoption of Security Council Resolution 435 demanding that Namibia be given its independence from South Africa in the face of the persistent opposition from the Pretoria government.

In February of 1977, the Management Committee instructed the Department for Church and Society to prepare a statement on human rights. Richard Niebanck was assigned to oversee its development with aims to articulate a Lutheran theological approach, to clarify the ethical issues, to indicate directions and strategies for church and public policy, and to lay the theological and ethical groundwork for future action.[22]

This was the first social statement to undergo the formal constituency review proposed in *By What Authority?* The first stage followed older patterns. Niebanck prepared a basic issue paper and then took it "on the road" for discussion at four seminaries—Chicago, Gettysburg, Northwestern, and Waterloo—and at the University of Iowa where George Forell taught. In addition, the paper was mailed to approximately one hundred others, including professionals in the fields of theology, political science, sociology, and economics. Based on the various responses, Niebanck prepared an initial draft of the statement, circulated it among those involved in the first round of review, and then, drawing upon their comments, revised his draft.[23]

The next stage was new. This second draft was circulated among a sampling of 237 congregations, selected from all thirty-three synods to represent diverse locations, sizes, and constituencies within the synods. Robert Strohl of the Division for Parish Services supervised the research and prepared the report.²⁴ Of these congregations, 113 agreed to respond, 19 declined, and 105 made no response. Yet by November 3, 1977, the date of Strohl's report, only 62, or 26 percent of the congregations originally sampled, had submitted reviews based on a one-time discussion held in meetings of five to ten parishioners. Another 21 congregations apart from the original sample also submitted reports, for a total of 83 congregations from 29 synods. Strohl included copies of the draft in the "Aids In Mission" (AIM) packet, a monthly mailing for pastors and lay leaders. From this mailing Strohl received 275 review forms, 180 from pastors and 95 from lay people.

Strohl identified several clusters of response. There was widespread support for a statement and considerable appreciation for congregational involvement. More than half of the congregational groups found the statement too general. Some wanted more scriptural undergirding for the argument without "prooftexting." Sixty-three groups thought the language was unnecessarily difficult. Finally, some pressed for greater elaboration of the argument for the link between rights and responsibilities.

The review had exposed the very problems that Niebanck confronted as he drafted a theological analysis of human rights. He recalls seeking a middle ground between the classic approaches of John Locke, who emphasized individual civil and political rights, and Georg Hegel, who considered social and economic rights dependent upon the state. Niebanck had also noted the difficulties of establishing rights on a scriptural basis.²⁵

In November of 1977 Strohl's report was presented to a group of consultants which made suggestions for further revisions.²⁶ The next draft was reviewed by the Conference of Synodical Presidents in January 1978. Later that month, the Management Committee approved a final version and an accompanying set of "implementing resolutions" for presentation to the 1978 convention.

At the convention, two hearings were conducted on July 14. By the time the statement reached the floor of the convention, it had garnered considerable support. Fry, who chaired the Management Committee, presented Susan Martyn, a member of the consultation, to introduce the statement.²⁷

During the floor debate, the most critical discussion centered on the citation of biblical texts to support the statement's theological argument. After Pastor Robert E. Goehrig, Jr., proposed that all biblical references be removed from the text of the statement and placed in the study documents, the chair ruled that the review committee, made up of department staff and consultants, take the motion under consideration. Then

Philip J. Hefner of the Lutheran School of Theology at Chicago called for the removal of the following two sentences in the section on "The Human and Human Rights": " 'Rights' is not a biblical category. There is no revealed body of rights."

John H. P. Reumann, a professor of New Testament at Philadelphia Seminary, called in a substitute motion for the replacement of the two sentences with the one: "There exists in the biblical revelation no neat, well-defined, definitive list of human rights." Reumann's motion was modified and adopted.[28] In effect, his sentence acknowledged the difficulty of deriving a fixed body of human rights from Scripture without minimizing Scripture's authority on the issue. Time for debate had expired, and the review committee was given other amendments to consider overnight.[29]

On the next day Fry and Lazareth presented a series of amendments recommended by the review committee and accepted by the convention,[30] the most significant of which was a new introductory paragraph for the section "The Human: A Theological Understanding" which outlined the intentions of the statement to base human rights on a biblical view of humanity. (See Appendix, "Human Rights.") Niebanck describes the statement as moving through three theological "moments": righteousness, justice, rights.[31] Righteousness is God's will that male and female, equally created in God's image, live in "co-humanity," which includes "responsible life in community with God and neighbor and faithful stewardship of the world's resources." "The provisional forms" of God's righteous will are discernible within the corrupted human heart as justice. Human rights are then "*moral* assertions of what justice demands in particular historical situations," as distinguished from the "*legal* guarantees" of civil, political, and economic rights.

The convention moved quickly to adopt the statement and, after some discussion, the set of more specific resolutions in particular areas of public policy.[32] Echoes of at least five other social statements reverberate throughout: "Race Relations," "Church and State," "Religious Liberty," "Sex, Marriage, and Family," and "Ecology." The implementing resolutions address the issues of the day more specifically, including institutionalized populations, refugees, undocumented aliens, torture, political oppression, economic rule, and the equality of men and women. The separation of the statement itself from its implementation reflects the prior reassessment of a social statement's purpose. Policy is contained in the statement and is neither limited to nor bound by the immediate context for its development. Rather, it is forward-looking. On the other hand,

149

the resolutions prevent the statement from functioning in a vacuum and direct its principles to specific historical circumstances.

"Human Rights" is a solemn statement of a position based on the Lutheran confessional tradition. It addresses the issues without aligning the denomination with any particular social, political, or economic ideology. It allows Lutherans themselves to disagree on the particulars of strategy for human rights, while also providing a platform for cooperative efforts with others. So, for example, the theological undergirdings of this statement supported the LCA's expression of abhorrence of apartheid in South Africa, while also leaving room for debate over whether apartheid has *status confessionis*, as proposed by the Lutheran World Federation in Dar es Salaam in 1977.[33] One resolution also set the agenda for the next statement by committing the church "to an intensive study of international economic relations and to the consideration of a major policy statement on that subject in 1980."[34]

"ECONOMIC JUSTICE: STEWARDSHIP OF CREATION IN HUMAN COMMUNITY"

When the Lutheran Church in America met in convention in Seattle two years later, "Economic Justice" was the single social statement on the agenda. In many ways this particular statement is the culmination of efforts throughout the LCA's history to articulate a theological approach to issues of justice. Appearing four years prior to the Roman Catholic Bishops' pastoral letter "Catholic Social Teaching and the U.S. Economy," "Economic Justice" remains a significant counterpoint among North American Christians.

Double-digit inflation and the subsequent rampant unemployment provided the immediate impetus for the statement. Those with low and/or fixed incomes were the least able to cope with violent fluctuations in the economy. In the same years, the disparities between the salaries of women and men engaged in the same work attracted criticism. When a second embargo on oil followed the one in 1973, North Americans again faced their economic interdependence with the OPEC nations. There was also growing concern over the influence of multinational corporations in the Third World.

Theologians in Latin America took the initiative to develop new forms of economic and political discourse that came to be characterized as "liberation theology." The conference of Roman Catholic bishops at Medellin, Colombia, in 1968 became the benchmark of the movement. Noting the cry of the impoverished and confessing the church's former blind support of social disparity, the bishops issued a statement declaring that God had a special preference for the poor.[35]

The theological repercussions of the Medellin conference spread far beyond the Roman Catholic Church as other supporters favored the demand that the Christian churches listen to the cries of the oppressed and actively combat the power of their oppressors. Many believed that liberation theology was a mode of expression which arose from the people themselves and was not based on theoretical constructs taken from classical, European theology. On the other hand, critics challenged the agenda of liberation theology, arguing that it was actually a programmatic form of Marxism couched in theological language.

By the late 1970s liberation theology had entered all theological considerations of political, social, and economic issues. The very terms *poor, oppressed, injustice,* along with their opposites, *rich, oppressor,* and *justice,* had become near-theological vocables.

Following the Chicago convention, the Church and Society staff began to prepare for the drafting of a statement. Richard Niebanck was given a sabbatical leave to study economic theory at the New School for Social Research. The Management Committee issued its formal request in March of 1979 with instructions to highlight the issue of expenditures for armaments.[36] Plans called for a number of regional consultations, each with a panel of experts, to be held during the initial drafting stage. A second draft was to be distributed by mail to people nominated by chaplains and campus pastors, and by the Consulting Committee on Minority Group Interests. Later, the draft was to be presented at two "Listening to People" conferences.[37]

By the spring and summer of 1979, the constituency review began but was unable to attract a wide response. Of the 350 congregations solicited, 135 agreed to participate, but only 32, or 9 percent of the sample, actually responded. Another 222 individuals answered the review form in an AIM packet. When Paul Johnson of the Division for Parish Services compiled the report, he noted that many had expressed doubt whether the church, and especially the clergy, had the expertise necessary for this topic. He also noted that lay people tended to respond from their life experience, and members of the clergy from moral and theological perspectives.[38]

Apart from complaints about its difficult language, the most severe criticism centered on what was perceived to be the underlying economic principles guiding the argument. Some reviewers believed that the draft contained an overly harsh criticism of consumer capitalism. Correspondingly, several thought the draft could be read to support socialism. Others commented that the statement polarized economic groups into the rich and the poor, paying little attention to the circumstances of the middle class. The attempt to describe the interdependence between the industrially developed and the less-developed nations had struck a raw nerve.

The drafters took Johnson's report to mean that the statement required much more work before it would be acceptable in convention. To concentrate on a major redrafting, staff members Lazareth, Niebanck, and George Brand secluded themselves at Princeton Theological Seminary for several days. After Niebanck would complete a set of revisions, his work would be examined by the other two. Following discussion, Niebanck would again incorporate their comments into the document.

The result was a draft of "Economic Justice" very similar to that presented to the convention. This version abandoned any attempt to describe the current situation, because that had been proven impossible to do without appropriating a specific economic ideology. Instead, economic relationships were defined in general theological terms, and the theological section was revamped to fit this definition. Paradoxically, the reliance on broad theological principles allowed the statement to speak more concretely to matters of economic justice without implying an allegiance to any particular economic system.

In February of 1980, the Management Committee recommended the social statement, with minor revision, for presentation at the LCA convention. Accompanied by Lazareth and others,[39] Amalie R. Shannon, who chaired the Management Committee, introduced the statement in Seattle. Delegates were given opportunities both at the plenary session and at several subsequent hearings to offer suggestions for revision.[40] The review committee, led by Lazareth, returned to the convention several days later with a series of editorial revisions which brought greater clarity and precision to the argument of the statement.

The depiction of private property had been the major point of contention at the hearings. Originally asserting that "private property is not an absolute human right,"[41] the sentence was modified to read: "The private ownership of property is a humanly devised legal right which can serve as a means for the exercise of that responsible stewardship which constitutes the divine image."[42] This shift was meant to allay fears that the statement refuted the private ownership of property and to align the section more closely with the total argument.

With a few minor exceptions, the statement as modified was adopted by the convention. (See Appendix, "Economic Justice.") Its subtitle, "Stewardship of Creation in Human Community," denotes its thrust and suggests its connection to "Human Rights." An economic system is defined as "a pattern of relationships, processes, institutions, and regulations, together with the values underlying them, by which the activities of production, distribution, and consumption are carried out in and among societies and cultures." The fundamental questions underlying any system are "political and social in nature" and not confined to the technical experts. The theological section then addresses such questions by employing the traditional distinctions between creation and redemption.

Justice is defined as "distributive love" required by God when many people must be served by limited resources. The content of justice is discovered only through the use of every "aspect" of human life—reason, intuition, politics, and morality—in the midst of human claims and counterclaims. Since sin intervenes at every point, justice determines that people are compelled to serve one another when they might otherwise refuse.

The statement sharpens the distinction between righteousness and justice that was suggested in "Human Rights" and constitutes an indirect criticism of liberation theologies and others which ignore the distinction or equate the two.[43] Righteousness refers to God's redeeming activity in Christ, whereas justice takes place "at the intersection of serving love and enlightened self-interest." Any equation of "human justice with divine righteousness" can only distort the meaning of God's redeeming work on the one hand and blind humans to their own self-righteousness and rationalizations on the other.

The final section, "Economic Applications," addresses the stewardship of meanings and values, government, economic justice, work, and property. In each instance, the statement suggests a sober balance between the need for structure to insure economic justice and the dangers of absolutizing any particular structure by identifying it with God's will. There is also a recognition that even rebellion might be required when all other efforts to effect justice fail.

Supplementing the body of the statement is a set of general implementing resolutions far different in character from those accompanying "Human Rights." These commit the church to study and apply the stated theological principles to its own "corporate stewardship."

"Human Rights" and "Economic Justice" stand together as milestones in the history of the social statements. Although born of the moment, they provided the church with theological principles and practical guidance for its work as an institution in society. They also allowed the church to address a broad range of issues without subordinating its evangelical ethic to any single political, economic, or ideological system of thought. Together they provided a basis for joining with others to take shareholder action against corporations doing business in South Africa. The hope has been that economic pressure would create the political ferment to ease restrictions on human rights.

Constituency reviews expanded the discussion of social issues and gave interested church members a voice in the preparation of statements. The paucity of responses suggested that theological analysis and social thought were not easy exercises for church members. Constituency reviews could also enhance political dissension within the church, one result of confronting the torturous issue of nuclear deterrence in the last years of the Lutheran Church in America.

NOTES

1. LCA, *Minutes . . . 1972*, 671.

2. LCA, *Minutes . . . 1978*, 15-16.

3. LCA, *Minutes . . . 1978*, 678-80.

4. Carroll, *It Seemed Like Nothing Happened*, 34.

5. See Virginia Lieson Brereton and Christa Ressmeyer Klein, "American Women in Ministry," in *Women in American Religion*, ed. Janet Wilson James (Philadelphia: University of Pennsylvania Press, 1980), 171-90.

6. The 1978 minute uses the term *contraception* wrongly, since conception has occurred.

7. LCA, *Minutes . . . 1978*, 100-1, 158, 160, 175.

8. See Cedric Tilberg, *The Fullness of Life* (DMNA/LCA, 1980), 21.

9. Other members of the committee are listed in LCA *Minutes . . . 1978*, 369.

10. Martin Heinecken, telephone interview with von Dehsen, 22 August 1987.

11. The status of this paper was debated. Department for Church and Society Minutes, 18 March 1975; Heinecken, telephone interview with von Dehsen, 22 August 1987; DMNA Management Committee Minutes, 18–19 September 1975. Gail Ramshaw Schmidt edited the paper. DCS Minutes, 12–13 May 1975.

12. DMNA Management Committee Minutes, 18–19 September 1975.

13. Cedric Tilberg, interview with von Dehsen, Glen Rock, N.J., 21 July 1987.

14. Ibid.

15. Cedric Tilberg, *Revolution Underway: An Aging Church in an Aging Society* (Philadelphia: Fortress Press, 1984), 52.

16. LCA, *Minutes . . . 1978*, 322-23. The proposal to study retirement policies led to the preparation of the retirement program *Ten to Get Ready*, by Betty and Umhau Wolf of the Division for Parish Services.

17. In his 1985 paper "Ministry with the Aging and the Older Adult in the Lutheran Church [in America]," Tilberg lists eighteen programs and emphases generated by the LCA Staff Team on Aging. Among them are an extensive pre-retirement program and an evaluation of the mandatory retirement policies for

LCA staff; pension and health benefit issues; parish programs on aging; and the National Lutheran Symposium on the Church and Aging in 1984. The social statement also led to the publication of Tilberg's two books: *The Fullness of Life: Aging and the Older Adult* (DMNA/ LCA, 1980) and *Revolution Underway*.

18. Heinecken, telephone interview with von Dehsen, 22 August 1987.

19. Tilberg, interview with von Dehsen, 21 July 1987.

20. Richard J. Niebanck, *Human Rights: Theological Perspectives*, a staff paper of the Department for Church and Society (DMNA/LCA, 1978), ii.

21. On July 28–29, 1977, Richard J. Niebanck and James Gunther represented the LCA at a consultation sponsored by the National Council of Churches on the Helsinki "Final Act," emphasizing a broad definition of human rights to include security, economics, and humanitarian concerns. Niebanck, Memo to Marshall, Senft, Lazareth, and the members of the Staff Team on World Community, 9 August 1977 (Department for Church and Society files, LCA).

22. William H. Lazareth, foreword, in Niebanck, *Human Rights*, iii. This paper was originally prepared as a study document for the delegates to the 1978 convention.

23. Ibid., iv.

24. "Report on LCA Constituency Involvement in Reviewing the Draft Statement on Human Rights: Congregational Groups," (Department for Church and Society files, LCA).

25. Richard J. Niebanck, interview with von Dehsen, Maywood, N.J., 27 August 1987.

26. The members of this consulting group were Rebecca Rae Anderson, Jane Baldwin, Rev. Thomas B. Miller, Ronald S. Christenson, Ralston Deffenbough, Rev. J. Patrick Flynn, Douglas W. Johnson, Lani Johnson, Amy B. Machen, Wolfram Kistner, Susan Martyn, Angela Metzger, Eberhard Scheuing, and Edward Schweitzer.

27. LCA, *Minutes . . . 1978*, 216-26.

28. Ibid., 226.

29. Ibid.

30. Ibid., 351-52.

31. Niebanck, *Human Rights*, 2.

32. LCA, *Minutes . . . 1978*, 353-62.

33. See Eckhart Lorenz, ed., *The Debate on Status Confessionis: Studies in Christian Political Theology* (Geneva: Lutheran World Federation, Department of Studies, 1983) and Paul H. Hinlicky's review in *The Lutheran Forum* (Advent 1984). For the interpretation given by Lutheran World Ministries on this point, see LCA, *Minutes . . . 1978*, 574.

34. The Church and Society staff had begun work the previous year. DCS Minutes, 10 February 1977, 10 March 1977, 16 May 1978.

35. See Deane William Ferm, *Third World Liberation Theologies: An Introductory Survey* (Maryknoll, New York: Orbis, 1986), 10-11. Ferm summarizes the essence of the conference's sixteen documents with two statements:

(1) By its own vocation Latin America will undertake its liberation at the cost of whatever sacrifice.

(2) The Lord's distinct commandment to "evangelize the poor" ought to bring us to a distribution of resources and apostolic personnel that effectively gives preference to the poorest and most needy sectors.

See also Deane William Ferm, *Third World Liberation Theologies: A Reader* (Maryknoll, N.Y.: Orbis, 1986), 3-11.

36. DMNA, Management Committee, Minutes, 22–24 March 1979, 12-13.

37. Ibid., 6.

38. "Report on LCA Constituency Response to the Draft Statement on Economic Justice," 19 October 1979 (Department for Church and Society files, LCA).

39. Rose Marie Newsome, Dennis Sullivan, and Joseph Walker.

40. LCA, *Minutes . . . 1980*, 130-37.

41. Ibid., 136.

42. Ibid., 190.

43. Niebanck makes this challenge more explicit in his book in the Christian Social Responsibility series, *Economic Justice: An Evangelical Perspective* (DMNA/LCA), 69-86.

9

DIFFICULT DECISIONS,
1981–1984

The final two social statements tested the denomination's mettle on the issues of nuclear war and death. "Death and Dying," adopted in 1982, was the legacy of two decades of study in biomedical ethics. "Peace and Politics," adopted in 1984, was shaped in the atmosphere of intense debate over President Ronald Reagan's defense policy, but was rooted in long-standing judgments about armaments and international relations. Each demonstrated some of the limits in denominational policy making. Both were passed in conventions preoccupied with the question of Lutheran merger.

"DEATH AND DYING"

Biomedical ethics (called "bioethics" in issues of research) had been under study throughout the years of the LCA and was a successor to the project "Man, Medicine and Theology" initiated in 1958 by ULCA's Board of Social Missions.[1] The National Council of Churches had helped to fuel interest by hosting conferences and generating publications. From the outset, the Board of Social Ministry was determined to provide information and ethical reflection on decisions surrounding the beginning and end of life and therapies for emotional and physiological disorders. The series "Studies in Man, Medicine and Theology," written by consultants, began appearing in the mid- to late 1960s,[2] and the board established its own committee to tend to this work.[3]

In one of its last acts and in response to a convention resolution in 1970,[4] staff members of the Board of Social Ministry organized a consultation on euthanasia in which Elizabeth Kübler-Ross, author of *On Death and Dying*, participated.[5] Meeting in Chicago on October 15–16, 1971, the consultants included representatives from the fields of medicine, hospital administration, ministry, mortuary science, and law.[6] The board's own *ad hoc* Committee on Death determined the need for consultation with theologians, and Aarne Siirala, Carl Braaten, Krister Stendahl and, from Smith College, Karl Donfried, met with staff members in New York in August of 1972. Church reorganization interrupted efforts to produce a publication on the topic for the Christian Social Responsibility series.[7]

The thicket of ethical issues only continued to grow with the new and ever-changing medical techniques and the court cases which reviewed their application. As the Division for Mission in North America shouldered the board's commitment to study, the Supreme Court's decision in *Roe* v. *Wade* in 1973 suggested that more guidance on abortion was needed than the few lines in the church's 1970 statement "Sex, Marriage, and Family." On invitation, Franklin Sherman wrote the small book *The Problem of Abortion—After the Supreme Court Decision* in 1974. Sherman described decision making on abortion as "a balancing of factors" determined by "whether or not one counts the embryo or fetus as sufficiently human to make the taking of its life in any way comparable to capital punishment or even murder."[8] Sherman would later play a major role in drafting the statement on death and dying.

By the late seventies, biomedical ethics had moved toward the center of the division's agenda with plans for the development of a broad social statement.[9] Two memorials to the 1978 convention from the Central Pennsylvania Synod, one on the value of human life, the other on cloning and genetic engineering, encouraged this emphasis.[10] At the same time, staff members did not agree on the theological or ethical framework. Staff member Elizabeth Bettenhausen, charged with the coordination of the division's work in this area, wrote a study paper in the fall of 1978 on *in vitro* fertilization, and told the Management Committee the next spring that "the ethical issues posed in new research and technology will challenge certain traditional theological positions inherent in social statements to date and will demand a more careful methodology in ethics."[11] She said in a recent interview that her opposition to the use of a two-kingdoms ethic derives from an epistemological critique of the way in which reason, without reference to the gospel and without representation from those whose lives are directly affected by an issue, is used to develop an ethical position.[12]

As events unfolded, plans for a statement in 1980 were aborted. Theological differences between Bettenhausen and Lazareth, now director of the department, had intervened. Bettenhausen's initial drafting of a statement and plans for a "constituency review" were halted in May of 1979, after she had announced her intention to accept a teaching position at Boston University and to leave the department in July. Once she left, no other staff was assigned to the project. When Lazareth himself left the following year to accept a position with the Faith and Order Commission of the World Council of Churches, the department had lost the two persons most involved in the project.[13]

Before leaving, Bettenhausen had convened a consultation on "bioethics" in April of 1979 at the Yahara Conference Center in Madison, Wisconsin. She had located some one hundred Lutherans at work in the fields of biological and medical research, medical services, and ethics. Participants prepared twenty-seven working papers for the conference and met in six consulting groups covering (1) reproduction, (2) genetic research, (3) human experimentation, (4) issues related to death, (5) allocation of resources (material and financial), and (6) responsibility and principles for decision making.[14]

When Paul Brndjar, former bishop of the Slovak Zion Synod, accepted the position as the new director of the department in 1980, he inherited a project that was understaffed and floundering, and a convention-mandated deadline for a social statement. He took the unusual step of asking Franklin Sherman to direct the project as a part-time consultant.[15]

Sherman first assembled some of the participants from the 1979 Yahara conference in Chicago in November of 1980 for what came to be called "Yahara II" to determine the scope of a statement or statements and to identify the appropriate publics and resources.[16] The conference chose to address the "person in the pew," including health care practitioners and patients and their families, along with the patient's "support community" of researchers, administrators, and policy makers. Secondarily, church policy would also be directed to the wider discussion of the issues. Conferees also accepted staff advice that creation and its stewardship ought to be the theological point of departure, and proposed the formulation of two statements, one on the beginnings and end of life (for the 1982 convention), and the second on health care (for 1984).[17]

After assessing the conference report, the Management Committee requested instead two social statements for the 1982 convention, one on theological perspectives and the second on death and dying.[18] By June of 1981, Robert Esbjornsen, professor of ethics at Gustavus Adolphus College, had drafted "Biomedical Ethics: Theological Perspectives," and Daniel Lee, his counterpart at Augustana College, "Biomedical Ethics: Death and Dying."

The constituency review conducted during the summer of 1981 not only attracted the highest number of respondents to date (143 out of a sample of 303), but also elicited appreciation from parishioners, many of them nurses and doctors, that their denomination was addressing such issues. Preferences were stated for the church's taking specific positions, even where members might disagree.[19]

In its next step, the staff took the various reviews to a theological consultation in New York in November of 1981, where consultants advised that energies ought to be focused solely on the preparation of "Death and Dying" for the convention. The staff concurred and anticipated drafting a more expansive statement on biomedical ethics for the 1984 convention, a goal that was never met.

Sherman and Lee continued to revise the statement. Paul T. Nelson, a doctoral candidate in ethics at Yale and a part-time consultant with Church in Society since 1981, served as their liaison with the department. Lee was asked to prepare a study document for convention delegates which was published after the convention in the Christian Social Responsibility series as *Death and Dying: Ethical Choices in a Caring Community*. The drafters next added a section of theological perspectives to the statement. After completion, the document was reviewed by staff and some of the consultants. In February of 1982 the Management Committee approved the draft unanimously after suggesting small stylistic changes.[20]

Two decades of work on biomedical ethics had produced more by way of discussion and study documents than by way of social policy. At the same time, this statement and the ones on sex, marriage, and family, and aging addressed the private sphere at a time when public policy was attracting the most attention among mainline Protestants. After this convention, issues of merger and then of reduced staff curbed the original plans for developing any further statements on the subject.

Amalie Shannon, who chaired the Management Committee, presented "Death and Dying" to the 1982 convention and explained its evolution. Sherman then summarized the statement and its implementing resolutions.[21] Next, delegates had an opportunity to discuss the statement at several hearings. As a result, the review committee returned to the plenary session with several modifications, including two additions to the resolutions: a statement on hospices, and the promotion of advocacy for those among the terminally ill faced with bankruptcy and for the just distribution of medical resources. With only a few editorial changes, the statement as proposed was adopted by the convention.[22]

The major argument over the statement did not come until two years after its passage. In Toronto in 1984, against the wishes of the Committee on Memorials, delegates forced the issue of amendment to eliminate on theological grounds, the depiction of "death as friend." Such action required an amendment to the denomination's bylaws, since provision had never been made for either changing or retiring social statements, except in the specific instance of the interim statement "Marriage and Family," adopted in 1964 and replaced in 1970.

The Virginia Synod had sent the memorial to modify the phrase "death as friend" to "death as merciful," since the intent of the original phrase was to recognize that in certain cases death brought release from torturous illness and also because the phrase contradicted the scriptural image of death as the enemy (1 Corinthians 15:26). The synod's memorial was adopted and the Executive Council instructed to prepare an amendment to the bylaws.[23]

"Death and Dying" does not focus on the technicalities of defining death but rather on the ethical dilemma associated with dying. (See Appendix, "Death and Dying.") The theological characterizations of death as "natural," "tragic," "friend" (later, "merciful"), "enemy," and "conquered in resurrection" offered biblical principles for making judgments in specific instances. In each case the statement recognizes the patient's role in making decisions about treatment, while also noting the more thorny cases when his or her judgment is impaired. The statement also asserts that life has meaning and hope even in suffering; calls for the support of those friends, relations, and medical professionals caught in the web of suffering; and describes the church's ministry of Word and Sacrament and of consolation.

Work in biomedical ethics did not end with the adoption of "Death and Dying." In 1984, under the editorial direction of Nelson, the division published the collection of essays *Abortion and Christian Conscience: Theological and Ethical Perspectives* after the Management Committee had determined that divergent views in the church prevented the agreement necessary for a formal resolution (see p. 114). Nelson also oversaw the development of another series of essays prepared in cooperation with the American Lutheran Church and later published in a collection edited by Edward Schneider, *Questions About the Beginning of Life.*[24]

"PEACE AND POLITICS"

The last social statement of the Lutheran Church in America was passed in Toronto in 1984 under a cloud of acrimony. The call for a statement on nuclear weaponry, deterrence, and "limited" nuclear war had been unequivocal. Differences over ethical analysis had surfaced two years earlier and was a portent of debates to come.

Anxiety and political disagreement had been exacerbated by recent events. Both the United States and the Soviet Union were developing lower yield, more accurate nuclear missiles which now made limited nuclear conflict possible, especially in Europe. In addition, the Reagan administration had countered the Soviet deployment of SS–20 mobile missiles targeted for Western Europe with the deployment of Pershing II and land-launched Cruise missiles directed at Eastern Europe and parts of the Soviet Union. These factors, coupled with the failure of the Senate to ratify the SALT II agreements and the weakening of *détente*, made nuclear conflict seem more likely than at any time since the 1962 Cuban missile crisis.

Twenty-one memorials addressing issues of war and peace in a nuclear age had been addressed to the 1982 convention. The departmental staff prepared a sense motion in response, which Ralph Eckard of the Office of the Bishop took to the Committee on Memorials. As modified and adopted in convention, the motion asserted:

> It is the sense of the delegates to the 1982 convention of the church to declare our support for a multilateral, verifiable freeze of the testing, production, stockpiling, and deployment of nuclear weapons and delivery systems as a step toward the eventual elimination of nuclear weapons and to work actively to achieve such a goal.[25]

Upon request, the chair had defined a sense motion as "a strong expression" of the convention's opinion when a convention is not yet prepared "to take action that will establish policy."[26] The statement also called upon the division to prepare a social statement and for a separate commission "to develop a contemporary theological/ethical study on these issues."[27]

Richard Niebanck's collateral paper "Peace, Power, and Might: The Church and Global Politics in a Thermonuclear World" was also recommended for study.[28] It employed the evangelical ethic to emphasize the complexity of issues and the nature of the moral and political dilemma created by the existence and possession of nuclear weapons.

This paper built upon previous work. There was, of course, the ULCA's 1960 statement "On the Problem of Nuclear Weapons," for which William Lazareth and O. Frederick Nolde had written the background study. "World Community," adopted by the LCA in 1970, was another resource. In 1979 Niebanck, along with George Brand, a pastor who held a doctorate in international relations from Columbia University and who had joined the staff in 1977, wrote a study on SALT II. While supporting the use of political means to limit the production and deployment of nuclear

weapons, they advocated neither unilateral disarmament nor an escalation in the number of weapons. Rather, following Nolde's and Lazareth's
approach, the study allows for the use of weapons for deterrence together
with negotiations for international arms reduction.[29]

In 1982 the department produced two other study papers. *Peace and
War: Some Theological and Political Perspectives* provided a topograph-
ical map of the debate among Christians. It drew the distinction between
human conflicts and God's war against sin, and between "temporal
peace"—the fruit of justice accomplished by politics—and God's eternal
peace—reconciliation with humanity. Brand wrote *Arms Control and Reduction in the 1980's: Problems and Prospects,* drawing upon McGeorge
Bundy's argument that deterrence is grounded in the "psychology of perceptions," the paradox that nuclear war in the present age can only be
averted by the possession of weapons and the apparent willingness to
use them.[30]

While many of these motifs would appear in the 1984 statement "Peace
and Politics," during the initial stages the drafting committee, made up
of members of the department, shared no consensus, but rather represented a range in perspectives and areas of expertise. Richard Niebanck,
knowledgeable in theology, ethics, and political science, was joined by
two students of international relations, George Brand and Katherine
Kidd, a doctoral candidate at the University of Pennsylvania; Paul Nelson,
an ethicist; and Paul R. Hinlicky, a doctoral candidate in systematic theology at Union. Paul Brndjar served as their moderator. Staff members
squared off immediately on three basic issues: (1) the nuclear freeze, and
a variant of that debate, (2) disarmament versus deterrence, and (3) the
pertinence of the "just war" theory in a nuclear age. Another controversy
centered upon whether the church ought to assume a "moral" or a theological position. Was a moral position so bound with the social climate
that it left no room for an independent theological perspective? Some
believed a statement should be an explication of theological principles
applicable to matters of nuclear conflict, while others maintained that
the statement should be more specific.[31]

Once the issues were defined in October of 1982, two staff members
were given leading roles. Niebanck was designated to manage the project
and to provide the first draft of a social statement. Hinlicky was assigned
to write a background study, *Christian Faith and the Nuclear Morass,*
which was eventually approved by the Management Committee for publication in 1983.[32] While Hinlicky spoke only for himself, his argument
reflected a growing consensus among the staff over the policy of deterrence. Niebanck's proposal for the social statement was approved by the
Management Committee on Armistice Day, November 11.[33]

By early 1983, as staff members reached greater agreement the contours of the statement took shape. Staff judged that the statement should include both an explication of the evangelical ethic and a statement of policy on the problem of warfare in a nuclear age. Similarly, they began to agree that the categories of the just war theory provided at least the vocabulary of the discussion, although there was still some disagreement over whether the theory itself was applicable.

In February Niebanck completed the first draft entitled "The Future of Temporal Peace: Politics and Might in a Post-Modern Age." Divided into three major sections, it begins with a careful analysis of the policy of deterrence, noting both the possibility that deterrence has contributed to the absence of a major war since World War II, and the risks, including a "flexible response," inherent in the presence of nuclear weapons. Next the statement considers theological principles on such points as the state's authority to use force to maintain peace and the applicability of the just war theory to nuclear conflict. The final section supports the peace movement as an independent expression of popular concern and recognizes political realities which commend a policy of deterrence.[34]

During the same months, preparations were under way for a symposium on contemporary issues of peace and war. Called by Bishop Crumley, the symposium was arranged by the Department for Church in Society and held in March of 1983. Lutherans were invited from colleges and seminaries and from all the synods to gather at the National 4H Center in Chevy Chase, Maryland, to hear and discuss presentations analyzing present tensions in East–West relations and offering ethical reflections. The gathering was intended to fulfill the mandate of the 1982 sense motion to stimulate study throughout the church and to contribute to reasoned and constructive public debate.

Speakers included Jaroslav J. Pelikan (Yale University), Moorhead Kennedy (Cathedral Peace Institute, New York), Zbigniew Brzezinski (President Carter's National Security Adviser), and Paul Warnke (Former Chief U.S. Negotiator on SALT II). In addition, four others, Eckehart Lorenz (Lutheran World Federation, Geneva), Heinz Vetschera (Institute of Strategic Studies, Vienna), Sven Kraemer (National Security Council), and Trutz Rendtorff (University of Munich) offered European perspectives.[35] Ties with these latter individuals had already been established when Brndjar, Niebanck, and Brand took early drafts of the statement to Tübingen, Munich, and West Berlin for discussion among Lutheran leaders.

While the participants appreciated the quality of the presentations, the symposium as a whole received mixed reviews. Some participants complimented the staff for the high quality of the presentations and for the opportunity to discuss these issues with people from other parts of the country. Other participants believed the event had been designed to present a "conservative" point of view and that the agenda was too cumbersome to allow sufficient time for discussion. A videotaped summary and study guide were sent to the synods to provoke wider discussion.

Later that year, the Roman Catholic Bishops joined the national dialogue by issuing the pastoral letter "The Challenge of Peace: God's Promise and Our Response." The bishops kept public their deliberations on earlier drafts and their negotiations with the Vatican. The distinction they drew in the latter between binding moral teachings and policy suggestions demonstrated the unique role of the magisterium in American Christianity.

By April of 1983 the next draft of the LCA statement, now called "Peace and Politics: God's Call to Temporal Peacemaking," was ready for constituency review. Again, Robert Strohl was charged with its design and execution. In a sample of 310 congregations, 190 agreed to participate and 96 actually submitted reviews.[36] Reactions varied, but indicated widespread disagreement. Twenty-seven congregational study groups supported the thrust of the statement, while two dozen opposed it. Some of these latter went so far as to recommend that the entire draft be scrapped and replaced. About one third held that the statement "lacked vision," and called for a "more prophetic" stance and a greater sense of urgency. Twenty-seven called for a closer link to the biblical witness and to theology. Nine called for more of a "world scope," while twenty-seven expected greater "ecumenical awareness." The statement was criticized for being vague by nearly one-third, for containing difficult language by about one-half, and for being "too wordy" by more than one-quarter of the study groups.

Responses from both congregations and individuals were also received through the July AIM packet and tended to confirm the sample. More than three hundred individuals had submitted comments. Following the constituency review, the proposed statement was evaluated at two "Listening to People" conferences. In February 1984 a draft of the social statement was presented to the Management Committee, where the range of opinion was as wide as it had originally been in the staff. After some debate and revision, the social statement "Peace and Politics" was approved for presentation at the Toronto convention.[37]

Never had opposition to a statement been more public. Joseph Sittler wrote an open letter in February that criticized four elements of the statement's argument: deterrence, verification, peace, and love and justice. Sittler also called for a "fresh mode" of moral reflection and argued

165

that the centerpiece in Lutheran doctrine ought to be the Word of God. He suggested that the creation of a "Commission of Theology and Ethics" would be an improvement over the different commissions and drafting groups put in place with each new statement. His suggestions are continuous with his long-standing criticism of the reigning evangelical ethic.[38]

In the month just prior to the convention, two public attacks were launched. First, Paul G. Johnson, himself a staff member of the Division for Parish Services, published "Deterrence and the Kingdom" in *Currents in Theology and Mission*, a journal edited by the faculty of Christ Seminary, Seminex.[39] Johnson, a proponent of nuclear disarmament, challenged the applicability of the doctrine of the two kingdoms to the issue of nuclear warfare by citing the economic drain and atomic waste inherent in a nuclear buildup and the failure of deterrence to prevent conventional warfare in either Grenada or Afghanistan. He proposed instead that the United States and the Soviet Union each construct a policy based on the kingdom begun by Jesus and assign their resources to the care of the poor, not the production of nuclear arms.

Meanwhile, the Lutheran Peace Fellowship, centered at Luther Northwestern Seminary, somehow obtained a list of the names and addresses of the convention delegates for mailing "What Is the LCA Saying about Peace and Politics? Some Comments on the Proposed 'Peace and Politics' Statement," a collection of critical reviews from theologians, pastors, and lay people.

The statement came before the convention on the morning of June 30 when Robert West, chairperson of the Management Committee, asked Philip J. Farley, senior research associate at the Center for International Security and Arms Control at Stanford University, to introduce the proposed social statement. Paul Nelson then presented an overview of its sections.[40] Two hearings held that afternoon gave delegates occasions for detailed discussion.

Debate on the convention floor began on the afternoon of July 3, once Brndjar had introduced some editorial changes.[41] Bishop Herbert W. Chilstrom of the Minnesota Synod moved to delete the assertions which claimed that the absence of any "nuclear exchanges" gave evidence that "the destructive potency of war" was widely recognized. His motion to weaken the argument for deterrence was adopted. After the defeat of several other motions, Krister Stendahl moved the deletion of several lines containing biblical references to God's use of aggression to punish injustice (Jer. 51:27; Micah 5:15; Rom. 1:18–32). This amendment, along with several others offering editorial changes, was adopted by the convention.[42]

166

Pastor Joy M. K. Bussert, a delegate from the Minnesota Synod and a newly elected member of the Management Committee, then moved and was supported by the majority of delegates to insert a paragraph in the section entitled "Judgments and Tasks" that condemned the "misappropriation of valuable resources" in the escalating arms race and affirmed the need for the global security necessary to pursue "progress against poverty and economic injustice."[43]

Pastor Ronald K. Johnson, another delegate from the Minnesota Synod, rose next to propose an amendment that would further undercut reliance on a policy of deterrence. After the statement's words "what it would be wrong actually to do, it is also wrong to intend or to threaten," he suggested four sentences:

> It is further the conviction of this statement that the strategy of nuclear deterrence cannot be embraced as one that adequately deters. Power believed to be a deterrent invites the response of a larger power. There is thus stimulated an ongoing escalation of the arms race that threatens total failure of deterrence. Therefore, we call upon the governments of the United States and the Soviet Union with their allies, to explore alternative strategies that would permit the world to move away from relying upon deterrence for peace and security.[44]

Discussion of this amendment resumed on the morning of the next day, the Fourth of July. After arduous debate, the amendment was defeated by a closely divided house, 319 in favor to 354 in opposition.[45] Pastor Robert L. Baughn, Jr., of the Central Pennsylvania Synod, then offered a series of four editorial amendments, two of which were adopted, the one labeling deterrence "appalling," (a substitution for "dangerous") and the other adding the judgment that "deterrence as a permanent policy is not acceptable."[46] Since time for debate again expired, Bishop Crumley, who recalls this debate as his most grueling experience as a presiding officer, ruled that subsequent amendments had to be submitted by midnight for consideration on the next day, the convention's final session.[47]

Early the next morning, the review panel and department staff labored over the proposed twenty-four amendments prior to the final day of debate. Of these amendments, two were adopted. The first was a minor change in wording. The second amendment was offered by Ronald Johnson, whose earlier amendment on deterrence had failed. He proposed successfully that the sense motion on the nuclear freeze adopted by the

1982 convention be inserted as policy in the section "Judgments and Tasks."[48]

At the end of the deliberations, three motions proposed an elaboration of the position on pacifism. After the first was defeated and the second ruled out of order, Pastor James A. Scherer of the Illinois Synod delegation proposed the insertion of a paragraph in the final section citing "both the Word of God and ecumenical sensitivity" as mandates for honoring "those who in obedience to Christ's command renounce all violence and commit themselves to the way of the cross as the only path leading toward reconciliation and peace," and for seeking "counsel and dialogue" with them.[49] When delegates adopted the motion, they accepted a statement that called pacifism "the way of the cross," while also affirming that faithful Christians could support deterrence as a necessary evil to restrain major powers.

At Bishop Chilstrom's request, Bishop Crumley counseled the convention on the authority of social statements, advising them that statements direct the policy of the church but are not binding on the consciences of individual members.[50] After his comments, the statement passed handily, with 557 of the delegates voting for the statement and 62 against it. George Forell was among those who claimed that without the inclusion of the freeze amendment, they could not have voted for the statement. Thirty-five opponents requested that their negative votes be recorded in the minutes.[51] Making no further changes, the delegates adopted the "Enabling Resolutions."[52]

The normative principles of the statement hinge on several theological judgments. Its title suggests the first; namely, that dominion over the earth is exercised through politics. Second, estrangement from God in sin nurtures fear and breeds hatred and violent aggression, the root cause of war. This section eschews the appeals to the just war theory that were made in earlier drafts, while still employing its language. The church's role is set forth as both modest in view of sin and bold in view of Christian freedom. "Peace and Politics" rejects any special authority for the church to advocate particular policies as if they had divine sanction. "Political stewardship" is exercised corporately by the church in society and individually by citizens, and obligates Lutherans "to contribute to the ongoing debates on matters that affect the survival and well being of the human family and all creation."

Delegates had agreed on many of the policy directions suggested, including a condemnation of the notion that nuclear wars could be won, that a "first strike" should be used to disarm the enemy, or that revenge might dictate retaliatory strikes. The statement also rejected policies intended for achieving nuclear superiority and the belief that such warfare might be warranted in an apocalyptic struggle between forces of absolute good and evil. Distinctions are kept between the political work necessary for "peacekeeping" and "peacebuilding" and the perspective Christians could bring to bear on their roles as "peacemakers." The final enabling resolutions gave instructions on the use of the statement within the church, in advocacy efforts, and as a message to world leaders.

"Peace and Politics" was the last of the denomination's social statements. As adopted, it offered the olive branch to warring factions within the church who disagreed over the policy of deterrence, the proposal of the nuclear freeze, and the proper expression of Christian conscience in the vocation of peacemaking. These Lutherans could not agree on a single prophetic cry that addressed both church and society amid the threat of nuclear war. Did such conditions warrant an appeal to absolutes in the formation of national policy and of individual conscience? Or did such conditions require a reasoned reminder that the work of peace continued to depend on perceptions of threat and political negotiation? While the various compromises made for internal inconsistencies, they also had insured the statement's passage. Church politics provided one more illustration of the temporal order as characterized in the evangelical ethic and of the challenges entailed in the always "political work of peace."

NOTES

1. Staff member Paul T. Nelson developed a chronology of prior efforts: "History of the LCA Bioethics Project as Background to Proposed Social Statement" (Department for Church and Society files, 1980).

2. American church historian Frederick Wentz oversaw the first series. BSM Minutes, 2 December 1965; 16–17 May 1966. Louis Almen of the Board of Higher Education supervised a subsequent set. BSM Minutes, 16–17 October 1967, 23-24, 101-6. Authors included Roy Enquist, Henry Wildberger, Carl E. Braaten, Bruce Carlson, and Aarne Siirala.

3. BSM Minutes, 3–5 October 1968, 61.

4. LCA, *Minutes . . . 1970*, 594.

5. Elizabeth Kübler-Ross, *On Death and Dying* (New York: Macmillan Co., 1969).

6. BSM Minutes, 27–30 October 1971, 102-8.

7. BSM Minutes, 22 March 1972, 109-10; 25–28 October 1972, 127-28.

8. Franklin Sherman, *The Problem of Abortion—After the Supreme Court Decision* (DMNA/LCA, 1974), 17.

9. DCS Minutes, 27 May 1977.

10. LCA, *Minutes . . . 1978*, 113-14.

11. DMNA Management Committee Minutes, 4–6 June 1979, Collateral Paper B1, 1.

12. Bettenhausen, telephone interview with author, 16 July 1987.

13. Memos from Bettenhausen to Lazareth, 6 December 1978, to Robert Strohl, 20 March 1979, to Lazareth, 20 March 1979; Memos from Lazareth to Strohl, 15 May 1979, to Kenneth Senft, 30 May 1979.

14. Papers are listed in DMNA Management Committee Minutes, 4–6 June 1979, Collateral Paper B1, 2-18.

15. Paul Brndjar, interview with von Dehsen, Montclair, N.J., 30 July 1987.

16. Those in attendance were J. W. Bennett, E. Corinne Chilstrom, James H. Dunlevy, Robert G. Esbjornsen, Dorothy Jaeger-Lee, Daniel E. Lee, Harvey Mohrenweiser, Joan Novak, David Petering, Guenther P. Pohlmann, Alvin S. Rudisill, Charles F. Schaffer, Franklin Sherman (presiding), David D. Swenson. From DMNA staff were Kenneth Senft and Richard Niebanck. DMNA Management Committee Minutes, 12–14 March 1981, Collateral Paper K, p. 1.

17. Ibid., 1-8.

18. Ibid., 2.

19. Robert R. Strohl, "Report on LCA Constituency Involvement in Development of a Proposed Statement on Biomedical Ethics" (Department for Church and Society files, 23 October 1981). "Listening to People" conferences were conducted at Mills College in California and Susquehanna University in Pennsylvania.

20. DCS Minutes, 23 November 1981; DMNA Management Committee Minutes, 18–20 February 1982, 2-3.

21. LCA, *Minutes . . . 1982*, 149-56.

22. Ibid., 255-64.

23. LCA, *Minutes . . . 1984*, 40-41, 225-26, 389.

24. Edward Schneider, ed., *Questions About the Beginning of Life* (Minneapolis: Augsburg Publishing House, 1985). Schneider wrote his doctoral dissertation under the guidance of George Forell at the University of Iowa as "An Examination of the Social Statements of the American Lutheran Church from 1961 to 1972 from the Perspective of the Theology of Luther and *The Augsburg Confession*" (1978).

25. LCA, *Minutes . . . 1982*, 309-11, 185-88.

26. Ibid., 204.

27. The ambiguity of the commission's mandate hampered its deliberations. After four meetings and the discussion of several papers written by commission members and consultants, plans for a publication were abandoned.

28. LCA, *Minutes . . . 1982*, 185-88.

29. George H. Brand and Richard J. Niebanck, *SALT II: Strategic Arms Limitation Treaty* (DMNA/LCA, 1979).

30. Brand also developed the staff's working definition of deterrence. He argued that for country A to deter country B from an unacceptable action, three conditions had to be satisfied: (1) country A conveys to country B a threat to inflict

severe punishment if country B commits a specific act; (2) country B would otherwise commit such an act; and (3) country B believes that country A would carry out its threat and therefore refrains from committing the act. George H. Brand, *Arms Control and Reduction in the 1980's: Problems and Prospects* (DMNA/LCA, 1982), 2, 4.

31. Summaries of opinions held by staff members are drawn from interviews conducted by von Dehsen with Paul Hinlicky (16 July 1987), Paul Brndjar (30 July 1987), Paul Nelson (24 August 1987), Richard Niebanck (27 August 1987), and Katherine Kidd (4 December 1987) and intermittent conversations with George Brand.

32. Paul R. Hinlicky, *Christian Faith and the Nuclear Morass* (New York: DMNA/LCA, 1984).

33. DMNA Management Committee Minutes, 10–13 November 1982.

34. "A Biography of 'Peace and Politics,' " a notebook collection of memos and drafts (DMNA, Church in Society files).

35. Other speakers at the symposium were John Langan, S.J. (Woodstock Theological Center, Washington, D.C.), Roger Molander (Founder, Ground Zero), James Johnson (Rutgers University), and Amoretta M. Hoeber (Principal Deputy Assistant Secretary of the Army).

36. "Report on LCA Constituency Involvement in the Development of a Proposed Social Statement on PEACE AND POLITICS" (files of Department for Church and Society, 1983).

37. DMNA Management Committee Minutes, February 1984.

38. "An Open Letter by Joseph Sittler," 20 February 1984, 2-14.

39. Paul G. Johnson, "Deterrence and the Kingdom," *Currents in Theology and Mission* 11 (June, 1984): 148-53.

40. LCA, *Minutes . . . 1984*, 141.

41. Brndjar, who had already resigned as director of the Department for Church and Society to accept a call in New Jersey to two congregations of the Slovak Zion Synod, had been asked to participate in the deliberations.

42. LCA, *Minutes . . . 1984*, 260-75.

43. Ibid., 275.

44. Ibid., 276.

45. Ibid., 276, 312.

46. Ibid., 312-13.

47. Although Crumley (interview with von Dehsen, 1 September 1987) was himself sympathetic to the original argument of the statement, he recalls making every effort to conduct a fair and open debate.

48. LCA, *Minutes . . . 1984,* 333-34.

49. Ibid., 335.

50. Ibid., 335-36.

51. For the list of those who requested that their negative votes be recorded, see ibid., 336.

52. Ibid. A concise summary of the convention's actions on the proposed social statement is provided in the second edition of a study guide prepared for convention delegates. Paul T. Nelson, *A Commentary on "Peace and Politics"* (DMNA/LCA, 1984), 21-22.

EPILOGUE

In its quarter century, the Lutheran Church in America developed an admirably coherent tradition in theological ethics. Taken as a body, the social statements exhibit an approach to social issues that is identifiable and that reflects Lutheranism's confessional heritage. The "evangelical ethic," as it was called,[1] was present from the outset, although it gained in visibility and elaboration after the first rush of statements in the 1960s. Along with its considerable accomplishments, this ethic also leaves work for any who would have American Lutherans address moral and social issues with a corporate voice.[2]

Proponents of the "evangelical ethic" speak of it as a compound of doctrinal elements. William Lazareth views it as the effort to express the interdependence of the personal ethic of Christians who are committed to "faith active in love" with the social ethic of all people of goodwill, Lutherans included, who seek justice. In traditional language, it is the interplay of "civil righteousness" with "Christian righteousness," a combination that honors God's ongoing work of creation by not confusing it with redemption, and yet draws upon the gospel-given freedom of Christians to take action in the murkiness of history.[3]

Richard Niebanck emphasizes that the evangelical ethic gives grounding to Christians freed in Christ for work within the social order. Christ's work of redemption does not catapult Christians out of the structures of the created order, nor does that gospel lead to antinomianism. Rather, it gives Christians the freedom to make judgment calls in their application of the Ten Commandments, which have the civil use of providing principles of justice along with the theological purpose of judging sinners.[4]

Niebanck, Lazareth, Cedric Tilberg, and others understood their work as "theological" and not "social" ethics, although the latter term has been used on occasion to indicate the application of theological concepts to the social order. The evangelical ethic establishes a frame of reference by drawing the analytical distinctions between God's different forms of rule in creation and redemption, between law and gospel, and between the present age and the age to come. The ethic also appeals to the use

173

of reason, thereby seeking to protect the social analysis conducted among Lutherans from the irresponsibility of ignorance, naïveté, or utopianism.

The foundations laid during the last years of the United Lutheran Church in America guaranteed the introduction of the evangelical ethic in the LCA, but not its staying power. The ethic took hold because it provided a guide during the church's early years through a brier patch of such issues of church and state as civil disobedience in support of civil rights, selective conscientious objection, and prayer and Bible reading in the public schools. It proved that Lutheran doctrine could illumine public issues. The persuasive teaching of theologians William Lazareth and George Forell in convention helped to set a precedent for the future.

The commitment to these teachings, achieved in convention after vigorous discussion in a variety of forums, gives the denomination unique standing in the history of American Lutheranism and of American Christianity. The status of "policy" for positions taken on social issues came to be reserved for statements which built their regulative directives upon the evangelical ethic. In this way, the denomination was able to steer clear of particularly political and social ideologies. Moreover, resolutions were not meant to have the same authority in governing and guiding the church, except when understood as extensions of policy statements. The practice in the last years of separating broad policy directives from specific "implementing resolutions" underlined this approach.

The accomplishments of the evangelical ethic also underscore the work yet to be done. The establishment of theological norms still leaves unanswered the ways in which reason is to function in actual cases of ethical decision making. For the most part, LCA delegates in convention did not debate theology, although on occasion they did argue over scriptural authority. Rather, they debated the regulative sections of statements because there, different ethical perspectives can lead to various conclusions.

Hence the paradox: while reason is affirmed, there is lack of clarity about its use, and gaps can occur at strategic moments in the application of the theological norms. Thus, for example, in the 1970 statement "Sex, Marriage, and Family," the assertion in the regulative section that "every child has a right to be a wanted child" has no basis in the normative section. Moreover, a second gap opens between the regulative principles and the actual process of making decisions in Christian life, since guidance for asking self-critical questions is often not supplied. Using the same statement as an example, no relative weight is assigned to the various "factors" surrounding the decision to have a child or to the "considerations" in a decision about abortion.

174

The nature of moral discourse within the Lutheran community needs tending, especially if the evangelical ethic is to be protected from becoming what Dietrich Bonhoeffer called "cheap grace." Arbitrary, individualized autonomy is never a substitute for Christian freedom. Precisely because Christians are held accountable to God's law in their civil relations, they need help in sorting through the competing issues which surround ethical decision making.

The LCA has explored the evangelical ethic most fully in matters of public policy. Fifteen of the nineteen social statements deal primarily with the responsibilities Christians face as citizens, while four examine the private sphere on such issues as sex, marriage, and family (1964, 1970), aging and the older adult (1978), and death and dying (1982). On the one hand, this focus on public policy is attributable to the burgeoning confidence, competence, and resources available to Lutherans who, in increasing numbers, have entered the mainstream of American life. On the other hand, such focus seeks to correct the narrow view of an earlier day when all social problems were attributed to failures of private morality. "Code morality," "legalism," and "third use of the law" have in the second half of the twentieth century become epithets for the presumed inadequacies of pre-World War II Lutheran social thought. Greater attention to moral discourse may enable Lutherans to respond more appropriate attention to matters both public and private.

The notion of policy has been elaborated in particular ways during the years of the LCA. Policy was meant to discipline the denomination in both its public witness and its internal organization and to guide its members. As Kenneth Senft would remind his staff in the Division for Mission in North America, denominational structures were themselves institutions under the order of creation. They were, therefore, subject to the civil use of the law to achieve justice.

And so, for example, for the sake of greater internal discipline, the division spearheaded programs within the denomination to express and extend the policy adopted in the 1964 statement "Race Relations." A churchwide inventory on race relations, proposed at the time of the statement's tenth anniversary, set in motion studies and goal setting. After the inventory (see p. 138) was reported to the 1976 convention, giving evidence of both the effort to develop "minority ministry" and the continued evidence of "injurious discrimination based on race," two years were devoted to the development of the statement "Goals and Plans for Minority Ministry 1978–1984," which the Chicago convention adopted in 1978. This set of directives attempted to make concrete the commitments in "Race Relations."

175

The 1978 statement outlined a set of goals to guide the church's internal workings and public voice. It called upon leaders to assess their attitudes and programs for eradicating racism and upon churchwide agencies and synods to provide resources for congregations, all in an effort to "exhibit a self-understanding consistent with the Gospel of what it means to be the church in a diverse culture." The statement also aimed to have forty congregations in areas with more than 50 percent minority group persons established before 1984. The document determined to make economic justice a focal point and to work with others to improve schools attended predominantly by minority group persons, to advocate federal government programs for the development of appropriate housing for all people, and to address deficiencies in the criminal justice system. Other goals included the recruitment and training of professional leaders to serve in minority settings and the encouragement of minority group persons to serve in professional positions in the church. The statement concluded with goals to increase the number of minority group persons who serve as delegates to the LCA conventions, who fill positions in churchwide agencies, and who are appointed to consulting committees.

In 1984 in Toronto the denomination voted "to renew and expand these commitments" in a statement entitled "Inclusiveness and Diversity, Gifts of God." Every aspect of the LCA's organization was examined to find ways to promote the true unity of the church and to make clear that cultural diversity, beyond the usual European variety, was welcomed. Although percentages had been named in the goals set in 1978, they were now even more explicit: the church was to become more inclusive of American/Canadian Indian, Asian, Black, and Hispanic persons by working for a 12 percent annual membership increase among them, for 25 percent of all new congregations to be located in communities where they lived and for a 20 percent representation of them on all committees of churchwide agencies.

The report, itself evidence of internal discipline, to the last convention of the LCA in 1987 details both the difficulties in meeting such goals and the progress toward them. It proves easier to alter publications and to redirect investments than to evangelize. The various churchwide agencies had increased the number of people from those ethnic groups on their committees, in many instances exceeding the established goal of 20 percent. Other means of expressing inclusiveness were only in the beginning stages of development, although dialogue with the historic Black denominations had yet to begin.[5]

In more recent years the denomination has sought to order its external witness through the development of state offices for public policy advocacy and through publications to inform Lutheran citizens about public issues on which the church has acted. The new offices supplemented the efforts of the Lutheran Council's Office of Governmental Affairs in Washington, D.C.

These more recent developments in policy suggest a final area for reexamination of the LCA's tradition. "Policy" *per se* is an idea that had its origins in the rise of national business corporations and then the national government around the turn of the century. The search for ways to rationalize and control behavior in far-flung and complex organizations fixed upon policy as the means to coherence. Within corporate culture, bringing order has always included periodic review and clear lines of accountability.

There is no particular reason why the developing Protestant denominations should not have borrowed "policy" from corporate culture as one means for bringing order to their own houses. Yet, in the LCA's family of denominations, only under conditions of denominational merger in the early 1960s and now in the late 1980s has all social policy faced its toughest review. In its last years the LCA made provision for the formal change of social statements, but earlier there were but few instances of periodic evaluation. It may be that the expansion of programs and structures for advocacy can also have the effect of making such review more threatening than it ought to be. At the same time, the manner in which policy was formulated attracted considerable attention and underwent significant change.

The presence of theological standards, without well-developed moral discourse, tended to make policy more dependent on politics in later years. Certainly, social statements will always be products of politics in the sense that they depend upon the art of compromise. Nevertheless, without greater emphasis on the art of ethical discourse, even political compromise will be stymied in church bodies if principles of representation come to mean that individuals are trusted to understand only the alleged interests of their own sociologically and biologically defined groups.

The tasks in the years ahead are enough to engage all the resources of Lutheranism. The LCA's evangelical ethic has plowed the ground, but the cultivation of thoughtful social policy in both its public and private spheres for the discipline of the church and the guidance of Christians needs yet more tending.[6]

NOTES

1. Helmut Thielicke uses the term *evangelical ethics* to distinguish his Protestant approach from Roman Catholicism in his *Theological Ethics*, edited by William Lazareth (Grand Rapids: Wm. B. Eerdmans, 1979).

177

2. For a striking analysis of the procedural questions raised in the formulation of social policy in the American Lutheran Church, see Charles P. Lutz, *Social Policy Development in the American Lutheran Church, 1960–1987* (Minneapolis: Office of Church in Society, The American Lutheran Church, 1987), pp. 17-26.

3. William Lazareth, telephone conversation with author, 20 November 1987.

4. Richard Niebanck, telephone conversation with author, 17 November 1987.

5. Report of the Churchwide Agencies to the LCA Convention, "Inclusiveness and Diversity: Gifts of God" (April 28–29, 1987).

6. The author is grateful to a number of individuals whose thoughtful responses during interviews informed conclusions reached here and elsewhere in these pages: Elizabeth Bettenhausen, telephone interview, 16 July 1987; Rudolph Featherstone, interview, Columbus, Ohio, 28 May 1986; Franklin Drewes Fry, interview, Summit, N.J., 16 May 1986; Paul Nelson, telephone interview, 12 October 1987; Richard Niebanck, interviews from 1985 to 1987; Bruce Marshall, interview, Northfield, Minn., 23 October 1986; Lloyd Svendsbye, interview, Minneapolis, Minn., October 1985.

APPENDIX:
SOCIAL STATEMENTS
OF THE LCA

All of the statements in the appendix except two are in the form circulated in the church after 1980. "Marriage and Family" (1964) was superceded in 1970 and "Vietnam" (1966) was no longer circulated after 1975.

In 1980 the LCA Convention in Seattle voted to edit the social statements, as they were reprinted, to reflect the guidelines on inclusive language developed by the Division for Parish Services. (Support for the development of such guidelines and for their application to official documents had been voiced at the 1974 and 1976 conventions and in a report from the Consulting Committee on Women and Men in September of 1979.)[1]

CONTENTS

NOTES

1. LCA, *Minutes . . . 1974*, 507; *Minutes . . . 1976*, 428; *Minutes . . . 1980*, 177.

AGING AND THE OLDER ADULT

Adopted by the Ninth Biennial Convention, Chicago, Illinois
July 12-19, 1978

Life is a gift of God, and aging is a natural part of living.

More positive attitudes toward the aging process and toward older adults are a profound need today. Men and women 65 years of age and over now constitute one-tenth of the population of Canada and the United States. A vast number of older adults are able and willing to function effectively throughout their lives, serving their congregations and communities, and adding their strength in the struggle to achieve justice for all.

AGING: PREJUDICE AND INJUSTICE

Too often negative attitudes within our society place unnecessary restrictions upon the freedom of the elderly. Frequently the media portray older adults as tottering, forgetful, slow-witted and helpless. Prejudicial attitudes result in injustice toward a large number of older people and deprive society of their talent, experience and wisdom. They are forced too readily into retirement, often eased out of responsible leadership positions in the church and community, too frequently "protected" from making life-affecting decisions, and in some instances made the objects of service activities that other well-meaning persons plan and administer.

People in our work-oriented society tend to view personal dignity largely in terms of occupational performance. As a consequence, loss of occupation or retirement frequently results in the loss of one's sense of dignity. While acknowledging the many problems that arise from unemployment or retirement, this church nevertheless affirms that human dignity has a far deeper foundation than work or status.

THEOLOGICAL AFFIRMATIONS

God's love for all persons is creative and unconditional. Human beings have dignity not because they have achieved success or the esteem of the world, but because they are made in the image of God. They are given the capacity to relate to God in responsible freedom.

However, in sinful rebellion against God, old and young alike frequently act unreasonably and irresponsibly toward each other. As one consequence, older adults often become the undeserving victims of prejudice and discrimination in the callous abuse of their dignity and rights.

The Christian faith looks at all of human existence, its joy and its suffering, in the

181

light of the cross and resurrection of Jesus Christ. It takes seriously both life and death, declares God's promise that the sting of death is overcome by the resurrection of Christ, and testifies that forgiveness and new life are granted to the faithful in daily and eternal fellowship with God. This Christian view of the aging process gives reason for joy and hope at every stage.

By God's action in Holy Baptism, we are commissioned to "lead a life worthy of the calling to which we have been called" (Ephesians 4:1). This calling — vocation — empowers us to live for others by faithfully serving our neighbors in love and justice. We receive varieties of gifts, which the Holy Spirit enables us to use in building up the body of Christ in witness and service in the world.

Older members of the church have skills, wisdom, and experience to share in exercising the universal priesthood of the baptized. The Spirit helps us to discern the special gifts and needs of the elderly, along with the related opportunities and obligations of Christians in society.

A chief way in which God deals with the human condition in society is to provide all people with civil authority in order to advance the well-being and to secure equal opportunity for the full development of all citizens. Persons are given reason and conscience to help them determine and seek what is just. For older adults, government shares in this responsibility with the elderly themselves, the family, the church, religious and voluntary organizations, business firms, labor unions and other social institutions and structures.

AGENDA FOR ACTION

This church affirms the God-given dignity of human beings of all ages. It emphasizes their right and responsibility to make important decisions and to choose ways in which to participate in the family, the church, and the community. It sees them as individual persons, each different from others in background, life experiences, talents, interests, and present circumstances.

This church understands that many older adults continue to learn, to be open to new ideas, to enjoy a wide variety of interpersonal relationships, including their sexuality, and to engage in constructive activity. But this church also acknowledges that it should respond with sensitivity and skill to the special needs of those who are ill, handicapped, lonely and discouraged.

This church sets forth the following agenda for purposeful action:

FAMILIES
Human beings, whatever their age, are to be viewed not as individuals in isolation from one another, but as persons in community. One basic expression of community is the family. In a time when "family" is frequently viewed in two-generational terms — father, mother, and their children — older members often find themselves set apart from the extended family group, treated as outsiders or invited guests, and deprived of the warm acceptance they cherish.

182

Whether or not there are severe problems in such areas as income and health, older adults may be even more distressed by a sense of alienation from life, especially if it involves unsatisfactory relationships with the younger generations. This tendency to alienation is often associated with such factors as family mobility, differing opinions regarding the rearing of children, and the smaller size of living accommodations. Tensions may be increased by the effect the disabilities of older persons may have on younger relatives, by difficult decisions that families must make, by lack of effective communication, or by feelings of inadequacy and guilt on both sides.

It is essential to the well-being of all that older men and women be given honor and loving respect, and that in this spirit they be acknowledged as full members of their own families, even if geographically separated, living in an institutional setting, or mentally or physically incapacitated. Every effort must be made to foster wholesome exchange of ideas, sensitive understanding, and mutual communication and helpfulness among generations.

CONGREGATIONS

This church should seek older women and men, as it seeks other persons, both as members and as full participants in all dimensions of parish life. Older members are called to share in worship, learning, witness, service and support according to their personal abilities and interests. The congregation is potentially well qualified to engage persons of all ages in activities and relationships which encourage understanding and fellowship across generational lines.

The congregation as a community of faith has unrivaled opportunity to assist people, including older men and women, when they experience changes in living arrangements, loss of social esteem or physical capacity, and illness. This is especially true when Christians face the death of spouse, other family members or friends, and ultimately their own death. Through its ministry of Word and sacrament, its educational ministry, its supportive fellowship and spiritual nurture, the congregation can help persons cope with such experiences.

The congregation, recognizing that both the positive and negative attitudes of society are found among kinfolk, should strengthen and provide resources to the family as it relates to its older members. It should help the family to cultivate love and respect and a sense of mutual responsibility across the generations, and to be a constructive healing force in all its relationships. The congregation should show equal concern for older persons who are isolated or alienated. Such men and women often have greater needs than do those with a supportive family. It is necessary, therefore, that they be provided with or alerted to alternate supportive relationships, including the congregation's own role as an "extended family."

In seeking to help older adults with their social and material needs, the congregation should concentrate on encouraging the community to provide essential services. Within this larger setting it can either offer or join with others in offering supportive programs. These may include visiting, telephone reassurance, home health care, chore service, transportation assistance, congregate meals or meals delivered in homes, financial help to meet special needs, senior center activities, and guidance to its people in using community resources. The congregation should make every effort to assure that its buildings afford easy access and free mobility for all persons, and, wherever advisable and feasible, make those buildings available for community programs.

In whatever is done, older women and men ought to carry an important share of responsibility for planning and operating programs. Every effort should be made to respect their dignity, and to remember that bedridden as well as healthy persons wish to be accepted members of society and are often capable of enriching or rendering service to others.

SYNODS
This church should advance the well-being of older adults by:

1) assisting congregations in their ministries with the elderly, using the skills and leadership of educational and social service agencies and institutions wherever feasible;

2) maintaining supportive relationships with church-related agencies and institutions that are engaged in this field;

3) advocating with provincial/state and local governments concerning the rights and needs of older persons;

4) advocating with provincial/state and local governments on behalf of church-related agencies and institutions to encourage the establishment of adequate levels of reimbursement for covered services provided by said agencies and institutions to eligible recipients;

5) availing themselves of and referring congregations and individuals to the resources of governmental and nongovernmental organizations working with the elderly, and cooperating with such organizations in mutual endeavor;

6) conducting training workshops for persons involved in ministry with older persons; and

7) providing guidance and leadership for programs, workshops and seminars on the aging process, avoidable factors that accelerate aging, attitudes toward older adults, and pre-retirement planning.

Each synod should assign responsibility for these tasks to a specific program unit, new or existing, and include older men and women in its planning and leadership.

SOCIAL SERVICE AGENCIES AND INSTITUTIONS
This church should affirm the ministries of social service agencies and institutions related to it which work with older adults. As it requires these agencies and institutions to meet the highest standards of health, safety, and service, this church encourages them in their efforts:

1) to assist synods to support area congregations in carrying out their ministries with older adults;

184

2) to design programs which assist older adults to continue to be integral members of society;

3) to provide supportive services — physical, emotional, social, spiritual — which enable older men and women to maintain independent living arrangements as long as feasible;

4) to provide services which protect older adults from abuse and exploitation, whether physical, emotional or economic;

5) to provide supportive services which enable ill or disabled older persons to receive sensitive care in the homes of their families, or in other residential settings;

6) to improve the physical, mental, emotional, and spiritual well-being of the elderly in institutionalized/specialized care;

7) to develop institutional living arrangements and programs that affirm the sexuality of older adults;

8) to place buildings in geographical locations and make structural provisions that assure maximum access to all persons;

9) to serve and employ low income older persons whenever possible;

10) to advocate public policies and regulations that assure that church-related and other voluntary agencies or institutions are not made the objects of discrimination when they endeavor to obtain public funds in return for services they provide to the community; and

11) to use academic resources in gerontology and other disciplines to help with these tasks.

HIGHER EDUCATION

This church encourages the colleges, universities, and campus ministries related to it in their efforts:

1) to motivate and equip faculty and students to see education as a lifelong process;

2) to extend opportunities for middle-aged and older persons to participate in formal educational programs;

3) to sponsor courses, seminars, and intergenerational activities regarding older adults and aging which involve faculty, students, alumni and the general public;

4) to enable the participation of faculty and students in church and community programs working with the elderly;

5) to assist in training personnel for agencies and institutions which render direct services to older persons; and

6) to use academic resources in gerontology to help with these tasks.

185

THEOLOGICAL SEMINARIES

This church encourages theological seminaries in their efforts:

1) to equip pastors and other professional leaders with information and skills with regard to aging;

2) to extend opportunities for middle-aged and older persons to participate in formal education programs;

3) to sponsor seminars, workshops, and related activities which foster constructive attitudes among faculty, students, alumni and the general public toward older persons and aging;

4) to enable the participation of faculty and students in church and community programs working with the elderly; and

5) to use academic resources in gerontology and other disciplines to help with these tasks.

RETIREMENT POLICIES OF THIS CHURCH

This church, in dealing with older adults, should be concerned to practice the best stewardship of human resources in its own employment and retirement policies.

PUBLIC POLICY

This church, both through the daily lives of its members and through its corporate actions, seeks changes in society toward a more positive image of aging and greater justice for the elderly. It views this endeavor as part of the promotion of justice for all people, and recognizes that many older adults are ready to serve as leaders and participants.

Therefore, this church declares itself in support of the following public policy goals:

1) Adequate income for all older persons, derived from an effective combination of personal resources, pension plans, continuing income from work, and government social insurance and income support programs.

2) Food policies and programs (including nutrition education) which benefit the elderly, especially the poor, the homebound, and the isolated.

3) Action and funding to help secure adequate housing of sufficient variety to offer alternatives in living arrangements for older adults, including those without the ability to pay the full costs.

4) A comprehensive health care program ensuring equity in access to services and facilities and freedom from fear of catastrophic medical costs; a program funded through fair and equitable means, with risks spread over the entire population.*

5) Responsible government fiscal policies which recognize the impact which

186

inflation has upon the elderly, and which seek to contain inflation by providing more efficient delivery of human services and by moderating federal spending for programs not directly related to human services.

6) Elimination or avoidance of injurious age discrimination in employment and retirement practices in government, business, and industry.

7) Exploration of ways by which business and other types of organizations may use the experience and counsel of older adults, and may develop more effective programs that prepare workers for retirement.

8) Structural provisions in public buildings that assure easy access and free mobility for infirm and handicapped persons, large numbers of whom are elderly.

9) Supportive services which enable persons to maintain independent living in their communities as long as feasible; and skilled care in institutions, including hospices, for all who require it, provided in ways that respect the dignity of the individual in the right of self-determination with regard to his or her own person so that family and community ties may be continued.

10) Legal assistance and law enforcement which protect the rights and provide for the safety of older men and women.

11) Educational programs, under private and public auspices, available to people of all ages.

12) Cultivation of constructive attitudes toward aging and the older adult in areas such as the communications media and educational institutions.

13) Encouragement of cultural institutions and programs to recognize older adults as part of their constituency — as volunteers, paid professionals, and audiences.

*Canada has such a program.

CONCLUSION

All persons have worth and dignity because they are created in God's image. This church calls upon its members and all elements of its corporate life to embody this truth in all their relationships, especially — in the context of this statement — those affecting older adults.

CAPITAL PUNISHMENT

Adopted by the Third Biennial Convention, Kansas City, Missouri
June 21-29, 1966

Within recent years, there has been throughout North America a marked increase in the intensity of debate on the question of abolishing the death penalty. This situation has been accompanied by the actual abolition of capital punishment in ten states and two dependencies of the United States, qualified abolition in three states, and in six states a cessation in the use of the death penalty since 1955. Although the issue of abolition has been widely debated in Canada in recent years, a free vote in Parliament on April 5, 1966, failed to end the legality of the death sentence. However, during the last two years or more, death sentences in Canada have been consistently commuted.

These developments have been accompanied by increased attention to the social and psychological causes of crime, the search for improved methods of crime prevention and law enforcement, efforts at revising the penal code and judicial process, and pressure for more adequate methods in the rehabilitation of convicted criminals. There has been a concurrent concern for persons who, because of ethnic or economic status, are seriously hampered in defending themselves in criminal proceedings. It has been increasingly recognized that the socially disadvantaged are forced to bear a double burden: intolerable conditions of life which render them especially vulnerable to forces that incite to crime, and the denial of equal justice through adequate defense.

In seeking to make a responsible judgment on the question of capital punishment, the following considerations must be taken into account:

1. *The Right of the State to Take Life*
The biblical and confessional witness asserts that the state is responsible under God for the protection of its citizens and the maintenance of justice and public order. For the exercise of its mandate, the state has been entrusted by God with the power to take human life when the failure to do so constitutes a clear danger to the civil community. The possession of this power is not, however, to be interpreted as a command from God that death shall necessarily be employed in punishment for crime. On the other hand, a decision on the part of civil government to abolish the death penalty is not to be construed as a repudiation of the inherent power of the state to take life in the exercise of its divine mandate.

189

2. *Human Rights and Equality Before the Law*

The state is commanded by God to wield its power for the sake of freedom, order and justice. The employment of the death penalty at present is a clear misuse of this mandate because (a) it falls disproportionately upon those least able to defend themselves, (b) it makes irrevocable any miscarriage of justice, and (c) it ends the possibility of restoring the convicted person to effective and productive citizenship.

3. *The Invalidity of the Deterrence Theory*

Insights from both criminal psychology and the social causes of crime indicate the impossibility of demonstrating a deterrent value in capital punishment. Contemporary studies show no pronounced difference in the rate of murders and other crimes of violence between states in the United States which impose capital punishment and those bordering on them which do not.

In the light of the above considerations, the Lutheran Church in America:

urges the abolition of capital punishment;

urges the members of its congregations in those places where capital punishment is still a legal penalty to encourage their legislatures to abolish it;

urges citizens everywhere to work with persistence for the improvement of the total system of criminal justice, concerning themselves with adequate appropriations, the improved administration of courts and sentencing practices, adequate probation and parole resources, better penal and correctional institutions, and intensified study of delinquency and crime;

urges the continued development of a massive assault on those social conditions which breed hostility toward society and disrespect for the law.

THE CHURCH AND SOCIAL WELFARE

Adopted by the Fourth Biennial Convention, Atlanta, Georgia
June 19-27, 1968

INTRODUCTION

"Social welfare" is a system of laws, programs and services which provide for the meeting of social needs in order to promote the well-being of people and the humane functioning of society.

Social welfare in the United States and Canada has developed under the auspices of governments, of churches and of voluntary associations. They provide a wide variety of health and welfare services and other related programs responding to human need. Each makes its contribution to the total social welfare system.

Neither churches nor voluntary agencies have the capability of dealing with massive, pervasive social problems arising in a highly mobile, rapidly changing society. Therefore, governments have rightly assumed increasing responsibility for meeting social need and dealing with its causes.

While the degree and kind of involvement of the churches and voluntary associations have changed, the significance of these nongovernmental activities in social welfare is not diminished.

The governments of both countries encourage the involvement of nongovernmental social welfare agencies and institutions, and solicit counsel based on their experience.

The changing scene requires that the Lutheran Church in America redefine its social welfare concerns in relationship to the present day within the context of its own self-understanding of its mission.

BASIC CONSIDERATIONS

1. Justice requires that the state promote the general welfare, further the well-being of every citizen, and secure equal opportunity for full development of all its citizens. This requires that the state provide means for self-fulfillment to those who cannot because of circumstance provide them for themselves.

2. The unique task of the church is to bear witness to God's Word. Such witness must always be in both word and deed, if the life of the church is to be consistent with its message. The imperative to serve leads the church into the broad range of activities identified with social welfare. The church rightly engages in social welfare because the gospel it proclaims impels Christians both individually and corporately to show con-

191

cern for persons and to serve them at their point of need and should be properly recognized.

3. In fulfillment of its role, government engages today in many social welfare programs which historically developed under the auspices of the church. Thus churches and governments often find themselves engaged in parallel social welfare activities.

4. The social statement of the Lutheran Church in America on "Church and State, A Lutheran Perspective" (1966) affirms the functional interaction between the two as desirable and right. Functional interaction between church and state contributes to the enrichment of all social welfare, and to the common good.

5. Since the services of governments are established by law, they may not be readily adaptable to new situations in times of crisis and rapid change. The churches, not being so limited, ought to adapt their services more flexibly to new situations. The church can react to social need also by seeking to influence the political and administrative processes which control the welfare services of government. Regardless of how pervasive and thorough public social welfare service may become, meeting social needs in a democratic society requires the resources of the whole community, including those of the church.

6. The church should explore new forms of service in its diaconic task since no particular form of service is scripturally or theologically determined.

7. As the church engages in social welfare services it is better able to acquire understanding of social problems which will assist it in influencing public policy to bring about social change and to further sound public social welfare services and programs.

8. Social welfare in the church is not limited to providing professionally conducted services, or to corporate efforts in social education and action. To be truly effective the church must encourage services which can be provided by congregations and their members in their outreach to their communities. Corporate instruments for social welfare may represent the church, but they do not absolve individual Christians from responsible services of love, either in their occupation or in their voluntary service.

9. This church affirms the sacredness of all services which further the common good in the helping, healing professions and in the political, economic and educational processes of society.

AFFIRMATIONS

1. This church reaffirms its belief that social welfare services carried on

through the church either in its individual or corporate expression are a joyous and self-less response of love growing out of faith in Christ.

2. This church in order to fulfill its service role should carry on continual study, research and experimentation in the field of social welfare.

3. This church should be flexible in its social policies and practices. The diversity and complexity of modern society are such that a variety of responses to any problem may be appropriate.

4. This church should be alert to the manner in which social need is met, whether by government, voluntary, church, or proprietary agency. Wherever practice or policy threaten the rights and dignity of those who require aid, the church should strive to bring about correction.

5. This church's concern may be expressed by the development of agencies and institutions when community need calls for them. They are not to be ends in themselves, but are to be seen as part of the total engagement of the church.

6. When this church establishes social welfare programs it may properly enter into agreements with federal, state and local government to receive payment for services rendered or to accept, on a nonpreferential basis, grants or long-term loans.

7. This church through its various jurisdictions should support social welfare services by providing opportunity for financial participation by its congregations and their individual members through both general benevolence and direct personal giving, in keeping with the established policies of the appropriate synod(s).

8. The social welfare services of this church should comply with the service standards set by government, professional agencies and the church.

9. This church should serve all people in its related social service programs.

10. This church in its social welfare activities should, so far as it is possible, involve those for whom service is intended in determining the services and the manner in which they are administered.

CONCLUSION

In contemporary society the church has tasks of service to perform in obedience to Jesus Christ, its servant Lord. It is he who placed upon his people the indelible mark of servanthood and gave them the mission to identify with all who are disadvantaged and suffer hurt. They bear this mark not to serve themselves but to give witness to Christ.

The foremost task of the church in social welfare is to proclaim the Word of God in such ways that it makes all of its members alert and responsive to human need at home and abroad and to the many faces of injustice. It should abhor and oppose all that erodes and destroys human dignity and deprives people of their God-given rights.

The Lutheran Church in America calls upon its congregations, synods, boards, commissions and agencies to re-examine their roles in the light of current social needs and to bring the redeeming and healing power of the gospel to bear upon those needs. It calls upon all of its people to give ungrudgingly of their time, talents and substance in support of those works of mercy and of service which witness to the truth they profess.

CHURCH AND STATE
A LUTHERAN PERSPECTIVE

Adopted by the Third Biennial Convention, Kansas City, Missouri
June 21-29, 1966

The relations between church and state in the United States and Canada are profoundly affected by significant changes which have been emerging in recent years in the organization of society. For one thing, in the pluralistic structure of both nations all religions, and the various secularistic philosophies, are claiming and receiving equal status socially and before the law. Furthermore, there have been dramatic changes in education and welfare and in concepts of the role of national government in these fields. Consequently, religious bodies, through their agencies of education and social service, are being invited to participate more fully than ever before in publicly sponsored programs and in the acceptance of public financing.

These essentially new circumstances require the churches of the United States and Canada to state in terms which are contemporary and relevant the distinctive functions of church and state, areas of common concern, and the possibilities and boundaries of mutual co-operation.

In response to this situation the Lutheran Church in America affirms both institutional separation and functional interaction as the proper relationship between church and state. We hold that both church and state, in their varied organized expressions, are subject to the will and rule of God, who is sovereign over all things.

INSTITUTIONAL SEPARATION

By "institutional separation" we mean that church and state must each be free to perform its essential task under God. Thus we reject those theories of relationship which seek the dominance either of church over state or of state over church.

The one, holy, catholic, and apostolic church manifests itself in the world through organized communities of Christian believers. The church militant is both a divine organism related to Christ and a human organization related to society. Its distinctive mission as an ecclesiastical institution is to proclaim the Word of God in preaching and sacraments, worship and evangelism, Christian education and social ministry.

"Civil authority," according to the New Testament, is divinely ordained. This does not imply that every particular government or governor enjoys God's approval; it means rather that "civil authority" which is manifested in the state is to be respected and obeyed as an expression of the sovereign will of the Creator.

195

This forbids any state from deifying itself, for its power is not inherent but is delegated to it by God to be employed responsibly for the attainment of beneficial secular goals. A government is accountable to God for the way in which it uses, abuses, or neglects to use its powerful civil "sword." The constant need of the state, therefore, is not for the church's uncritical loyalty and unquestioning obedience but for the prophetic guidance and judgment of the law of God, which the church is commanded to proclaim, in order to be reminded of both its secular limits and potentialities. The distinctive mission of the state is to establish civil justice through the maintenance of law and order, the protection of constitutional rights, and the promotion of the general welfare of the total citizenry.

FUNCTIONAL INTERACTION

"Functional interaction" describes a process which takes place in areas in which church and state, each in pursuit of its own proper objectives, are both legitimately engaged. We believe that such interaction is appropriate so long as institutional separation is preserved and neither church nor state seeks to use its type of involvement to dominate the other. We, therefore, reject theories of absolute separation of church and state which would deny practical expressions of functional interaction.

The church, solely through the free exercise of its divine mandate, relates to the interests of the state in such ways as 1) offering intercessory prayers on behalf of the state and its officials; 2) encouraging responsible citizenship and government service; 3) helping the state to understand and holding the state accountable to the sovereign law of God; 4) contributing to the civil consensus which supports the state in fulfillment of the duties of just government; and 5) championing the human and civil rights of all citizens.

The state, on the other hand, by fulfilling the duties of just government, relates to the interests of the church in such ways as 1) guaranteeing religious liberty for all; 2) acknowledging that the rights of humanity are not the creation of the state; 3) maintaining an attitude of "wholesome neutrality" toward church bodies in the context of the religious pluralism of our culture; 4) acting on a nonpreferential basis if providing incidental benefits in recognition of the church's civil services which also make a secular contribution to the community; and 5) acting on a nonpreferential basis if offering financial aid for educational or social services which church agencies render for the secular benefit of the community.

CONCLUSION

In summary, we affirm the sacredness of the secular life of God's people as they worship, witness, and work in God's world. We advocate the institutional separation and functional interaction of church and state. This position rejects both the absolute separation of church and state and the domination of either one by the other, while seeking a mutually beneficial relationship in which each institution contributes to the common good by remaining true to its own nature and task.

This statement, addressed particularly to the situation of the church in the United States and Canada at the present time, is not intended to provide guidance with regard to all the issues arising from church-state relations. Its purpose, rather, is to set forth a basic theological stance within the context of which discussion may continue, policies may be formulated and specific actions may be taken.

CONSCIENTIOUS OBJECTION

Adopted by the Fourth Biennial Convention, Atlanta, Georgia
June 19-27, 1968

War and military service are and always have been a cause of division among people of conscience. Many choose to bear arms, recognizing that in a sinful world force is often required to restrain the evil. Others, unable to reconcile the inhumanity of war with the demands of love and justice, refuse to participate in particular wars or in any armed conflict. Still others either enter the military or seek deferred status without having resolved the basic ethical dilemmas facing them.

Lutheran teaching, while rejecting conscientious objection as ethically normative, requires that ethical decisions in political matters be made in the context of the competing claims of peace, justice, and freedom. Consequently, one need not be opposed to participating in all forms of violent conflict in order to be considered a bona fide conscientious objector. It is in responsible grappling with these competing claims that a person should consider participation or nonparticipation in the military.

Consistent with this, the responsible, conscientious choice of the individual to participate or not to participate in military service or in a particular war should be upheld and protected. The office of soldier, like all other temporal offices, is to be held in esteem by all. At the same time, the conscientious objector should be accorded respect and such freedom as is consistent with the requirements of civil order.

Governments have rightly seen fit to provide legal status for conscientious objectors, allowing them the privilege of performing alternative service in lieu of military duty. In granting such status, governments recognize that conscientious objectors may make a more valuable contribution to their nation in alternative service than they would if imprisoned or otherwise penalized.

Furthermore, the moral considerations which underlie the stand of the conscientious objector can have a salutary influence upon a nation. The ethical sensitivity and human concern represented in conscientious objection have a value that far outweighs any potential risk to security involved in granting legal exemption. It is better for the general well-being that the conscientious objector be given more than the stark choice between compromised integrity and imprisonment.

However, legal exemption for the conscientious objector is a privilege, not a right, which a just government grants in the interest of the civil good. This does not imply that governments are required to exempt persons from any legal obligation. Governments must reserve the right not to grant, or to revoke, the privilege of legal exemption in situations of clear danger to the public order.

The fact that some persons may falsely exploit conscience to defend irresponsible disregard for the obligations of citizenship does not excuse the church from its responsibility of defending the bona fide conscientious objector. The church must exercise special care in judging the spirit and motives of those who may call upon the church for safeguarding in such a position.

Recognizing both the heart-searching of many persons confronted with the possibility of military conscription and the broader considerations of justice and public order, the Lutheran Church in America adopts the following affirmations:

1. This church recognizes its responsibility of assisting its members in the development of mature, enlightened and discerning consciences. It calls upon its pastors and agencies of Christian education and social ministry to continue in their efforts to cultivate sensitive persons who can act responsibly amid the complexities of the present day.

2. This church stands by and upholds those of its members who conscientiously object to military service as well as those who in conscience choose to serve in the military. This church further affirms that the individual who, for reasons of conscience, objects to participation in a particular war is acting in harmony with Lutheran teaching.

3. Governments have wisely provided legal exemption for conscientious objectors, allowing such persons to do other work of benefit to the community. While such exemption is in the public interest, the granting of it does not imply an obligation on the part of government to provide legal exemption to anyone who finds a law to be burdensome.

4. In the best interest of the civil community, conscientious objectors to particular wars, as well as conscientious objectors to all wars, ought to be granted exemption from military duty and opportunity should be provided them for alternative service, and until such time as these exemptions are so provided, persons who conscientiously object to a particular war are reminded that they must be willing to accept applicable civil or criminal penalties for their action.

5. All conscientious objectors should be accorded equal treatment before the law, whether the basis of their stand is specifically religious or not. It is contrary to biblical teaching (cf. Romans 2:15f) for the church to expect special status for the Christian or religious objector.

6. This church approves provisions whereby persons in the military who become conscientious objectors are permitted reclassification and

reassignment. This church urges that these provisions also be extended to the conscientious objector to a particular war.

Consistent with these affirmations, the Lutheran Church in America directs a member who is a conscientious objector to send a written statement of those convictions to the member's pastor, to the synod bishop and the secretary of the church. Pastors of the church are directed to minister to all in their care who are conscientious objectors.

DEATH AND DYING

Adopted by the Eleventh Biennial Convention, Louisville, Kentucky
September 3-10, 1982

Today it is commonplace to speak of the triumphs of modern medicine—achievements such as open heart surgery and organ transplants, dialysis machines that substitute for the kidneys, pacemakers that regulate the beating of the heart, and vaccines that have made once-dreaded diseases almost forgotten words. Each of these discoveries has saved countless lives and relieved much suffering. None of this, however, has changed the fact that death still occurs. The new technologies do not always cure but sometimes only prolong the dying process, at times with great suffering. The irony of modern medicine is that with the new technologies that vastly expand the range of what it is possible to do has also come the anguish of deciding when it is appropriate to use these capabilities.

Nowhere are these ethical dilemmas more pressing than with respect to death and dying. A terminal cancer patient who is experiencing great pain suffers cardiac arrest; should the patient be resuscitated? A newborn infant with massive and multiple birth defects is unlikely to survive without surgical intervention; is such intervention appropriate? A family member with a life-threatening illness refuses to undergo treatment; should treatment be administered in violation of his or her expressed wishes? In these and countless similar situations, we confront not only the grief and anguish always associated with death and dying, but also new and difficult moral decisions that call for prayerful reflection and the support of a caring community.

THEOLOGICAL PERSPECTIVES ON DEATH AND DYING

Perspectives on death and dying within the Christian tradition, both in its biblical origins and in its subsequent development, reflect several contrasting and complementary themes:

Death as Natural. Death is frequently viewed as a natural part of the life cycle. Like all other creatures, human beings have a limited life span. "The years of our life," the psalmist observed, "are threescore and ten, or even by reason of strength fourscore" (Psalm 90:10). The fact that our span of life is limited serves to remind us that we are finite. We are created by God; we are not God. Both living and dying are part of the dynamic processes of the created order, which biblical faith affirms as being good. The story of Abraham's death reflects this view: "Abraham breathed his last and died in a good old age, an old man and full of years, and was gathered to his people" (Genesis 25:8).

Death as Tragic. Death may also be experienced as an unwelcome event that involves a tragic dimension. Sometimes this is because death seems untimely, as in the case of the death of a child, a youth, or an adult in the prime of life. Or its unwelcomeness may be due simply to the desire to continue living rather than depart life, a desire that in its own way gives eloquent testimony to the goodness of the life that God has created. Sometimes the reluctance to die arises from dread of the suffering which may accompany the dying process. Thus it is in keeping with a wide range of human experience that the psalmist prays for deliverance from mortal illness: "Turn, O Lord, save my life; deliver me for the sake of thy steadfast love" (Psalm 6:4).

Death as Friend. When dying involves prolonged suffering, death can be experienced as a deliverance, and in this sense as a friend. This does not imply that one should deliberately end life to avoid suffering, for the Christian witness is that meaning and hope are possible even in deepest adversity. It does imply that death, when it brings relief from suffering, can be understood and accepted as merciful.

Death as Enemy. Even though death must be viewed as part of the created order and can sometimes be a friend, the sinfulness of the human condition makes death an enemy. As the apostle Paul puts it, "The sting of death is sin" (I Corinthians 15:56). The alienation and estrangement that are pervasive in our lives make us unready to face death, an anxiety that may be heightened by fear of what lies beyond the grave.

Victory over Death. The New Testament message of Christ's victory over death speaks directly to this alienation and anxiety. Through Baptism, the believer is buried with him "into death, so that as Christ was raised from the dead by the glory of the Father, we too might walk in newness of life" (Romans 6:4). The new life of faith enables the Christian to face death with courage and with the assurance of forgiveness. The promise of the resurrection of the body and eternal life provides comfort and reassurance that death is not the end.

Whether death is viewed as natural or as tragic, as a friend or as an enemy, all who experience death-and-dying situations can be certain of God's love. Thus the apostle Paul asserts, "For I am sure that neither death, nor life, nor angels, nor principalities, nor things present, nor things to come, nor powers, nor height, nor depth, nor anything else in all creation, will be able to separate us from the love of God in Christ Jesus our Lord" (Romans 8:38-39).

ETHICAL DECISION-MAKING

Careful and prayerful reflection in the immediacy of the situation is an essential ingredient in a responsible decision-making process. At the same time, Scripture, tradition, and the shared wisdom of Christian people provide important resources for making these decisions.

While the exact nature of death-and-dying situations can never be anticipated fully, it is possible to identify interpretive principles that are useful in shaping our response. These include the following:

1. Life is a gift of God, to be received with thanksgiving.

2. The integrity of the life processes which God has created should be respected; both birth and death are part of these life processes.

3. Both living and dying should occur within a caring community.

4. A Christian perspective mandates respect for each person; such respect includes giving due recognition to each person's carefully considered preferences regarding treatment decisions.

5. Truthfulness and faithfulness in our relations with others are essential to the texture of human life.

6. Hope and meaning in life are. possible even in times of suffering and adversity—a truth powerfully proclaimed in the resurrection faith of the church.

The decision-making process involves not only the question of what principles should be used in responding to death-and-dying situations but also the questions of who should make such decisions. If the person is capable of actively participating in the decision-making process, respect for that person mandates that he or she be recognized as the prime decision-maker. At the same time, to relegate such decisions solely to the individual facing death is to deprive that person of love and care. Therefore, it is appropriate that the physician, family members, close friends, the pastor, and other members of the health care team play a supportive role.

If the person in question is not capable of active participation, the situation is somewhat more complex. In some cases, the person's clearly stated preferences, made before he or she lost the capacity to participate, are on record; respect for that person requires that these preferences be given recognition. In other cases, no preferences are on record because the person never gave expression to his or her preferences while still able to do so, and is now too weakened to respond. If the situation involves a child under the age of majority, who is therefore legally incompetent, or a person who is mentally impaired and hence unable to participate fully in the decision-making process, a shared decision-making process is preferable. Collective wisdom is likely to result in better decisions, and no one should be left to bear alone the full burden of deciding. Participants in this decision-making process may include family members, the physician and other health care professionals, the pastor, and others close to the person. If it is not possible for those immediately involved to reach a consensus, a hospital ethics committee, if one exists, can be an important resource. Appeal to the courts should be avoided unless so doing is the only way to protect individual rights or to resolve the controversy.

WITHDRAWING AND WITHHOLDING TREATMENT

Among the most difficult decisions which confront family members and others in death-and-dying situations are those that involve withdrawing or withholding medical treatment. Opinions differ as to whether there is a significant ethical difference between withdrawing a treatment (e.g., a respirator) that has already been initiated, and simply deciding not to administer it in the first place. Both, essentially, are decisions not to treat.

The situations in which these treatment decisions arise vary widely. At least three different types of situations can be identified, each of which demands a different response:

A. The Irreversibly Dying Person

The first type of situation involves persons whose disease is progressive and for whom no effective therapy is available. As the final stages of the dying process occur, there comes a time to recognize the reality of what is happening by refraining from attempts to resuscitate the person and by discontinuing the use of artificial life support systems. To try desperately to maintain the vital signs of an irreversibly dying person for whom death is imminent is inconsistent with a Christian ethic that mandates respect for dying, as well as for living.

205

This does not, however, in any way preclude supportive care intended to maintain comfort and otherwise respond to the needs of the dying person. Indeed, quite the opposite is the case; when no cure is available, the responsibility to extend loving care not only continues but assumes even greater importance. This includes not only controlling physical pain, but also responding to the fear, guilt, and anger, the sense of isolation, the blocked communications, and the family stress that are often experienced by the dying.

B. Burdensome Treatments

In some cases there are forms of therapy which offer prospects for sustaining life but which themselves involve considerable discomfort, thereby necessitating a choice between quantity of life and quality of life for the patient. Examples of this type of situation include persons with widespread malignancy who are experiencing extensive side effects from chemotherapy and terminally ill children whose lives can be sustained for a greater period of time if they are hospitalized, but who will be separated from their familiar home environment. In such cases, the issue is whether it is preferable to have a greater number of days that are overshadowed by the rigors of therapy or a lesser number of days that are more peaceful, i.e., whether quantity of life or quality of life should be accorded priority.

Factors to be considered in making these decisions include the following:

1. The probability that a particular form of medical treatment will help sustain the life of the patient

2. The length of time that the life of the patient is likely to be sustained

3. The anticipated risks and side effects of the treatment

4. Other forms of treatment available, if any, and their relative advantages and disadvantages

5. The patient's adjustment to hospitalization or to the treatment

6. The extent to which the treatment will interfere with the person's most cherished activities

7. Available support systems at home or in alternative institutional settings

Second opinions and consultations are often useful in clarifying and assessing these factors.

C. Chronically Ill Individuals

The foregoing should not be taken to imply that chronically ill persons should be allowed to die because their lives are judged to be not worth living or because they are viewed as burdensome or useless to society. Whether the person in question is a newborn infant with serious birth defects or an aged person whose capacities have begun to wane, the Christian response in such cases must be a strong presumption in favor of treatment. Exceptions might arise in cases of extreme and overwhelming suffering from which death would be a merciful release, or in cases in which the patient has irretrievably lost consciousness.

Just as abandoning the chronically ill to die is inconsistent with Christian conscience, so also is abandoning the family members who, along with the patient, must bear the psychological, social, and economic costs of chronic illness. Responding to these needs involves the stewardship of time (e.g., offering to share in the responsibility of

206

caring for a chronically ill person) as well as seeking to make adequate financial resources and supportive services available, whether by public or private means. Finally, to assert that all lives are worth saving does not eliminate the necessity of establishing priorities when available medical resources are inadequate to treat all who are in need. In these tragic situations, it is inevitable that the priorities that are established, regardless of what they might be, will result in reduced levels of treatment for some, perhaps even to the point that death occurs earlier than would be the case if adequate resources were available.

REFUSING TREATMENT

If the patient has the prime decision-making role, the question then becomes one of refusing treatment for oneself, rather than withdrawing or withholding treatment from another. Since our responsibilities for stewardship of our own lives do not differ significantly from our responsibilities for the lives of others, the general guidelines outlined above are pertinent here also. Thus, for example, one may in good conscience refuse burdensome treatments in some situations.

A further question, however, also arises: Should persons be allowed to refuse treatment in situations in which such refusal is not supported by these guidelines? Or should they be treated in violation of their wishes? Here the principle of respect for individual self-determination comes into play. To treat a patient in violation of his or her deeply held, carefully considered, and clearly expressed preferences is to do violence to that person just as surely as would physically assaulting that person or deliberately destroying his or her property. This is as true in the case of an incompetent patient who has made his or her preferences known while still competent as it is in the case of a competent patient who can actively participate in the decision-making process.

At the same time, it must be emphasized that pain and other factors often distort the decision-making process, resulting in expressions of preference that may not represent a person's true wishes. In such cases, it may be appropriate to administer treatment (by authority of court order, if necessary) if so doing would sustain the life of the patient.

In all cases—including those situations in which a person's considered judgments are unmistakably clear—there is a continuing responsibility to care for and to extend the warmth of human community to that individual. A decision to allow refusal of medical treatment must never become an excuse for abandoning that person.

USE OF PAIN-KILLING DRUGS

In certain instances, some drugs administered in order to control pain experienced by terminally ill patients also have the effect of hastening the dying process, thus securing a better quality of life at the expense of quantity of life. As with burdensome forms of therapy, it is appropriate to ask whether there are alternative courses of action that do not pose this conflict—i.e., whether there are available means of controlling pain that would not hasten death. If there are not, the choice between quality and quantity of life cannot be avoided. In cases of great suffering, administering pain-killing drugs is justifiable even if this hastens the dying process. At the same time, adjustments in administering such drugs should be made so as not to

207

deprive the patient of consciousness prematurely. In all cases, recognition should be given to patient preferences, when they are known.

ACTIVE EUTHANASIA

Deliberately administering a lethal drug in order to kill the patient, or otherwise taking steps to cause death, is quite a different matter. This is frequently called "active euthanasia" or "mercy killing" (as contrasted with the cases discussed above, which involve withholding or withdrawing medical treatment, thereby allowing death to occur from a disease or injury).

Some might maintain that active euthanasia can represent an appropriate course of action if motivated by the desire to end suffering. Christian stewardship of life, however, mandates treasuring and preserving the life which God has given, be it our own life or the life of some other person. This view is supported by the affirmation that meaning and hope are possible in all of life's situations, even those involving great suffering. To depart from this view by performing active euthanasia, thereby deliberately destroying life created in the image of God, is contrary to Christian conscience.

Whatever the circumstances, it must be remembered that the Christian commitment to caring community mandates reaching out to those in distress and sharing hope and meaning in life which might elicit a renewed commitment to living.

CARING FOR THE LIVING AND FOR THE DYING

Health care includes not only attempting to cure disease and repair injury, but also caring for and relating to the patient as a person. As noted above, in the case of a terminally ill person for whom no cure is available, the responsibility to care not only continues, but assumes even greater importance, so that life may be lived to the fullest until death occurs.

Moreover, the responsibility to care includes extending care to the family and to all those who are involved in such situations. Hospice programs (which provide a wide range of supportive services for patients and their families) and other supportive care programs represent useful and constructive ways of assisting the patient and family members in relating to the human dimensions of death and dying and subsequent bereavement. Such support for family members is needed in cases of sudden death, as well as prolonged terminal illness.

Health care professionals as well as family members have a responsibility to be truthful in relations with patients. Information must be shared so that the person can understand the disease and the options for treatment. Being informed of terminal illness is also essential so that one can prepare for death.

In death-and-dying situations, the Church's ministry of Word and Sacrament through its members and ordained ministers is of great significance. Remembrance of Baptism renews the Christian's sense of unity with Christ and the Church, and the Sacrament of Holy Communion serves as a reassurance of Christ's living presence and offers hope for the life to come. Simply to be with those for whom death is approaching—to pray with and for them, to listen and to respond, to comfort and to console—is also an essential ministry.

A commitment to caring community must also give recognition to the humanity of health care professionals, who are frequently asked to bear tremendous burdens. They, too, have a need for grief therapy sessions and other supportive programs, which in turn will enable them to minister more effectively and compassionately to patients and their families and friends.

A particular responsibility of each individual is making treatment preferences known, after careful consideration, so as to facilitate the decision-making process and relieve the burden on others. Living wills (signed and witnessed statements completed while a person is still in sound mind indicating treatment preferences) represent one way of doing this. Other areas of broader responsibility for patients and family members include considering the possibility of organ donation as a means of sharing life with others, authorizing an autopsy, and the donation of the body for scientific purposes.

FORGIVENESS AND THANKSGIVING

There is much that we do not know. We do not know when a debilitating disease may strike, what course that disease might take, and when death will occur. And there is much that we do not understand. Sometimes the death of a child or the large measure of suffering that may accompany the dying process seems to make no sense at all. Our finitude not only involves the fact that our life spans are limited; it is also reflected in the limitations of what we know and can understand.

Moreover, in responding to the dilemmas that are thrust upon us in death-and-dying situations, we sometimes make the wrong decision, or at least are uncertain as to whether we have made the right one. And we are often woefully inadequate in extending compassion and understanding to our fellow human beings. Even in the best of circumstances, our sins and shortcomings are manifold.

But this we know: God is merciful and forgiving. Thus, by grace, we can both experience forgiveness and forgive others, as God forgives us.

We also know that God may be closest to us in times of adversity, for then the pretensions that alienate us and the diversions which preoccupy us are stripped away. It is then that we learn to rejoice again in the marvelous gift of life, and the privilege of sharing this life with family and friends and all those we have known and loved. Thus even at the moment of death we can proclaim with the psalmist:

> O give thanks to the Lord, for he is good;
> for his steadfast love endures for ever! (Psalm 107:1)

IMPLEMENTING RESOLUTION

The Lutheran Church in America recommends to its congregations and their members, synods, agencies, and institutions, the following as appropriate ways of implementing the principles set forth in the statement "Death and Dying."

I. Congregations

A. Provide an educational program that includes sessions on death and dying, so as to encourage members to reflect about these issues within a Christian context.

B. Sponsor training sessions to help members learn how to minister to the chronically ill and to those in death-and-dying situations, and to members of their families.

209

    C.   Encourage the development of mutual support groups within the congregation.

    D.   Join with other congregations and community groups to establish and maintain supportive care programs, including hospice care.

II. Churchwide Agencies, Synods

    A.   Prepare study material on death and dying to be used in educational programs.

    B.   Provide continuing educational opportunities and supportive services for clergy and laity to help them relate effectively to death and dying.

    C.   Encourage the development of hospice programs and other supportive care programs designed to respond to the human dimensions of death and dying.

    D.   Advocate with federal, provincial/state and local governments legislation and administrative regulations that advance the best interests of persons with respect to dying and death.

    E.   Advocate and support public and private measures designed to relieve the economic burden of terminal illness and to promote the just distribution of medical resources.

III. Church-Related Health Care Institutions and Social Service Agencies

    A.   Review and discuss institutional policies in terms of the guidelines outlined in the social statement.

    B.   Introduce and maintain programs designed to help health care professionals deal with death and dying.

    C.   Introduce and maintain programs designed to help patients and members of their families relate to death and dying.

IV. Educational Institutions (Seminaries and Church-Related Colleges)

    A.   Design college courses and programs on issues related to death and dying.

    B.   Provide seminary courses and programs to train future pastors and lay professionals for their ministry to the dying and to members of their families.

    C.   Cooperate with the synods in offering continuing education for clergy and laity in this area of concern.

V. Individuals

    A.   Prayerfully examine the ethical questions related to death and dying and make treatment preferences known to family members and to others as appropriate (e.g., by completing a living will).

    B.   Share time and other resources with those whose lives are affected by chronic illness or by death and dying.

    C.   Consider the possibility of organ donation as a means of sharing life with others.

ADDENDUM TO SOCIAL STATEMENT ON DEATH AND DYING

Adopted by the Eleventh Biennial Convention
of the Lutheran Church in America
Louisville, Kentucky
September 3–10, 1982

The Twelfth Biennial Convention of the Lutheran Church in America (Toronto 1984) adopted a memorial from the Virginia Synod directing "that all references in the Death and Dying Statement that call death '(a) friend' be changed to 'merciful'."

ECONOMIC JUSTICE

STEWARDSHIP OF CREATION IN HUMAN COMMUNITY

Adopted by the Tenth Biennial Convention, Seattle, Washington
June 24-July 2, 1980

INTRODUCTION

God wills humanity to exercise justice in its stewardship of creation. Holy Scripture declares that the earth is the Lord's, and that persons created in God's image are divinely authorized to care for this earth and to share in its blessings. Since human community is dependent on responsible stewardship, God commands that persons deal equitably and compassionately in their use of the earth's limited resources in order to sustain and fulfill the lives of others.

It is in obedient gratitude for all the gifts of God that we in the Lutheran Church in America commit ourselves in faithful love to struggle for economic justice as an integral part of the witness and work of God's People in the world.

ECONOMY IN SOCIETY

The word, "economy," is derived from the Greek words which mean the ordering of the household. In this basic sense, economy denotes the activity of persons in the management of all the resources (natural, human, and manufactured) of this world.

An economic system is the pattern of relationships, processes, institutions, and regulations, together with the values underlying them, by which the activities of production, distribution, and consumption are carried out in and among societies and cultures.

Economic policies and institutions develop through social custom and political decision. The allocation of the resources, burdens, and benefits of the economy is variously done: by traditional habits, by individual choice in the marketplace, by governmental regulation, by the action of corporations, or by all of these. Likewise the institutional constraints on economic activity are made by these means separately or in combination.

Economic activity is embedded in the total life of a society. Relations of production and distribution reflect the prevailing patterns of power as well as the values by which a society lives. The material allocations within a society are both an effect and a cause of the basic character of that society. The economic choices of the members and institutions of a society reflect what a society is and influence what it is becoming.

The fundamental questions underlying any economic system are therefore political and moral in nature. There are always technical questions that are peculiar to the operation of any given system, but the basic issues are not technical in character. For example, who may work? What should motivate our labors? By whom and how should it be decided what to produce, where to distribute, and how much to consume? Who determines, and how, the "fairness" of prices, profits, wages, benefits and strikes? How do we balance economic production and environmental protection? Do our economic practices reflect or reinforce child exploitation, sexism, ageism, racism, or anti-Semitism? The answers, never final, emerge qualified and compromised from the field of contending interests, powers, and moral claims.

The organization of economic life has undergone vast changes throughout the course of history, and no economic "system" has ever shown itself to be permanent. The appearance of new conditions, the development of new technologies, and the evolution of social values and political structures have all occasioned the alteration or replacement of economic institutions and relationships.

It is in such a world of continual change, amid graphic evidence of both progress and exploitation, that the Holy Spirit calls the church to bear witness to God's sovereign reign in our midst. As the Lord of history God acts in society to judge and fulfill the daily efforts of all people in their economic theory and practice.

THEOLOGICAL FOUNDATIONS

All persons are intended to respond in worship and work as one human family to the Creator's love: to propagate, nurture and extend human life and enhance its quality; to protect and use wisely the world's resources; to participate with God in the continuing work of creation; and to share equitably the product of that work to the benefit of all people.

In a world broken by sin the Creator lovingly enables the doing of justice. Into such a world God calls the redeemed in Christ to be advocates and agents of justice for all.

THE IMAGE OF GOD

Human life depends totally on a loving Creator. All persons are made in God's image for a life of trust, obedience, and gratitude.

Life under God is also meant to be life in community. There is no humanity but co-humanity, for one cannot be human alone. It is only together that persons can realize their creation in God's image. This image is reflected as persons respond in love and justice to one another's needs. Male and female persons are created equally in the image of God. (Gen. 1:27) It is in the basic human relationships of domestic, political, and economic life that persons share in their common humanity. God's love encompasses all people, and God intends that stewardship be practiced for the benefit of the entire human family.

Created in the image of God, persons are together stewards of God's bounty. They are accountable to God for how they use, abuse, or neglect to use the manifold resources — including their own bodies and capacities — which God has placed at their disposal. Reflecting God's cosmic dominion as Creator, they are called to care for the earth and "have dominion over," but not callously dominate, every living thing. (Gen. 1:28)

WORK

Work, the expending of effort for productive ends, is a God-given means by which human creatures exercise dominion. Through work, persons together are enabled to

214

perpetuate life and to enhance its quality. By work they are both privileged and obligated to reflect the Creator whose work they are.

Although sinful rebellion issues in burdens of toil and alienation, the forgiving and renewing Lord holds out the possibility of work as useful and satisfying, prompting the Psalmist's prayer, "Establish the work of our hands." (Ps. 90:17)

Work is thus meant for persons in community, not persons for work. While participation in the community of work is meant to enhance personal well-being, the identity of persons created in God's image is neither defined by the work they do nor destroyed by the absence of work. What a person *does* or *has* does not determine what one *is* as the personal creature of a loving Creator.

Christian identity is also not to be equated with the work Christians do. As new persons in Christ, Christians have been set free and empowered to exercise their vocation through many roles, occupations among them. However, Christians do not equate baptismal vocation in God's kingdom with economic occupations in the world.

JUSTICE

Justice may be described as distributive love. It is what God's love does when many neighbors must be served with limited resources. Justice is the form of God's creating and preserving love as that love is mediated by reason and power through persons and structures in community life. Injustice dehumanizes life and prevents full participation in co-humanity. Justice is therefore viewed simply as that which people need to be human.

God mandates the doing of justice. (Micah 6:8) The specific content of that justice, however, is not directly revealed but is discovered as life is lived amid claim and counterclaim. The discernment of justice involves every aspect of the human being. It is a task of reason, requiring the counting, measuring and classifying of factors that admit to such analysis. It is intuitive, involving the capacity for empathy. It is political, involving the struggle for power among competing groups. Above all, it is moral, involving the fundamental human capacity to know what enhances and what destroys the being and dignity of the person. That capacity, conscience, grows and is nurtured in the creative interaction of persons and groups, in the recollection of and reflection on past experience, and in the confronting of new situations.

Therefore the doing of justice is the proper stewardship of the social and material resources of creation in which our co-humanity in God's image is being realized.

Social justice refers to those institutional and legal arrangements which promote justice for all the members of society.

In addition to being the way in which God's providential love is expressed socially, justice is also the way in which sinful persons are required to do for others what, in their self-centeredness, they would not otherwise do to meet their neighbors' collective needs.

Because human beings, both individually and collectively, are self-centered, self-serving, and self-justifying, their defining and doing of justice are inevitably tainted by the rationalization of special interest. This sinful rationalization often leads to such errors as the pitting of benevolence against justice and the confusion of justice with righteousness.

Social justice should not be pitted against personal benevolence (often called charity) or corporate benevolence (often called philanthropy); but neither should benevolence be substituted for justice. In its true sense, benevolence is the loving response directly to others in need; in its false sense, it is the vain attempt to purchase a good conscience and to avoid the demand for justice. Rightly understood, benevolence and justice complement each other as different forms of the Creator's providential love.

Neither personal nor corporate benevolence can accomplish what a society is required to do for its members under justice; but a society cannot remain sound if it leaves no room for benevolent acts.

Justice and righteousness, as these terms are used in this statement, are not to be confused or identified with each other. Righteousness denotes the redeeming activity of God in Christ which effects the forgiveness of sin, new life, and salvation. It frees and empowers God's faithful servants to act lovingly and justly in the world, not merely out of prudent self-regard, but also sacrificially for their neighbors' sake.

The attempt to equate human justice and divine righteousness distorts Christ's Gospel and undermines God's law. In the name of liberty, such self-righteousness enslaves; in the name of life, it kills; in the name of abundance, it lays waste. God's holy wrath is provoked when humans presume to rule society by a spurious "gospel," thereby weakening the possibility of realizing justice, peace, and civil order under God's law.

Justice takes place at the intersection of serving love and enlightened self-interest. All sinners, including Christians, are still able as the corrupted image of God to act justly out of such self-regard; and forgiven Christians are empowered to move beyond such self-regard. By the power of Christ working in them, they are freed to enlarge the conventional limits of justice.

While the advancement of justice involves the interplay of countervailing power, it depends finally upon the degree to which the members of a community are either willing or constrained to moderate their acquisitiveness in the interest of the common good.

Justice is a painful process, serving as both the prerequisite for and the fruit of civil peace. Although never fully completed, struggles for justice draw people into the ongoing work of approximating God's will in this sinful world.

ECONOMIC APPLICATIONS

God gives to human creatures the freedom and capacity to devise the means of exercising the stewardship that has been entrusted to them. They may therefore establish such social and legal institutions as will facilitate the life of mutual responsibility for which they have been created. Such humanly-devised means are legitimate so long as they do not usurp the place of God as Lord and owner of all things or thwart the will of God for the well-being of the whole human family.

THE STEWARDSHIP OF MEANINGS AND VALUES

God enables persons to employ ideas as tools of analysis and evaluation. The fashioning and use of conceptual tools is never finished. New historical situations may require new modes of diagnosis and prescription. The refinement of appropriate concepts is a vital part of the constructive work of seeking justice.

216

An ideology is a set of linked ideas by which a society, social movement or interest group seeks to explain, give coherence to, and justify a given pattern of behavior or a prescriptive vision for society. An ideology may be used to elicit commitment to preserving the social *status quo* or to changing it.

An ideology can be a useful means for the securing of political cohesion within a society or for mobilizing people in support of constructive change. It can also be used deceptively to mask injustice and to elicit an ultimate commitment which, besides being idolatrous, may make people insensitive to the violation of basic human rights.

No ideology can legitimately be held to be redemptive or represented as embodying God's saving righteousness.

Christians recognize stewardship as including the right use of meanings and values in the just ordering of society and economy. Such ideological stewardship must, however, prevent any system of values from laying an ultimate claim on persons as the bearers of God's image.

As part of the stewardship of meanings and values the following principles are offered as guidance for responsible action.

GOVERNMENT

In a sinful world God intends the institutions of government to be the means of enforcing the claims of economic justice. Government should neither stifle economic freedom through excessive regulation, nor abdicate its responsibility by permitting economic anarchy. Legitimate governmental activity normally includes such functions as: protection of workers, producers, and households from practices which are unfair, dangerous, or degrading; protection of the public from deceptive advertising and from dangerous or defective products or processes; encouragement and regulation of public utilities, banking and finance, science and education; environmental protection; provision for the seriously ill and disabled, needy, and unemployed; and establishment of an equitable system of taxation to support these functions. Compliance with these and other legitimate governmental activities should be affirmed, even as their improvement and correction are sought through appropriate political means.

In extreme situations, when governmental institutions or holders of political power engage in the tyrannical and systematic violation of basic human rights, and when the means of legal recourse have been exhausted or are demonstrably inadequate, then non-violent direct action, civil disobedience, or, as a last resort, rebellion may become the justifiable and necessary means of establishing those conditions within which justice can again be sought and enjoyed.

ECONOMIC JUSTICE

Economic justice is that aspect of social justice involving the material dimension of social relationships and the social activities of production, distribution, and consumption of goods and services. Economic justice denotes the fair apportioning of resources and products, of opportunities and responsibilities, of burdens and benefits among the members of a community. It includes the provision for basic human need, fair compensation for work done, and the opportunity for the full utilization of personal gifts in productive living.

Economic justice includes the elements of equity, accessibility, accountability, and efficiency.

Understood as equity or fairness, economic justice does not mean economic equality. It is rather the result of a discerning of, and response to, the various needs of the members of a society, respecting differences without being partial to power or special interest. Equity implies a sense of the common good and a care for the diversity of gifts and human resources that contribute to it. At the same time it provides for those minimal necessities which, in a given social and cultural setting, are prerequisites for participation in society; and it provides for those members of the society who, because of circumstances not of their making, cannot provide for themselves.

Accessibility includes both the formal entitlements to political participation and legal redress, and such substantive entitlements (e.g., nutrition, shelter, health care, basic education, minimum income and/or employment) as are needed for entrance into the social and economic community. It also includes the provision of the means by which the members of a community may participate in decisions which affect the quality of the common life and that of future generations.

Accountability implies that economic actors must be held answerable to the community for the consequences of their behavior. Government properly establishes the legal means whereby people may secure compensation for injury incurred, as a result of economic decisions which have not taken account of their likely impact on personal and community well-being.

Efficiency requires a responsible use of resources that is genuinely productive by minimizing waste. This productivity is conserving not only of material resources and time, but also of human resources and the environment. The economy should be structured to permit the calculation of efficiency so as to take account of social and ecological waste.

Persons should be permitted and encouraged to participate in fundamental as well as market decisions governing the economy. Members of a society should be co-determiners of the quality of their economic life. Such co-determination, requiring differing structures appropriate for differing situations, is the basic right of persons whom God has created in co-humanity as responsible stewards.

Stewardship requires careful forethought. Planning is vital to the stewardship of material resources at all levels of human life: personal, familial, communal, and political. Planning on economic matters is more than technical. Questions of basic human value are involved in both specifying economic goals and devising the means of achieving them.

Planning should therefore be sufficiently pluralistic in character to assure the possibility of self-correction and prevent domination by one or a few special interests. It should be done on a scale and level of social life which provide for the greatest practical degree of participation and co-determination.

God has implanted in the human creature the capacity and initiative to define the problems of material existence in community and to effect positive change. No person or community should relinquish that initiative or capacity, and social and political institutions should be designed to encourage such initiative at the local and intermediate levels of society. A society is healthier when its members are encouraged to participate responsibly in determining their own lives rather than being only the passive consumers of goods and services.

WORK

Even in the present state of sinful estrangement, God's intention remains that work be done and its fruits be enjoyed by the whole human family. The division of labor according to efficiency and the diversity of human gifts, along with the social relations of productive activity, are means by which life in co-humanity may be both extended and enriched.

Work that is beneficial to society glorifies the Creator. Those who perform such work are to be esteemed for their contribution to the common good. They are not to be judged by whether or not the work is remunerative, or by the amount of remuneration. Vast disparities of income and wealth are both divisive of the human community and demeaning to its members.

Exclusion of persons from the community of work is a denial of the opportunity of realizing the divine intention for co-humanity.

Humanly-devised economic arrangements which, in their operation, tend both to exclude some persons from the community of work, and subsequently to stigmatize such persons for not working, constitute a double affront to the Creator and to persons created in God's image.

PROPERTY

The concept of property is a legal means of determining responsibility for the use of resources and humanly-produced wealth. Property may be held by individuals, by business corporations, by cooperative or communal self-help organizations, or by government. In whatever manner it is held, property is held in trust and its holder is accountable ultimately to God and proximately to the community through its constituted authorities for the ways in which the resource or wealth is, or is not, used.

While the holder of wealth-producing property is entitled to a reasonable return, as determined contextually by the society, the holder of such property may not assert exclusive claim on it or its fruits. Justice requires that wealth be both productive and contributory to the general well-being through both the provision of new opportunities and the alleviation of human need.

The private ownership of property is a humanly devised legal right which can serve as a means for the exercise of that responsible stewardship which constitutes the divine image. Private property is not an absolute human right but is always conditioned by the will of God and the needs of the community. The obligation to serve justifies the right to possess. The Creator does not sanction the accumulation of economic power and possessions as ends in themselves.

CONCLUSION

We affirm the inseparability of the economy from the whole of human life. The criticism and reshaping of economic relations and institutions is a fundamentally moral task in which Christians should be actively involved. Economy, rightly understood, is the God-given stewardship of life.

In Christ the People of God are freed and enabled individually and corporately to participate in the quest for greater economic justice and the achievement of the conditions of human well-being. As a worldwide community of brothers and sisters, the church can summon the human family to care for the earth responsibly while God yet gives us time.

IMPLEMENTING RESOLUTION

This church calls upon its ministers and congregations to engage in an intensive study over the next biennium of the social statement, "Economic Justice: Steward-ship of Creation in Human Community," with a view to ascertaining the content of this church's corporate stewardship within the present historical setting. Such study is to consider both the institutional allocation of the material and human resources of this church internally and the work of public advocacy by this church externally.

This church directs its program agencies and offices to facilitate such study through programs appropriate to their several mandates. Such work should to the extent possible be planned and executed through such means as the Staff Team on World Hunger Concerns and the Staff Team on Fiscal Support. Each churchwide agency shall report to the 1982 convention of this church the results of its study and action, as well as its future intentions in the field of economic justice.

Efforts are to be made by appropriate agencies of this church to equip both the ministers and the laity to understand and apply the orientation and principles em-bodied in this statement through such means as:

1) Seminary and college curricula;
2) Continuing education for pastors;
3) Conferences for parish lay leadership;
4) Church school curricula; and
5) Faith and Life Institutes

The Division for Mission in North America shall advise this church as to appropriate ways of implementing this statement both through advocacy in the public sector and through consultation and shareholder action in the private corporate sector.

The administrative offices of this church, in consultation with the Division for Mis-sion in North America, shall study this statement with a view to the application of its principles to this church as a manager of resources, employer, fund-raiser, investor, and purchaser and provider of goods and services.

The Division for Mission in North America shall continue the work of issue-clarification and the constructive criticism of ideology begun during the preparation of this statement. It shall continue to involve the lay persons of relevant expertise and experience who were engaged in the development of this statement as well as others whom it may identify.

The Division for Mission in North America, through its program, Advocacy for Global Justice, shall identify and act upon the global and domestic implications of this statement as they impinge on the reality of world hunger.

This church shall endeavor to implement this statement through its inter-Lutheran and ecumenical involvements, both in North America and worldwide.

THE HUMAN CRISIS IN ECOLOGY

Adopted by the Sixth Biennial Convention, Dallas, Texas
June 30-July 6, 1972

Society today is confronted by a profound crisis and challenge in the world of humans and of nature. God so orders creation that everything in it is related to everything else. All physical components and all organisms, including human beings, are purposefully woven together in ecological systems or ecosystems, such as forests, grasslands, the oceans, as well as the planet earth. When any part is tampered with, exploited or destroyed the effect is felt in other parts and eventually in the whole system. The ecological crisis consists in the radical violation of the systems God creates. The challenge to human beings is the way in which they deal with this crisis; it will have profound significance for all of life in our time and for generations to come.

A. FACETS OF THE CRISIS

GROWTH RUNNING WILD

This is an age of rampaging growth—growth in production and consumption, sales and profits, population and power. Unchecked population increases exponentially (for example, $2 \to 4 \to 8 \to 16 \to 32 \to 64 \to 128$); technological and economic expansion often takes place even more rapidly. Because of increasing population, increasing consumer demands, and increasing technological achievements, the engine of the economy races on, running wild. But, with all this growth—scarcely questioned by the popular mind—come also rapidly increasing pollution, depletion of non-renewable resources, population pressures, social injustice, and deterioration in the quality of life. Since the earth is finite, with a limited supply of air, water, and places to dump refuse, there is an inevitable breaking-point beyond which even the most sophisticated technology cannot rescue us.

POLLUTION

Pollution of air, water, soil, and sound is a daily experience for nearly every North American. Individuals, municipalities, industries often poison their environments with only a minimum of restraints, hardly considering the impact of their practices on human beings and the rest of the natural world.

The serious solid waste problem, for example, results not only from governmental and industrial neglect but from the public's desire for the convenience of a throw-away style of life. Pollution is also a global problem. The currents of the atmosphere and the oceans carry harmful substances from contaminated areas to the most remote places of the earth. This is particu-

1. Ecology: "The totality or pattern of relations between organisms and their environment." *Webster's New International Dictionary.*

221

larly serious with long-lived pesticides, radioactive fallout, and ecological damage caused by war.

DEPLETION OF NATURAL RESOURCES

Breathable air and drinkable water, the resources most critical to life, are diminishing in quantity and quality. There is an irreplaceable reduction of minerals, open spaces and forests because of the insatiable human demand for raw materials and room for factories and housing. Technology's best efforts to develop new food sources are frustrated by the pace of population growth, the diminution of arable land, and the injury done to the productivity of soil by some chemical applications. These and other forms of resource depletion cause severe damage to plants, animals, and human beings as they push hard on the limits of the earth's ecosystems.

POPULATION PRESSURES

If there were no more people in the world than in the time of Christ, estimated to be about ¼ billion, the destructive effects of pollution and exhaustion of resources would be minimal. Since population has grown exponentially, experts project that if this trend continues in the same manner, the earth's population, about 3.7 billion in 1971, will rise to about 7 billion by the year 2000—a dangerously crowded planet.

Although the population growth rate in Canada and the United States is less than in many other lands, even in these countries the anticipated increases will cause severe problems. Most frightening, however, is the effect of North American growth upon the rest of the world. The United States alone, with only six per cent of the world's population, is responsible for at least one-third of the world's consumption of nonrenewable resources.

Population pressures enormously complicate all other facets of the ecological crisis. The stark fact is that, if the responsible decision of people does not result in population limitation, the ghastly alternatives of famine and disease, crime and violence and war will do it in their own ways.

SOCIAL INJUSTICE

The human crisis in ecology is an enormously complex and urgent problem. It is understood only when the dimension of social injustice is taken seriously. When the poisons of pollution and the explosion of population take their toll, the impact falls most heavily upon the poor, certain minority groups, and others who are already oppressed by many of the most crushing problems of today. The unequal distribution of wealth and resources both within and among nations results in injustices which cry out for redress. Too often an overemphasis on the private sector has diminished the ability of government to work effectively for justice. Too often the power of technology has been used by some nations and by some groups within nations to dominate others, thus widening the chasm between the "haves" and the "have nots." The struggle for the earth's resources and the tensions of urbanized living will become increasingly potent causes of domestic violence and international war. The issues of social injustice are profoundly involved in the ecological crisis.

B. A HUMAN CRISIS

THE UNDERLYING CAUSE

The underlying cause of the ecological crisis is not natural forces but human arrogance and rebellion against God, what the Christian faith calls sin. Because humans alone are responsible before God, they alone are capable of sinning. By seeking to serve themselves rather than God and their neighbors, human beings both individually and corporately forsake their humanity as responsible, relational beings. Likewise, they choose to perceive the nonhuman world not as possessing God-given integrity of its own, but as existing primarily for their use and benefit, or merely as the stage upon which they live their lives. Some of their disruptive influence, to be sure, results from their ignorance or from changing circumstances, from their inability to foresee the eventual consequences of well-intentioned actions. Nevertheless, whether through sin or ignorance, human beings violate their selves, their neighbors, and the whole of creation.

TOWARD NEW VALUES

There is little hope of arresting the mad rush toward ecological disaster unless a very large number of persons and institutions *renounce* certain values which have long dominated civilization. Defining "the good life" in terms of creature comforts and material "progress," many people in all strata of society cherish such assumptions as the following: that the earth's resources belong to humanity and are inexhaustible; that prosperity is a reward for diligence and character, and poverty is caused by the indolence of the poor; that maximization of profit, economic growth and technological expansion is inevitably good; that the threat of intolerable population pressures is exaggerated; and that human ingenuity, working through science, technology, and present social structures, can resolve the ecological crisis without decisive changes in values and institutions. These old values, reflections of sin and ignorance, flout ecological facts and tear the fabric of interrelatedness which is of the essence of God's creation. They must be renounced in favor of new values which give priority to quality of life rather than to quantity of things, characterized by responsibility in human community and enlightened care of the earth and its resources.

In the task of discovering new values and nurturing commitment to them, the church has a crucial role to play. Moved by faith in its Lord, love for neighbor, and concern for justice, the church joins with others in facing the baffling problems of the ecological crisis and searching for solutions which are true to these new values. It is grateful for constructive changes which have been taking place in society and in its own life, and for persons and groups whose labors have brought them about. The church sees itself called to work as an instrument of God for a maximum of justice and reconciliation in a sinful world. Recognizing the ambiguity of all decision-making, it speaks and acts trusting in God's grace.

C. IMPERATIVES FOR ACTION

In obedience to God and in response to the urgency of the human crisis in ecology, this church sets forth the following imperatives for action:

1. *Reaffirmation of the biblical doctrine of creation.* Scripture portrays creation as a continuing manifestation of God's love and sovereignty. God acts to establish and preserve a just and ordered life, to enable every part of the world, in proper relation with all other parts, to perform the function for which it is made.

Human beings are part of the vast ecosystem of the planet earth. They cannot live their lives against that system; they must live within it. They must respect the integrity of the nonhuman world, including its inorganic components.

Only when this is remembered dare we speak of whatever uniqueness human beings may have: uniqueness in their capacity to respond to God in faith and to their neighbors in love, and in their corresponding capacity to rebel against God, alienate themselves from their neighbors, and deal selfishly with the rest of creation. God's commission to humanity to have "dominion" over the earth and "to till it and keep it," calls for responsible stewardship of the earth and all living things, to work for the fulfillment of all creation and for justice in the human community. But human beings too often have distorted this commission into a license to exploit the world and other human beings.

This means that we live ecologically among our neighbors as well as within nature. Humankind is a relational unity; every person lives both in history and in nature. Degradation of any person degrades all persons. The individual cannot find personal integration and peace apart from struggling for the integration and peace of all humankind. For this reason, radical changes are called for in our attitudes and actions as we meet the distinctively human dimensions of the ecological crisis.

In its preaching and sacraments, worship and evangelism, education and social ministry, the church is called to teach this biblical understanding of human beings and nature as God's interrelated creation.

2. *Development of ecological life styles which are sensitive to the needs of human beings and the nonhuman world.* This calls for personal, family, and societal behavior patterns which reduce pollution and the wasting of resources, for example, using recycled products when ecologically feasible, practicing selective buying, and regulating habits of consumption according to ecological criteria. It also calls for this church, in its structure, policies, and actions, to demonstrate concern for the interrelatedness of people within its own life and in the world.

3. *Serious questioning of the philosophy of material growth which has been virtually unchallenged in modern society.* Some economic growth seems necessary if a more equitable distribution of wealth is to become possible.

Such distribution will not be achieved automatically by economic growth; it will be accomplished only by basic economic reforms, such as changing tax structures, providing incentives, optimizing energy use, and reordering priorities, both public and private. Technology is essential to the solution of some ecological problems, but it must be controlled. The task of encouraging growth in quality of life by securing a dynamic equilibrium between consumption and available resources is complex and controversial. This church should guide its members to examine their own "growth" attitudes, and should stimulate and participate in critical interdisciplinary examination of society's dedication to material growth.

4. *Challenge to popular beliefs.* Many erroneously believe that science and technology will resolve the ecological crisis without decisive changes in social structures. On the contrary, many technological advances, despite their benefits, have multiplied problems—pollution, depletion of resources, and unforeseen damage. Therefore, among other strategies, political action is needed to bring technology fully into the service of genuine quality of life. To assist existing governmental agencies, advocacy groups might be formed. Consisting of competent people from appropriate fields, such advocacy groups—independent of both industry and government—would evaluate new technological developments in terms of their direct and indirect environmental impact.

5. *Concern for the social costs of actions of industry and government.* What effect, for example, do decisions regarding the disposal of industrial effluents or municipal sewage have upon lakes, rivers, and oceans—ultimately upon human beings, wildlife, and vegetation? This church supports efforts to monitor the performance of regulatory agencies at all levels of government; tax reforms which discourage polluting and encourage safe environmental practices; and legislation which requires greater accountability of private and public enterprises to their appropriate communities. Financial costs of improved ecological procedures should be allocated in such ways as not to overburden those least able to afford them.

6. *Earnest attention to population control.* Population control differs from family planning in that it bases family-size decisions on the capacity of the world to support children rather than the desire of parents to have them. It is imperative that every effort be made to achieve control by voluntary incentives. If voluntary appeals prove ineffective, however, the danger from population growth is so ominous that there will be societal pressures for compulsory control. The possibility of coercion by law involves complex questions of social ethics and personal conscience which the church and society must study with great care.

7. *This church's economic policies and practices.* This church shall witness to the affirmations of this statement in its own economic policies and practices in such areas as employment, purchasing of goods and services, investments, and responsible use of its human and financial resources.

225

Especially in carrying out its investment policies the church should, within the criterion of fiduciary responsibility, exercise priority for considerations of ecological and social justice.

8. *Public Action.* This church and its members should take public action which protects, restores, and enhances the natural and the specifically human environments. They should express their convictions to officials of government in behalf of constructive environmental policies and practices, and should cooperate with other churches and organizations which have similar objectives. This church and its members should pursue the same goals in business and industry through personal contact with corporate leaders, scrutiny of investment and employment practices, participation in stockholders' meetings, selective purchasing of goods and services, and making public statements of criticism or commendation. This church should involve decision-makers in government and industry in faith-and-life dialogues to enable them to share insights into the crucial ecological issues which they face.

9. *Application of all these imperatives to the relationships among the nations of the world.* This church should cooperate with other churches and with governmental and nongovernmental organizations in dealing with international ecological problems. New global dimensions are lifted up by the LCA Statement on World Community (1970):

> It is no longer possible for one nation to consider its use, or abuse, of resources within its own borders—for instance, air and water—as its exclusive concern. The time has come for all nations to cooperate in the coordination of conservation efforts within their respective territories, as well as to establish the rule of law governing resources of oceans, polar regions, and outer space—"the international public domain." The latter task, a beginning of which has already been made, includes the establishment of agreements which protect international resources from uncontrolled private or national exploitation, the guarantee that such resources shall not be used for warlike purposes, and the development of genuinely international agencies empowered to enforce the agreements.

The issues of international social justice are an integral part of the human crisis in ecology. Fair distribution of resources and power, equitable standards of living, reduction of global pollution, just resolution of the tensions that make for war, the building of peace on earth—all the problems of world community are inescapably the problems of every nation and every citizen. Their solution, however, will require special considerations and sacrifices by the people of Canada and the United States.

D. A CALL

In light of the above imperatives for action the Lutheran Church in America calls upon its members and all elements of its corporate life to develop and pursue courses of action, appropriate to their respective responsibilities and capacities, which will promote environmental protection and social justice.

HUMAN RIGHTS
DOING JUSTICE IN GOD'S WORLD

Adopted by the Ninth Biennial Convention, Chicago, Illinois
July 12-19, 1978

God calls the church in every time and place to proclaim righteousness, to struggle against injustice, and to care for creation. It is therefore fitting that we in the Lutheran Church in America, as one embodiment of God's people in the world, declare our understanding of human rights and take our stand with all who work and suffer to advance freedom, equality, and justice in ways that more truly reflect God's intention for humanity.

THE PRESENT SITUATION

This is a time of rapid and radical change in every aspect of human existence. Such change is simultaneously awakening new hopes for a greater degree of justice for people and rendering the achievement of such justice increasingly problematic.

Dramatic achievements of human imagination and skill hold out the possibility of the virtual elimination of such chronic scourges as starvation, ill health, congenital defects, and ignorance. Men and women throughout the world dare to dream of a life for themselves and their children that is increasingly free of poverty, oppression, and disease.

Justice and human rights have become a concern that transcends national boundaries. The Charter of the United Nations, the Universal Declaration of Human Rights, and numerous international agreements reflect the reality of this worldwide concern. The specialized agencies of the United Nations work quietly for the achievement of justice. Many voluntary organizations strive to expose injustice and to work positively for its elimination. The worldwide Christian community is becoming increasingly engaged in both direct ministry to oppressed persons and groups and in public advocacy for justice.

At the same time oppression appears to be more widespread and systematic. There are countless refugees from political tyranny and economic hardship. Imprisonment and torture are commonplace in many countries irrespective of ideology or political alignment. Persons of conscience, rather than being valued as resources to the community, are frequently treated as subversives by those in power. Privacy and due process are violated in the name of security. The practice of religion is often curtailed or prohibited, and the faithful are harassed, imprisoned, or even killed. The use of terror by both governments and private groups constitutes a serious threat to human rights.

Inequitable economic relationships deny to millions the basic necessities of

227

dignified life. For the majority of the world's people starvation and disease are commonplace. Even in wealthier countries pockets of chronic poverty exist.

In all parts of the world there are institutionalized populations — in mental hospitals, nursing homes, and prisons — who languish without advocates. Many persons held in these circumstances are the very young or the very old; many, having little knowledge of their rights, are the objects of continuing victimization.

Racism, sexism, and discrimination against the handicapped — whether enforced by official policy or by cultural mores — are realities throughout the world.

The increasing vulnerability of a complex, interdependent, and technology-based world society is accompanied by increasing concern about security against disruption, sabotage, or destruction by private groups or alien governments. This legitimate concern for maintaining conditions of order and peace can easily become an obsession. There appears to be a growing culture of fear that pits the interests of security against those of human rights. The national security state, with its reliance on might and, frequently, on repression rather than civil consensus, is more the rule than the exception in the community of nations.

There is a growing concern that the human ability to shape persons through increasingly subtle behavioral, physical, and genetic manipulation may tempt humanity to exchange freedom for a security based upon total control. The election of such a course could alter radically the future of the human race.

There is the concurrent warning that the utter contamination, exhaustion, or destruction of the resources of the planet will deprive future generations of their rights.

The continuing polarization of East and West reinforces an ideological polarization in the understanding of human rights, pitting a false collectivism against an equally false individualism.

THE HUMAN: A THEOLOGICAL UNDERSTANDING

In the face of this present situation we in the Lutheran Church in America declare our theological view of what it means to be a human being in order to state what we understand to be the rights of human beings. What follows is a statement of what we hold to be true in light of the divine Word about God and all humankind. This statement is cast as a confession of belief about God's intention for creation, followed by a confession or litany about our fallen state, which only those who have been laid hold of by God's Word can make. It speaks here of all humans, including Christians in the Body of Christ and within this church. Our confession of God's presence in the world likewise is a statement of faith; it also deals with all peoples in the Creator's world. Finally, we set forth a gospel affirmation of our vocation in Christ by which we are liberated and empowered to join in the struggle for human rights.

THE CREATOR'S INTENTION
We confess that God calls persons into being (Gen. 1:26, 27). Female and male

228

persons are equally created in God's image. They live by God's word of address to them; they are constituted by the relationship that word creates. Persons are created in and for co-humanity. The individual is not prior to the group, nor the group to the individual.

God's righteous will for persons is that they serve their Creator through responsible care for one another and for the creation (Micah 6:8; Ps. 8:6). We thus understand God's intention for "the human" to include responsible life in community with God and neighbor and faithful stewardship of the world's resources. No resource is the unqualified possession of the person or persons holding it. All is held in trust for the benefit of the whole human community and of future generations (Deut. 24:19ff).

The human struggle for justice is an ongoing one. The provisional forms of God's righteous will become evident in response to the concrete needs of people at particular times in history. The changing demands of justice are discerned in part by the inner witness of God's law in the human heart (Rom. 2:13-16). They are continually tested in social living.

A right is what justice requires in response to a particular human need.

It is necessary to distinguish between human rights and the legal entitlements and protections which flow from them. Human rights are *moral* assertions of what justice demands in particular historical situations. Civil, political, and economic rights are *legal* guarantees that have been established by governments.

Rights are formulated either positively or negatively. Some rights are entitlements to particular things or conditions which enable responsible life in community. Other rights are protections against the arbitrary and unjust use of power.

God has created persons in one human family (Acts 17:26). It is God's intention that persons should discover their mutual rights and responsibilities as they live together in community. Thus, individuals in community are prior to rights and duties. The proper end of rights and responsibilities is to serve the legitimate needs of persons in community.

Although persons differ as to endowments and circumstances, they are of equal worth before God. They are equally entitled to the things and protections they need to live in meaningful relation to God and neighbor.

Rights and responsibilities are interrelated. In exercising their rights, persons are responsible for the promotion of their neighbors' rights as well. Power of whatever kind carries with it responsibility for the protection and advancement of human rights.

OUR FALLEN STATE
We are willful, rebellious creatures. We are all equally guilty before God (Rom. 3:9-18). We do not fear, love, or trust God above all else, nor do we serve our neighbors as we ought. We are grasping, self-deceiving, and self-serving. We mask our appetites and privileges under the term, "rights," and we often perceive as

"charity" our grudging accession to our neighbors' rights. We define our rights and duties as best suits our advantage. We are covetous and greedy; if we are not exploiters ourselves, we benefit from the exploitation done by our ancestors or by those agents of power to which we pledge our loyalty.

We hold onto the wealth entrusted to us as if it were ours by right for our private enjoyment (Amos). We assert ultimate title to what God entrusts to us, taking up arms to defend our possessions against a world hungry and in want. We substitute a self-congratulating charity for the justice that God demands.

We make law and order ends in themselves or the means of preserving our privileged position.

We create invidious distinctions among persons, declaring some to be more human than others in defiance of the Creator who loves all equally. We erect barriers which separate race and race, sister and brother, poor and rich, in rebellion against God's holy will. We shut people out; we shut people in; we stigmatize; we stereotype.

We devour the resources of God's earth while millions go without sustenance, shelter, or other basic necessities.

We consume and contaminate with little thought for the rights of our children and future generations.

We allow our respect for institutions to degenerate into unquestioning obedience, especially when such respect serves our own self-interest.

As a church we often help to reinforce injustice. Our institutional arrangements frequently reflect prevailing patterns of oppressions; and the use we make of our corporate power seldom challenges the social *status quo*.

God's word of address to us becomes a word of judgment from which we flee (Gen. 3:8-10). The cry of those we oppress goes up to God, becoming the word of our condemnation.

THE CREATOR'S PRESENCE
The Creator lovingly preserves the world, however estranged it may be, through human works of civil righteousness.

We confess that within this fallen world God remains present and active, contending against our abuse of one another and of the power and resources entrusted to us. The Creator encourages and enables us and all people of good will to do works of justice. Human imagination, empathy, and mutuality are God's gifts which enable us to create and to preserve a measure of peace, justice, and community in this fallen world.

In the cries of outrage against injustice God's own voice of judgment is heard; in the political struggle against illegitimate rule, God's power is manifest, in the struggle to break down barriers of race, age, sex, and class, God is at work. Though ambiguous and mingled with the evidence of sin, these marks of God's governance give hope to the downtrodden and encouragement to all who strive for justice.

230

The Creator's presence is also discerned in the witness of the divine law, though obscured and distorted by sin, in the hearts of persons. God helps persons to know and to do what is civilly right, if not out of justice, then out of prudent self-regard. This limited capacity for justice, while it will not save persons ultimately, can preserve them temporally.

The capacity for prudence and justice can establish reasonable conditions for the promotion of the common good of all the world's people.

OUR VOCATION IN CHRIST

God has redeemed us by the Cross and Resurrection of Jesus the Christ, has incorporated us into Christ's Body, the church, and has called us to loving service in the world. God calls us to serve, both corporately and individually, in the ongoing struggle for justice and human rights.

Corporately as the church, and individually as Christians, we participate in this struggle not out of a love of power but by the power of the divine love for the whole world. In Christ we have been freed from a preoccupation with our own rights in order to give ourselves to the securing of justice for our neighbors in the worldwide human family.

For this task we do not claim special competence or insight. Frequently we require instruction from the knowledge and experience of persons who are not themselves Christians. Our identity lies not in our knowledge but in the New Being that is ours in Christ and in the lively hope that is ours for the fulfillment of God's promises.

We are empowered by God's Spirit to perform our vocation in the world under the sign of the Cross. In the Cross we see God's power victorious in apparent defeat; by that Cross we are able, in the face of the evil that permeates the world and ourselves, to persist in the struggle for justice, bearing witness that God has not abandoned this fallen creation.

As God's liberated people, we are free to advocate the rights of persons without fear or favor. We have a special duty to be skeptical and vigilant about the exercise of power by governments and institutions and to be humble and self-critical about our own interests and attitudes.

When temporal authority performs its legitimate function of securing human rights, we can thankfully support it (Rom. 13:1-7; I Peter 2:13f); when it does not, we can just as freely work for its reform or replacement and, if need be, disobey or resist it (Rev. 13), accepting the consequences of such action.

Because our Christian community is worldwide and transcends differences of nationality, political ideology, culture, physical condition, and race, we can be effective partners in the task of strengthening the growing world constituency of conscience which, with increasing effectiveness, is calling to account the holders of power, both public and private, for the deprivation of human rights. Both within our own countries and around the world we have the God-given responsibility to contribute to a powerful and effective community of caring for all who suffer injustice. We are especially called upon to work for the rights of those "forgotten ones" who are otherwise without voice or power.

231

THE HUMAN AND HUMAN RIGHTS

There exists in the biblical revelation no definitive body of human rights. Rights are historically and politically expressed through the stewardship of God's gifts of reason and power for the sake of justice in community.

A right is usually stated without qualification. In its application, however, it frequently comes into conflict with other rights and human necessities. Such situations are to be considered after, not before, a right has been articulated.

On the ground of God's revealed disposition toward and intention for the human family, and in the light of reason and experience, we submit the following assertions regarding facets of human reality and some of the principal rights implied by them at this time.

In specifying these rights, we choose to develop the basic aspects of human relationship which undergird the Ten Commandments.

HUMANS HAVE BEEN CREATED FOR DIVINE RELATIONSHIP.

All have the right to worship, or not to worship, without constraint or coercion by government or private agency.

No state, group, or person may command ultimate devotion or obedience. Persons have the right to protection against all such usurpations of the Place of God.

All have the right to celebrate, practice, and witness to faith through communal and public acts of devotion and service without fear of interference or persecution.

Governments have no right to legislate in matters of religious belief, but they may legitimately legislate in balancing the claims of the free exercise of religion and the safety and welfare of the general society.

HUMANS ARE CREATURES AND CREATORS OF SYMBOL AND MEANING.

All have the right to free expression through verbal and nonverbal communication, to participate in the exchange of ideas, and to create works of art.

All have the right of defense against communication considered to be debasing of human dignity and inciting to destructive or immoral behavior.

No one has the right to control the mind, will, or conscience of another person.

All have the responsibility to create and communicate meaning in a spirit of civility with a view to preserving personal liberty and promoting the common good.

HUMANS ARE FAMILIAL AND POLITICAL BEINGS.

All have a right to a personal identity and a spiritual heritage.

All have the right to protection against abuse, exploitation and neglect.

All children have the right to parental care and affection.

Parents are entitled to respect, affection, and care from their children.

Families are entitled to protection from forces that would tear them apart.

Older adults are entitled to the opportunity to continue as participating members of society.

Older adults should not be denied, because of circumstances beyond their control, adequate housing, sustenance, or health care.

Future generations have a right to their share of the world's resources and to a legacy of justice and meaning.

The state exists to secure and promote the rights of its citizens through prudent and just legislation, administration, and adjudication.

Communities have the right to establish institutions for the purpose of achieving the conditions of security and welfare and of controlling their goods and their temporal destinies.

Persons have the right to participate in the determination of how, by whom, and to what ends they will be governed.

All have the right to equality before the law and to protection from the arbitrary use of power.

HUMANS ARE PHYSICAL CREATURES.
All are entitled to the basic necessities of healthful physical existence and/or to the means of securing them.

All are entitled to the protection of life and physical well-being.

No person or agency has the right to inflict gratuitous pain upon a person.

HUMANS ARE SEXUAL BEINGS.
Human sexuality is a gift of the Creator for the expression of love and the generation of life.

Through sexuality, God enables persons to give of themselves, and to receive from others the gifts of personal comfort, joy, faithfulness, and commitment.

Sexual union is intended by God as a means of achieving communion between men and women within the covenant of marriage.

Persons are not intended to be a means to the end of selfish gratification.

No one has the right to debase sexuality by abstracting it from personal relationship, by making it a commodity for consumption, or by using it as a commercial inducement.

HUMANS ARE STEWARDS OF CREATION.
God has given the wealth of creation as a trust for the benefit of the whole human family in an interdependent world.

All have a right to those resources and opportunities required for full participation within the society, economy, and political system.

All have the right not to be reduced to a status of dependency upon charity or largess.

233

All are entitled to equal access to the opportunities and resources of a society.

All are entitled to a healthful environment.

No person, business enterprise, government, or other human agency holds ultimate title to the resources it controls. Private property is not an absolute right. Goods and abilities are held in trust from God and are to be allocated and used for justice in community.

All have the right to be heard by those who make decisions affecting the quality of their life.

All have both the right and the responsibility to participate productively in the economy in ways that contribute to the advancement of justice and well-being for the total society and all its members.

Workers have a right to participate with employers in determining the just return and the conditions of labor.

No one has the right to deprive neighbors or future generations of life by selfish and profligate consumption.

HUMANS ARE NAMED-PERSONS.
All have the right to a good name and reputation.

No one has the right to defame another person or to advance one's own interests through the misuse of another's name.

No public or private agency or individual may stigmatize a person through the misuse of personal information.

CONCLUSION

We confess that humans are created in God's image. God intends human beings for divine relationship and for community with one another in mutual service. Human beings have rights in order to fulfill the intention of their Creator.

Our concern for human rights arises from God's call to the faithful to participate in the care of creation and in the advancement of justice.

In responding to that call, we work in partnership with all persons and communities of good will to seek, articulate, and advocate the rights of all persons, particularly those without voice and power of their own. We seek to strengthen a constituency of conscience that transcends national boundaries and other arbitrary human distinctions.

When the powers of this world work to reduce the bearers of God's image to the status of spectator, prisoner, or victim, may we be empowered to bear witness to that lively justice which is God's holy intention for the entire creation.

IMPLEMENTING RESOLUTIONS FOR HUMAN RIGHTS SOCIAL STATEMENT

Adopted by the Ninth Biennial Convention
of the Lutheran Church in America
Chicago, Illinois
July 12-19, 1978

1. Employment, Income, Housing, Health Care, Education, and Nutrition

This church commits itself to the public policy goals of employment, adequate income, decent housing, health maintenance and care, nutrition, and education as fundamental rights of every citizen of Canada and the United States. This church shall work for the creation of a public will to support these goals and shall advocate measures to effect them, including enactment of appropriate enabling legislation.

2. Institutionalized Populations

This church, in cooperation with common Lutheran agencies and other groups and organizations, shall study the needs of institutionalized persons in the United States and Canada. Particular attention shall be given to the imprisoned, patients in mental hospitals, and persons in schools for the mentally retarded, hospitals, and nursing homes. This church shall advocate measures to make institutional life more humane. It shall devise strategies of ministry of and advocacy in behalf of institutionalized persons. It shall advocate alternatives to institutionalization for meeting human needs, insofar as these needs are better met through such alternatives. All persons, especially the elderly, have the right to informed consent in decisions relating to their medical care.

3. Refugees

This church affirms that refugees are entitled to consideration for admittance to the United States and Canada irrespective of the ideology or political alignment of the regime from which they have fled. This church shall advocate this principle before the governments of the United States and Canada; and it shall support the same principle in the policy and procedures of the Immigration and Refugee Service of the Lutheran Council in the U.S.A. and the National Committee for Canada/LWF.

4. Undocumented Aliens

This church acknowledges its responsibility of ministering to and advocating the human rights of undocumented aliens now in Canada and the United States. This church further recognizes the plight of such persons as a symptom of global injustice, and commits itself to the search for such long-term policies as may eliminate the necessity of the displacement of people.

5. Children

Noting that 1979 has been designated by the United Nations as the International Year of the Child, this church commits itself to seek, in cooperation with common Lutheran agencies and other organizations, appropriate policy goals and implementing legislation to advance the rights of children wherever necessary.

235

6. Torture
This church expresses its abhorrence of the deliberate infliction of pain on human beings. It declares its support of organizations and groups, including churches, which are striving to call nations to account for the practice of torture and to create a public climate of opinion which strives for the abolition of torture in all its forms.

7. Political Oppression
This church declares its concern for the human rights of persons in all parts of the world. It recognizes that its response to the deprivation of human rights will vary from place to place, and time to time, depending upon such factors as the presence of a sister church of strength in a particular country, the call from such a church for assistance, and the susceptibility of the regime and political system to overt pressure by Christians and others in behalf of human rights.

This church, out of concern for justice in all parts of the world, declares its opposition to all governmental policies and actions which suppress human rights. It declares its continuing critical solidarity with those who struggle for a just society in countries, including our own, which may deny human rights.

This church expresses its thanksgiving to God for recent signs of progress toward self-determination in Namibia, and pledges itself to support in appropriate ways its sister churches in that country as they participate in the transition toward independence and majority rule.

8. Economic Rule
Recognizing that the inordinate exploitation and consumption of the world's resources deprives the world's majority of such basic rights as those to nutrition, housing, work, and fair compensation for work and/or resources, this church commits itself to the continued advocacy of worldwide economic justice. Specifically, it commits itself to an intensive study of international economic relations and to the consideration of a major policy statement on that subject in 1980.

9. Voluntary Action
Recognizing that the achievement and protection of human rights is not the result solely of government action and law, but that supportive consensus and effective advocacy and monitoring are required on the part of citizens and groups, this church commits itself to search for more creative and effective human rights strategies in North America and throughout the world, in cooperation with Lutheran and ecumenical agencies, and in partnership with secular organizations about human rights.

10. Equality of Women and Men
This church affirms the principle of justice and equality for women and men, and supports legislation which will implement this principle. Therefore, this church declares its continuing support of the proposed Equal Rights Amendment to the Constitution of the United States and urges its congregations and agencies to mobilize support for its ratification.

IN PURSUIT OF JUSTICE AND DIGNITY: SOCIETY, THE OFFENDER, AND SYSTEMS OF CORRECTION

Adopted by the Sixth Biennial Convention, Dallas, Texas
June 30-July 6, 1972

A. THE PRESENT SITUATION

The growing incidence of lawlessness within North American society is the cause of widespread bafflement, anger, and fear on the part of law-abiding citizens. Unchecked criminal behavior, especially in its more violent forms, hastens the destruction of that minimal trust which makes social living possible, and erodes public confidence in those governmental institutions charged with the task of establishing civil peace and justice.

The civil community looks to its agencies of law enforcement and criminal justice to deter lawless behavior, to prosecute law-breakers, and to facilitate the socialization of offenders. When functioning effectively, these agencies serve to reinforce lawful conduct and contribute to public confidence that security is being maintained.

There is a growing but still too limited public awareness of the counterproductivity of present methods of criminal justice. Offenders frequently do not recognize the validity of sanctions which often are applied unequally and the legitimacy of the agencies by which these sanctions are administered.

The problems are manifold. Courts are often overloaded and consequently slow or unduly hasty in administering justice. In the United States the bail system and pre-trial detention result in disproportionate hardship for persons who are poor and/or members of minority groups. Long delays in prosecution of alleged offenders result in both the unjust incarceration of the innocent and the going free of the guilty when witnesses disappear and evidence becomes unavailable. The facilities where persons charged with crimes are "warehoused" are all too often places devoid of human concern and services. Racial and ethnic animosity among inmates and between inmates and correctional personnel reinforces feelings of total alienation within the offender population.

The popular assumption that confinement is normally the most appropriate penalty for criminal behavior has proven itself fallacious. Jails and prisons have too often become schools of alienation and violence. Those persons who survive them constitute a growing pool of disaffected men and women possessing neither the skills nor the motivation for effective social living. Nevertheless, much of the public looks approvingly upon the segregation of offenders from the communities to which they must eventually return.

The socially-destructive results of "warehousing" offenders are compounded by the fact that a disproportionate number of the persons so

237

confined are young, poor, and members of minority groups. Thus, in addition to reinforcing alienation and lawlessness in individual inmates, confinement facilities contribute to the widening of dangerous cleavages within the general society.

Two prominent notions underlie the perpetuation of the system of incarcerating offenders. The first of these is the feeling that the community is somehow safer if offenders are removed from it. The public has yet to take with sufficient seriousness the fact that most prisoners will eventually return to the community in many cases with a reservoir of bitterness and hostility. A person is in no sense made more human by being isolated from society.

The other notion is that solitude and deprivation are in some sense "redemptive." While some exceptional men and women may indeed have come into a fuller personhood within the situation of imposed hardship in prison, their self-discovery has not in all cases motivated them to adjust to what they perceive as an unjust society. In all too many cases prisons have produced persons either utterly passive or utterly enraged.

For society to seek increased security and order by means of a larger and more efficient prison system is for it to sow the seeds of its own destruction.

Similarly counterproductive is the treatment too often accorded first and/or younger offenders. Subjecting such persons indiscriminately to the traditional machinery of criminal justice can amount to schooling them in crime rather than in productive citizenship. Competent diagnostic procedures are all too often inadequate or completely lacking.

Finally, it needs to be clearly said that in North American society it is the poor who bear the brunt of society's ire toward the lawless. Organized and "white collar" crime have the poor as their chief victims. Yet the persons who commit such crimes often escape the hardship borne by the poor offender. It should come as no surprise that many younger or poor or minority persons feel less and less obligation to a social and political system containing such rank structural injustice.

B. A THEOLOGICAL PERSPECTIVE

There are several relevant insights which theology can bring to bear upon the agencies of criminal justice and their reform.

1) Distinctions among persons are relative, provisional, and subject to divine judgment. Distinctions between groups within society should be made only for purposes of social utility and well-being. The distinction between the "criminal" and the "law-abiding" elements within a society is one example of such conventional social classification.

The human condition of radical estrangement from God manifests itself in the constant tendency on the part of societies to absolutize these provisional distinctions. Particularly demonic is the inclination of societies to treat those whom it has defined as criminals as altogether alien to the human

238

community and deserving, therefore, of total separation from normal social life.

Thus deprived of their humanity, criminals may become the object of sadism and scapegoating on the part of the general society or may become prey to the "good works" of persons and groups who would use offenders as a means to their own salvation.

The fact that our Lord Jesus Christ was defined by the society of his day as a political/religious criminal, and that countless witnesses to Christ were likewise so defined, should cause Christians to resist the temptation to diabolize persons whom society has declared to be outside the law. Christians will also be reminded that champions of a larger measure of social justice have often been defined as enemies of society. To acknowledge this fact is in no sense to romanticize the criminal; it is rather to recognize that the social system which defines crime is itself capable of criminality. A society may be as much in need of correction as the individuals who deviate from its norms.

2) Civil institutions* have as their proper function the facilitation of community life, the guaranteeing of the fundamental rights of the community and its individual members, and the creation of a social order that is both secure and humane.

It is necessary to maintain a distinction between redemption in the Christian sense and socialization in the civil sense. Thus, theologically speaking, it is not the function of civil institutions to "redeem" persons. Crime and sin are not synonyms. Crime is behavior so defined by civil authority. As such it is relative and subject to redefinition. Criminal penalties should be established to deter lawlessness and to correct the lawless; when they cease so to function they must be altered or superseded.

Sin, by way of contrast, is estrangement from God and is shared by all persons alike. The work of redemption from sin belongs to God alone. Any civil institution which presumes to encroach upon the inmost selfhood of the person for the purpose of "redeeming" him or her has usurped the place of God and become demonic.

The task of civil institutions which relate to criminal justice is to facilitate the socialization of offenders in such a way as to preserve their dignity and the safety of the general community as well. These institutions cannot be seen, or be permitted to see themselves, as agents of "redemption." The idea of punishment as a vehicle of "redemption" must be abandoned; and such strategies as may be found to replace punishment must be predicated upon a theory of justice and human utility and not upon "redemption."

3) Lutheran social ethics has traditionally laid heavy stress upon a) effective social/political institutions dedicated to the maintenance of civil peace and

---

*Institution: a legally established system within a society, together with its own rules and procedures, dedicated to the performance of a set of designed functions.

239

the achievement of justice for the whole society and its individual members; b) conscientious and competent office-bearers to staff these institutions; c) a public climate that is supportive of these institutions and their personnel; and d) the accountability of these institutions before the law of God to the community which they are to serve.

Social institutions, like the persons who construct and operate them, have an inherent tendency to become self-serving. It is for Christians, along with other persons of good will, to be wary of this tendency and to take measures to arrest it.

The various institutions of criminal justice stand in need both of the support and the criticism of the general public. Support includes the generation of a climate that is hospitable to appropriation of the necessary resources for positive change. The tendency within the public to make scapegoats of these institutions should be vigourously resisted. The malfunctioning of an institution can be as much the result of public apathy and neglect as of self-serving administrators and anachronistic methods.

The institutions of criminal justice cannot be expected to become the bearers of the cure for their own illness and that of the general social illness as well. Society tends at once to expect too much of the institutions of criminal justice and to allocate too few resources to them for needed improvements.

C. POLICY GOALS

It should be the policy of the United States and Canada, and of the various political jurisdictions within them, to undertake a comprehensive reform of criminal justice procedures and institutions. The reform must be based on the understanding that the primary goal in the treatment of offenders is habilitation, not punishment. The personal dignity and safety of all offenders and persons charged with crime must be preserved, adequate legal representation afforded them, and justice afforded without such delay as to be in itself an injustice.

The strategy of reform should include at least the following elements:

1) There should be a comprehensive revision of criminal codes, the selective removal of certain classes of behavior from the category of crime, and the provision of alternative procedures for dealing with such behavior.

2) The correctional system should be viewed as a continuous process with the emphasis on treatment in the community and incarceration reserved for control of offenders who are judged dangerous or violent. Whether confined or not, whether processed by a criminal or non-adjudicative system, offenders should remain in touch with their home community where the mutual adjustment of community and offender must eventually take place.

3) Youthful and first offenders should be treated separately from the general

240

offender population. Insofar as possible they should be afforded alternatives to the traditional process of criminal justice. Financial resources should be made available to facilitate comprehensive, community-based and non-institutional treatment for the youthful and first offender.

4) A greater effort must be made to recruit professional, paraprofessional, and volunteer staff reflecting the ethnic, generational, and class composition of the offender population.

5) In-service training programs should be available for upgrading staff, and personnel policies should encourage recruitment of paraprofessionals, both paid and volunteer.

6) Offenders serving sentences should have maximum opportunity to participate in the governance of their own affairs collectively by means of the democratic process, within the context of the institution and its population.

7) Meaningful education, training and work should be available with more than token payment for productive work. State and federal laws restricting the sale of prison-made products should be modified or repealed.

8) Adequate grievance procedures should be available to inmates.

9) Local jails should be replaced by facilities competently staffed and suited to the needs of the communities they serve.

10) Communities must develop strategies of support and encouragement to offenders and ex-offenders. Laws barring ex-offenders from certain categories of employment should be eliminated. Government, business, labor, and industry should cooperate at the community level so that ex-offenders have equal access with others to available employment.

11) More resources, both public and private, must be allocated to the study of the nature and causes of criminal behavior, the evaluating of the effectiveness of correctional programs, and the devising of strategies that contribute both to the prevention of lawlessness and the effective socialization of the offender. It is recognized that it may be necessary to provide some of these public resources through supporting additional taxation; however, these resources could be considered as an investment toward reducing social costs.

D. STRATEGIES FOR THE CHURCH

The church and its agencies have an inescapable responsibility in the facilitation of genuine reform of criminal justice.

1) Congregations of the church have a crucial role to play in creating a climate of community feeling hospitable to the establishment of community-based programs and facilities for offenders and ex-offenders.

2) Congregations have the responsibility, together with others within the community, of stimulating public interest and concern about local jails and

the persons housed there. While working for alternatives to the jail, congregations and their social ministry committees should seek to provide human support and assistance to the incarcerated and press for optimal professional and correctional services.

3) Church-related social agencies should join (and where necessary, form) community teams to establish multi-faceted programs for offenders, ex-offenders, and their families. These programs, which should be publicly-funded, should employ a wide range of professionals and para-professionals, including where possible ex-offenders. The church has a key role to play in the recruitment and encouragement of these personnel.

4) The church in all its parts should declare itself open to the employment of ex-offenders. Such persons should be encouraged to apply for both nonprofessional and professional positions, including the ordained ministry. The colleges and seminaries of the church should explore the feasibility of establishing educational programs, possibly leading to careers within the church, for offenders serving sentences.

5) The local congregation should take the lead in fostering a public "caring about" the agencies of criminal justice. The church should support efforts at reform of the penal code, reform of the courts and establishment of non-adjudicative options for certain classes of offenders (especially the youthful and first offender), and the reform and/or replacement of present criminal facilities.

6) The church should assist the public to understand the special problems besetting correctional personnel, and provide them with the support they need in working justly and compassionately with those in their care.

7) The church should challenge its young people to consider careers in criminal justice as a worthy exercise of Christian vocation, and to see in such careers an opportunity to become system-change agents while serving intense human need.

8) Finally, in keeping with the social statement, "Capital Punishment," adopted in 1966, the church should work for abolition of capital punishment or oppose its reinstatement where it has been suspended.

E. CONCLUSION

Crime and criminals are in part reminders of the failure of society to establish justice for all its members. For untold generations societies have sought to remove these reminders of failure from sight and/or to subject them to extreme punishment. It is for the church, together with all people of good will, ever to remind society and government that such a strategy of removal and punishment is neither prudent nor just. Only when the offender is dealt with as a member of the community who must return to it will there be any real hope for a criminal justice system that is both just and effective.

MARRIAGE AND FAMILY
1964

D. That pending further action by the 1966 convention of the church, the 1964 convention adopt the following Statement on Marriage and Family as a guide to the congregations of the church:

1. Marriage is that order of creation given by God in love which binds one man and one woman in a lifelong union of the most intimate fellowship of body and life. This one-flesh relation, when properly based on fidelity and love, serves as a witness to God's grace and leads husband and wife into service one of the other. In their marriage, husband and wife are responsible to God for keeping their vows and must depend upon his love and mercy to fulfill them.

2. God has established the sexual relation for the purpose of bringing husband and wife into full unity so that they may enrich and be a blessing to each other. Such oneness, depending upon lifelong fidelity between the marriage partners and loving service one of the other, is the essential characteristic of marriage. Marriage should be consummated in love with the intention of maintaining a permanent and responsible relation. Continence outside of marriage and fidelity within marriage are binding on all.

3. Procreation is a gift inherent in the sex relation. In children the one-flesh idea finds embodiment. Children bring great joy to marriage and reveal how God permits men to share in his continuing creation. Married couples should seek to fulfill their responsibilities in marriage by conceiving and nurturing their children in the light of Christian faith.

4. Husband and wife are called to exercise the power of procreation responsibly before God. This implies planning their parenthood in accordance with their ability to provide for their children and carefully nurture them in fullness of Christian faith and life. The health and welfare of the mother-wife should be a major concern in such decisions. Irresponsible conception of children up to the limit of biological capacity and selfish limitation of the number of children are equally detrimental. Choice as to means of conception control should be made upon professional medical advice.

5. Marriage, as ordained by God, is a lifelong indissoluble union con-

summated through consent and coitus. Any breaking of the marriage bond involves sin and suffering. Forgiveness and reconciliation are incumbent upon all within marriage, and especially upon Christians. The church should extend its counseling services in an effort to maintain and strengthen families when they face difficulties threatening their unity.

6. Where marriage failure and divorce occur among Christian people, the church should recognize its involvement in the failure and seek to lead all concerned to repentance and forgiveness. If it proves impossible or unwise in the light of Christian love and concern for the welfare of all involved to reconstitute the marriage, then the church should continue, insofar as possible, to minister to each person involved.

If the question of the remarriage of a divorced person arises, pastors and congregations of the Lutheran Church in America should make their decisions on the particular circumstances in each case, being guided by the following considerations:

a. While it is the Christian teaching that marriage is a lifelong, indissoluble union and that divorce and remarriage do violate God's order, nevertheless, God in his love does accept the sinner and deals with him according to his need. The church has recognized that marriage may be a remedy for sin and has seen in such Bible passages as Matthew 5:32; 19:9; and 1 Corinthians 7:15 the possibility of remarriage, but it also knows that the final basis of decision is loving concern for man in his actual situation.

b. The divorced person seeking remarriage must recognize his responsibility in the breakup of the former marriage. He must give evidence of repentance and have made an effort to overcome his limitations and failures. He must have forgiven his partner in the former marriage, and he and his intended spouse must give assurance that he will fulfill his obligations to those involved in his former marriage.

c. The divorced person must give evidence of his Christian faith by his witness in the church and must have received adequate counsel and training in preparation for marriage. He must be prepared to undertake the full responsibilities of marriage in dependence upon God.

7. The church should provide opportunities for its pastors and lay leaders to prepare themselves to meet their responsibilities in ministering to families and young people contemplating marriage. This involves seminary training, in-service training opportunities, college courses, and special courses and institutes for lay leaders. Study material based on the view of marriage set forth in these Summary Statements should be provided.

8. Congregations should provide opportunities for study courses and other activities in preparation for marriage. Help should be given through activities strengthening and enriching the life of existing family groups. Each pastor should require regular counseling periods with couples before marriage. In part this may be done with groups, but private and individual conferences should also be required.

9. Congregations and youth auxiliary and student groups of the church should continue to carry on educational programs regarding the special problems in mixed marriages. The inevitable compromise or denial of the evangelical faith, and the social and cultural problems usually accompanying such marriages, should be thoroughly explained.

10. The wedding service is a service of the church in which the atmosphere of reverence and worship should be maintained. The recognized service of the church should be used, and only such activities as are in conformity with the Christian view of marriage and in keeping with a service of worship should be permitted.

11. The home as the best channel for Christian nurture, education, and evangelization should receive renewed emphasis by all agencies of the church. Baptism, as God's act of accepting the child into the church in response to which parents have far-reaching responsibilities, should receive its proper stress in Christian teaching and practice. In preparation for baptism, parents should receive special counsel and instruction as to their duties and opportunities in the rearing of their children. The church should prepare and encourage the use of materials to stimulate and help parents in their task of Christian nurture.

12. In order to develop the highest standards of pastoral practice regarding marriage and family life, synods should hold conferences of pastors for discussion and clarification of the pastoral practices envisaged in this study.

13. Christian citizens should seek the enactment of uniform and constructive marriage and divorce laws. Such laws should encourage the procedures of adjustment and reconciliation rather than adversary litigation.

> Respectfully submitted,
> Alfred H. Stone, *President*
> Luther H. Redcay, *Secretary*
> Harold Haas, *Executive Secretary*

PEACE AND POLITICS

Adopted by the Twelfth Biennial Convention, Toronto, Ontario
June 28–July 5, 1984

INTRODUCTION

Peace is the will of God. So the church confesses in every time and place, and so it prays: "For the peace from above, . . . for the peace of the whole world, . . . and for the unity of all . . . ." Announcing the reign of God, the church awaits with eager longing the appearing of the kingdom when God will "bind heaven and earth in a single peace." As they look forward to Christ's coming again, Christians attend to their stewardship of God's creation — keeping, building, and making peace in the sinful world.

In the present nuclear age, we of the Lutheran Church in America seek to discern the shape and dimensions of the political work of peace in the light of that peace which is our gift in the gospel and our task as a church in society. We offer this statement as a framework for that discernment and action. By it we bear witness that the political work of peace in the world is preeminently God's work of creation and preservation; and by this statement we commit ourselves to the politics of peace.

This statement is presented in fulfillment of the mandate of the Eleventh Biennial Convention (1982). It stands in continuity with prior statements by this church, notably "Church and State: A Lutheran Perspective" (1966), "Conscientious Objection" (1968), "World Community" (1970), "Human Rights" (1978), and "Economic Justice" (1980). It carries forward the witness of the predecessor church bodies as set forth in convention resolutions and statements, most notably "The Problem of Nuclear Weapons" (United Lutheran Church in America, 1960).

THE OCCASION

The vital urgency of preventing nuclear war challenges the imagination and will of every nation to pursue the political work of peace. The possibility of a nuclear catastrophe and the extermination of the human family is a preoccupation of men and women everywhere. The devastation of a nuclear war would be both immediate and long-term. In the shadow of the nuclear peril, in a fragile and interdependent world, people are confronted as never before by the urgency of forging the political means to deal with international conflict in ways that are preventive of violence and productive of justice.

War has been regarded by politicians and strategists as one means of conducting international relations, as "politics by other means." As such, war has been seen as having limited objectives, as manageable, and as subject to rules generally agreed upon. Political rulers have considered armed might to be the essence of state power, and regarded external security in terms of the capacity to settle conflict through military victory.

The advent of total war overwhelmed these restraints and limits. The two world wars were waged for unconditional ends and by largely unlimited means. The revulsion at the indiscriminate carnage of these wars moved world opinion to demand not the legal restraint but the outlawing of aggressive war as a crime against humanity.

Since the beginning of the nuclear age a profound transformation has been taking place in the understanding and practice of politics among nations. Considered to be politically meaningless, as well as morally unthinkable, nuclear war is widely rejected because it is a crime against humanity. Furthermore, policies based on the notion of nuclear superiority with first strike capability are seen as inherently destabilizing.

For all these reasons, weapons of nuclear war are generally deemed to be means not of waging but of preventing, a war the deadly effects of which could be total and permanent. It is the political use of nuclear weapons through possession, not the military use through war-fighting, that has thus far informed the policies of the nuclear powers. Yet the deterrent use of nuclear weapons may be endangered by the development of smaller weapons of more limited destructive capacity or the prospect of an arms race in outer space. It is widely feared that the capacity for "limited" nuclear war-fighting may seriously weaken the will to prevent nuclear war. Thus the structure of nuclear deterrence is changing, affected by both political and technological developments. It is the unpredictability of these developments that is leading many to call for strategies that will lessen the risk of war, and policies that will broaden the areas of common interest between the nuclear superpowers. Negotiated arms control and reduction, seeking a stable deterrence at the lowest possible level of risk are principles regarded by many in the strategic community as vital to keeping the peace. An unchecked arms race is widely rejected as a reckless imperilment of the human community.

Yet the keeping and building of peace is more than a matter between the United States and the Soviet Union. There is as yet no effective will to halt, or even control, the worldwide proliferation of nuclear weapons; and the international traffic in conventional arms is fueled by an expanding demand and the eagerness of supplying countries to earn foreign credits. The result is an increasingly dangerous world in which unstable regimes and terrorist groups possess a destructive potential beyond the control of the two principal nuclear antagonists.

At this time people everywhere are confronted by a profound challenge: to fashion a security which will ensure and policies which will guarantee the survival of the human family and the possibility of a life that is both safe and just. Thus, peace must be both kept and built. This crowded and dangerous world must discover nonviolent ways both of managing and of moving beyond the many deeply rooted antagonisms which divide peoples and states. Christians, who know the peace and security of life in Jesus Christ, are called by God to participate fully in this perilous but necessary quest.

THEOLOGICAL AFFIRMATIONS

Peace: The Promise of God

We confess, teach, and proclaim that God created and still preserves the world for peace with God and with itself. Made in the image of God, people are to live not in isolation and enmity but in co-humanity with one another. In this gift, all people have the task of exercising living dominion over the earth in a life of thanksgiving, praise, service, and obedience to their Lord. God's peace in creation was the condition of wholeness and harmony in which God first beheld the world and saw that it was good (Gen. 1:31), when all creation worshiped God. The peace of God's reign, infinitely surpassing the peace of creation, is the *shalom* of Christ's triumph over the present age, the Sabbath-rest of the people of God (Heb. 4:9-10).

In the present fallen world, the Holy Spirit creates the community of persons reconciled in Christ to be a witness both to the peace of God's creation and to God's promise to the world of reconciliation in Jesus Christ. As members of that community, we celebrate in hope the peace of God's reconciliation; the peace of the knowledge of God (Isa. 11:9); of vindication of God's people (Mic. 4:6-8); of harmony among all creatures (Isa. 11:6-9); in which nations will study war no longer (Mic. 4:1-3; Isa. 2:2-4); in which harassment and molestation will cease (Mic. 4:4). It is a peace in which God will remove all sorrow and suffering (Rev. 21:3-4). It is the peace of the reign of God, announced in word and deed by Jesus of Nazareth (Luke 6:20-23; 7:22) and proclaimed by the apostles (Luke 10:8-9; Acts 19:8; 20:25). It is the peace with God given by Christ to the believing fellowship (John 14:27), lovingly shared by Christians one with another (Gal. 6:16; Rom. 16:16), and experienced by the faithful amid this sinful age in anticipation of the day of Christ's final triumph (1 Cor. 15: 18-26).

Peace with God is the present possession of those who have been justified by faith in Christ Jesus (Rom. 5:1), the result of God's reconciling grace in Christ (2 Cor. 5:18-19). Inasmuch as faith and promise belong together (Rom. 4), in Christ God and the rebellious enemies of God are reconciled. They are reunited by Christ's death and victory (Rom. 5:10). In overcoming enmity between God and humankind, Christ's atonement overcomes enmity among peoples, making peace by the blood of Christ's cross (Col. 1:20), thereby uniting them in one new people, the Church (Gal. 3:28; Eph. 2:14-16).

In every age the daughters and sons of God in Jesus Christ have seen peacemaking through the love of enemies (Matt. 5:44) as the fruit of faith, the task to which they are divinely called and in which they are declared blessed (Matt. 5:9). Reconciled to God through Christ, they are entrusted with the ministry of reconciliation (2 Cor. 5:18-19), the proclamation of God's peace to all people (Luke 2:10-14).

Peace with God is a gift that is not of this world (John 14:27), which the world can neither give nor take away. Yet those to whom it is given are sent into the world (John 20:21; Matt. 28:19-20), not removed from it (John 17:5). Christians see in the struggle and suffering of the present world a deep yearning for the consummation of God's reconciling peace (Rom. 8:18-25). Subjected in hope to this convulsion and pain, the world is the place of God's work. We look confidently for the coming of God's reign and the victory of God's reconciliation.

Sin: The Root of War

War is evidence of the disorder of sin which infects the human family. While the external causes of war (including aggression, economic exploitation, racial and national pride, the ambition of rulers, and the desire for revenge) are many and complex, the root of war is sin — the willful rejection of God's lordship and worship of the creature rather than the Creator (Rom. 1:28-32). Because of this rebellion, all of creation is disordered, at war with itself, and humans are pitted against each other. God's question to the disobedient Adam, "Where are you?" (Gen. 3:9), and God's question to the murderous Cain, "Where is your brother?" (Gen. 4:9), together are addressed to every generation of humankind, for in sin we have become strangers to one another.

Estrangement and enmity among persons and nations are nurtured by fear. Having claimed for itself a privileged position, a nation or group lives in fear of those whom it has suppressed or excluded. Racists fear those whom they have declared inferior; exploiters fear their victims; nationalists fear national enemies; totalitarian rulers fear the free; and religious fanatics fear heretics and infidels. Moreover, the weak and victimized fear the strong. Fear often breeds hatred, and hatred, violent aggression.

Christian faith declares that aggression and its consequence, vengeance, are violations of the will of God. Often draped in a mantle of moral or religious right, they are

249

the deadly expression of the sinful lust for domination and the compulsion to self-justification. Aggression may involve the violation of the commands against both murder and theft; and vengeance compounds both. So Scripture declares vengeance as being reserved to God alone (Lev. 19:18; Deut. 32:35; Rom. 12:19), and enjoins the limitation of punishment for injustice (Gen. 4:14-15; Exod. 21:24). The church views war as a catastrophic consequence of sin against which God summons us all to strive. In the face of "rumors of wars" (Matt. 24:6), the church calls for repentance by the nations and makes intercession for them all.

The Creator's Presence in the Political Work of Peace

The human longing to build peace is evidence that the Creator has not abandoned the creation. It is because humans sense the absence of peace that they can decry the evil of war. It is because they sense the absence of order that they can deplore disorder. It is because they know, however dimly, what justice is that they can become outraged by injustice. The divine law is written upon their hearts, and their consciences testify to God's creative "yes" (Rom. 2:15).

God's "yes" in creation is thus not swallowed up in the chaos and violence of sin. Rather, it remains in the form of God's loving preservation of humankind (Gen. 3:21; Hos.11:8-9) and God's advocacy on behalf of the poor and the weak (Ps. 10:17-18; 68:5; Isa. 1:17). God cares for the helpless by means of good officebearers (Ps. 72:1-14), and holds the unruly and oppressive powers accountable for their oppressive acts (Ps. 82:1-3).

The human capacity for politics is further evidence of the "yes" of God's creating and preserving love. In political work, humans participate in the work of God in the restraint of aggression, the resolution of disputes, and the establishment of justice. Politics is the task of protecting and caring for the common life. Thus peace is the basis, sense, and goal of politics. The Creator is present in the politics of peace.

Whereas peace with God in Christ is the priceless gift of the reign of God, temporal peace is the work of God's preservation, a task which all are commanded to undertake. Temporal peace, the work of politics, is a task which Christians honor and to which they are especially summoned. It is in the political realm that Christians are privileged to employ their reason in service to God and neighbor (Rom. 12:1-2; 13:7). It is in the performance of political obligation that Christians exercise their freedom, a freedom from all obligation except to love the neighbor (Rom. 13:8).

An eminently social task, the politics of peace is conducted through institutions and by individuals. Civil authority and the institutions of government are principal means of God's preserving love (Rom. 13:2-3). God intends the officials and institutions of government to be both protective and productive, preventing and penalizing lawlessness (Rom. 13:4; 1 Pet. 2:13-14) and advancing human welfare (*Large Catechism*, 150). The church declares that all holders of civil office are accountable to God for their public stewardship.

The nonviolent management and resolution of conflict are the essence of politics and the work of just government. Resort to violence signals a failure of politics. Under such conditions, force should be used only to restore the conditions necessary for politics. Such force is to be wielded by the legitimate authority (Rom. 13:4; Matt. 26:52), lawfully and with restraint (Luke 3:14).

The legitimate use of deadly force stands under God's command of love for the weak in the deterrence of aggression, and love for the enemy in the case of hostilities. The discernment of love in such cases is filled with ambiguities, and requires the full participation of the citizenry in critical reflection and moral discourse.

The lawful possessors of the means of deadly force are often tempted to employ them in ways which by virtue of being premature, disproportionate, or indiscriminate are unjustifiable. To be justifiable, the application of military force must be undertaken as a last resort and only by legally constituted authority; and it must be waged in a way that is proportionate to the wickedness to be resisted and respectful of the noncombatant civilian. A Christian may evaluate any war in terms such as these, and must decide conscientiously whether his or her participation is ethically justifiable (*Augsburg Confession* XVI). We recognize the profound ambiguities which members of the armed forces often face in this regard, and support them in the conscientious exercise of their office.

Political societies are frequently tempted to perceive their security primarily in terms of military might, rather than conceiving of it as grounded in the politics of peace. Reliance on arms alone can create a dangerous insecurity. Security is ultimately the work of politics.

The Church's Proclamation
The mission of the church, the proclamation of the Word of God, contributes to the politics of peace by declaring that all are equally sinful before God and, therefore, that no nation enjoys a special righteousness or possesses the divine authority to rule over others; that human accountability is ultimately to God alone; and that earthly power itself stands responsible to God under justice.

The gospel declares to all that in Christ the enmity between God and humankind has been overcome, and that the new creation is the destiny God offers to all nations. It is the power of God's reconciliation in Christ that propels Christians into the world to make peace between enemies. They join in the political stewardship to which all are called as the expression of their hope in Christ Jesus, bringing as their specific insight the love of enemies.

As the community of forgiven sinners, the church provides a context for moral and political discourse in the civil community so that all may be equipped for responsible action in the world for the sake of many neighbors. Our theology of the cross of Christ forbids illusions regarding the possibility of establishing permanent peace and a perfect society in this age. Confident, however, in God's promise of peace, the church proclaims this hope so that all may persist in the politics of peace, trusting in the loving Creator's presence, and looking forward to the unveiled reign of God.

Although we have no special authority as a church to advocate particular policies as if they were divinely sanctioned, our political stewardship, individually as citizens and corporately as a church in society, obligates us to contribute to the ongoing debate on matters that affect the survival and well-being of the human family and all creation. This we must do both boldly and modestly — boldly, in the freedom for which Christ has set us free; modestly, in view of our sin, limited vision, and the ever-changing character of the world.

JUDGMENTS AND TASKS

We declare it to be our conviction that, while conflicts and violence are abiding features of this sinful world, war is not inevitable, is not to be sought, and is never to be blessed as a means of resolving disputes. While the weak must still be defended with power backed by might, and while nations may unhappily be forced to respond to aggression by limited military means, yet the normal use of force must be its political use through military non-use.

We declare without equivocation that nuclear war, with its catastrophic devastation of the earth, is contrary to the good and gracious will of God for the creation.

251

Accordingly, we condemn the notion of "winning" a nuclear war, and any military policies or rhetoric which may be predicated on it. We judge nuclear policies of either superpower intended to achieve the capacity for a disarming "first strike" to be inherently destabilizing and evil. An actual first strike would be the most inhuman form of aggression imaginable. A retaliatory strike solely for the purpose of revenge would be no less outside the limits of common morality.

We reject as imprudent and dangerous, policies designed to achieve nuclear superiority. An unchecked arms race is as "unwinnable" as nuclear war itself. It is dangerous folly to imagine that one of the superpowers could prevail by impoverishing or terrorizing the other. Only a balance at the lowest level of risk, not attempted blackmail through nuclear superiority, can facilitate mutual security.

We denounce as evil and as a form of aggressive violence any attempt to destroy a political adversary through destabilization. Such destabilization would be both disproportionate and indiscriminate in its human damage.

We reject the notion that the conflict between the nuclear superpowers is an apocalyptic struggle between absolute Good and absolute Evil. While there are profound differences between the political values of the Western and Eastern systems of government, and while honest comparative moral evaluation of the character and behavior of political regimes is called for, to absolutize these historical differences is theologically heretical and politically irresponsible. Such prideful absolutizing invites policies of total war unrestrained by morality or prudence.

We reject the notion of national messianism in which a particular nation-state pridefully declares it to be its historic calling to "save" the world from political, social, or religious "error," making the world over into its own likeness.

We reject the illusion that any nation can isolate itself behind walls of military might and economic protectionism. Notions of security and well-being founded upon political and economic isolation are incompatible with the reality of global interdependence, and foster suspicion and hatred among nations.

We likewise condemn the misappropriation of valuable resources by any nations of the world to an escalating arms race that impairs our financial ability to foster economic and political justice at home and abroad. We affirm that there is no national security without global security. And there can be no global security without serious progress against poverty and economic injustice. Justice and security go hand in hand; without one, the other cannot long endure.

While it is doubtless unavoidable that the East-West rivalry will reverberate in the politics of the third world, we deplore the violence which that rivalry has exacerbated and prolonged. The superpowers' frequent manipulation of regional conflict and their support of ruthless, tyrannous regimes in their respective spheres of influence stand in painful contrast to the good they could be doing to alleviate misery and promote human development.

We deplore the worldwide traffic in arms, the expanding demand for sophisticated weapons in the third world, and the eagerness to supply it by many industrialized countries. We are especially alarmed by the proliferation of nuclear weapons. The unchecked continuation of weapons trafficking can only further endanger the entire world community. As this church said in 1970:

> It is of vital importance that all nations give sustained attention to the inappropriateness of massive arms as a means of maintaining national security, a critical appraisal of their arsenals in the light of such considerations, and a restudy of national needs and goals with a view toward the reallocation of resources for peaceful purposes.
> (World Community)

Directions of Policy: Peacekeeping

It is an outrage that under present conditions, in order to exist together, the United States and the Soviet Union, with their allies, must confront each other with the possibility of mass slaughter. Yet that is precisely the situation of the two superpowers today. We hold, therefore, that nuclear deterrence involves us all in a sinful situation from which none are exempt.

For deterrence to succeed in preventing the catastrophe of nuclear war, there must be a credible threat to use nuclear weapons in retaliation for aggression. It is the conviction of this statement that such actual use of nuclear weapons would, even in retaliation, constitute mass murder. What it would be wrong actually to do, it is also wrong to intend or threaten. Yet insofar as aggression (one's own as well as the other's) is restrained by the possession of nuclear weapons (which includes the threat to use them in retaliation), nuclear deterrence remains at the present time as the lesser of evils. Yet evil it is and remains.

Therefore, we call upon the governments of the United States and the Soviet Union with their allies to forge more stable and less evil means to assure peace and security in the world. While they work toward such a time, the possession of nuclear weapons solely for the purpose of deterrence may be judged as tolerable yet appalling; however, deterrence as a permanent policy is not acceptable. In the interim, distress at this sinful situation in the face of God's will for peace should motivate all in the United States and the Soviet Union to persevere in pursuit of alternative strategies for peacekeeping and common security. As was affirmed in 1970:

> It is clearly time for a rethinking of the meaning of national security. In view of the overkill capacity now possessed by the super-powers, national security can no longer be defined in terms of either nuclear superiority or even nuclear stalemate. The common threat which such weapons hold for all humanity teaches that their continued development can only undermine security. It is now necessary both to create an international legal framework within which arms control can be brought about and to help nations perceive that their safety must be conceived in more than military terms.

> A beginning has been made in the construction of the necessary legal framework. This effort should be intensified, should become increasingly multinational in character, and should include all weapons of mass destruction. In the meantime, the United States should be encouraged to undertake such unilateral initiatives as may contribute to a climate more hospitable to the limitation of arms. (World Community)

We recognize that the East-West rivalry, while subject to change, will be a principal feature of international politics for an indefinite time to come. We therefore encourage the nurturing of an East-West relationship which excludes the notion of "win-lose," seeking instead to find increasing areas of common interest and endeavor, and to discover fields other than the military for competition which would be of benefit to the entire world community.

It is of vital importance for the near future that nuclear deterrence be stabilized at the lowest possible level of risk. Such stabilization requires the political recognition by both parties of the reciprocity of the deterrence situation. Reciprocity means that what is to be deterred is not only the other's capacity for aggression, but also one's own. Each side must restrain its own capacity for aggression to the satisfaction of the other. This requires evaluation of proposed technological advances to determine whether they enhance or diminish stability. On this basis, the negotiation of mechanisms of deterrence which are stable and keep the peace is conceivable, forming the basis for mutually assured security.

We encourage the steadfast pursuit of arms control and arms reduction agreements

253

between the nuclear superpowers, especially agreements which forestall the shifting of the arms race to destabilizing new technologies and areas, such as outer space.

We call for arms control agreements that are substantial, equitable, verifiable, and progressive. Such agreements should provide for an increasing mutual "transparency" of the military policies and actions of the superpowers by means of the regular exchange of information and ongoing consultation. We regard such provisions for mutual confidence-building to be necessary to progress toward mutually assured security between the nuclear superpowers.

We call for a multilateral verifiable freeze on the testing, production, stockpiling and deployment of nuclear weapons systems as a step toward the eventual elimination of nuclear weapons. We urge the leaders of the United States and the Soviet Union to take steps in the search for greater trust and understanding among nations.

Recognizing that a regional conflict could become a factor precipitating direct hostili- .ties between nuclear superpowers, we call upon the United States and the Soviet Union to institute regular consultative procedures for the joint assessment of potential or actual regional conflicts where the two powers may have overlapping and/or conflicting interests; to develop an early warning system for the prediction of violence; and to develop emergency procedures for the restraint and containment of hostilities and the expeditious, nonviolent resolution of disputes.

Peacekeeping is the prevention of war. It involves preventing, moderating and resolving conflict. Peacekeeping further requires peacebuilding, the political production of conditions in which nations and people are assured a common future of security in a world of conflict and uncertainty. Peacekeeping is minimally based upon mutual threat; but mutual threat alone is hardly sufficient as the means of peacekeeping over the long run. The understanding of East-West nuclear relations in terms of mutually assured destruction must be replaced by that of mutually assured security.

Directions of Policy: Peacebuilding

Peacekeeping must be seen in the context of peacebuilding. Peacebuilding as a political task refers to the wide range of positive measures nations and peoples may take to expand common interests, facilitate cooperation, generate mutual amity and goodwill, and create a community which transcends geographic borders and national differences. Peacebuilding aims at the establishment of the conditions of justice among people which, in turn, minimize hostility and the likelihood of violent conflict.

Peacebuilding is a constructive enterprise having many aspects. It involves negotiations between nations. A vital role is played, in this context, by nations such as Canada in offering their good offices for the mediation of conflict and the pursuit of peace. It also involves the willingness of nations to permit increasing opportunity for such nongovernmental contacts as cultural and humanitarian exchange, trade, and international travel. It presupposes a sufficient degree of security to permit space and freedom for the development of a variety of common interests not directly related to international politics. Such links, in turn, may contribute to an atmosphere favorable to further constructive policies and actions on the part of governments.

Peacebuilding also involves a growing commitment by governments to the support of international institutions and of world law. It is time for the members of the world community, and the nuclear superpowers in particular, to renew their commitment to support and work through international institutions for both the peaceful settlement of disputes and the advancement of human well-being. In addition, the international standards of human rights, to which most nations have subscribed, should be viewed as a challenge to common humanitarian endeavor, and not as weapons to be used in polemical rhetoric.

Regional consultative arrangements which bring together security, economic cooperation, and humanitarian concerns should be encouraged. Such arrangements could facilitate movement from peacekeeping to peacebuilding.

Human rights and economic justice are inextricable parts of peacebuilding and global security. Notwithstanding the predominance of the East-West bipolarity, both peacekeeping and peacebuilding should be seen increasingly as concerns of the entire world community, to be dealt with multinationally, through effective institutions. Global security and welfare, while distinct, are inseparable concerns in which all the world's people have a direct stake. The nuclear superpowers are morally accountable to the entire family of nations for their leadership in the keeping, and building, of world peace.

Citizens everywhere have a responsibility to participate actively in the keeping and building of peace. They are called, by virtue of their God-given humanity, to care for creation and for the whole human community, beginning with their immediate family, neighborhood, and workplace. Peacebuilding requires both the acquisition of knowledge about human affairs and the commitment to the civil, nonviolent, and constructive resolution of human conflict. We in North America must remind ourselves that the security of our cherished institutions of political democracy is not alone a matter of military might, but even more a matter of our willingness to participate in their working effectively for the sake of human justice. Political democracies must demonstrate their commitment to freedom and social justice in both their domestic and their international policies.

Peacemaking: The Vocation of Christians

For the Christian, peacemaking is the love of enemies and the reconciliation of the estranged. Christians are called both to testify to the active presence of God in the political work of peace, and to participate in the task of peace. Gifted with the promise of God's reconciling peace, Christians are empowered to join in the work of temporal peace in the present world of sin, conflict, and constant change. They are called to affirm the temporal ends of politics and government, and to perform political work as an expression of the hope that is in them, especially when fear and despair threaten to paralyze the human community.

As members of the ecumenical community of faith, transcending time, place, nationality and culture, Christians are challenged to bring to political work a perspective not limited to narrow self-interest. They are challenged to assist the civil community to perceive its security and well-being as interwoven with the security of all people everywhere. As people who understand themselves to be stewards of God's gifts, Christians are challenged to teach, by word and deed, that the gifts of life in community are a trust to be cared for and handed on to succeeding generations.

Christians, along with the rest of the civil community, are to participate constructively and critically in the ongoing work of the politics of peace. They claim no superior knowledge and no zone of purity for themselves. Rather, they bring to the common task of peace the love of enemies that is their gift in Christ. They are thus free, as forgiven sinners, to embrace the moral ambiguity of political life and, relying on Christ alone, to exercise their baptismal vocation in the world for the neighbor's sake — even the neighbor who is an enemy. Empowered by the love of God in Christ, the works of Christian love are not determined in conformity to a prescribed ideal, but are shaped by the neighbor's actual needs.

The Word of God requires of us such self-examination that we envision the possibility of selective conscientious objection to specific policies. This church is respectful and supportive of such witness on the part of those who act in conscience and courage.

> This church stands by and upholds those of its members who conscientiously object to military service as well as those who in conscience choose to serve in the military. This church further affirms that the individual who, for reasons of conscience, objects to participation in a particular war is acting in harmony with Lutheran teaching. (Conscientious Objection, 1968)

Both the Word of God and ecumenical sensitivity demand that we recognize and respect the tradition of those Christians who call for a radically different approach to discipleship. We honor those who in obedience to Christ's command renounce all violence and commit themselves to the way of the cross as the only path leading toward reconciliation and peace. We gratefully acknowledge our need for counsel and dialogue with those who pursue this alternative approach to peacemaking.

No one is exempt from civil and political obligation or from critical participation in the process of policymaking, whether as citizen or officeholder. All have a stake in, and a responsibility for, policies that advance peace; and all share the burden of guilt for the failure of the politics of peace. All are obligated to function as morally self-critical participants in the political society and its institutions; and all are responsible for contributing a self-critical dimension to the functioning of the institutions themselves.

All Christians are required to examine their actions conscientiously in light of their obligation to be peacemakers and their responsibilities to their neighbors. In a sinful world, when order, justice and peace are threatened by aggression, Christians may bear the civil sword to protect their neighbors and to restore peace. Even so, love for the aggressor or enemy requires that lethal force be used in a way proportional to the evil being resisted, and respecting the life of the innocent. In matters of war and peace, as in all of life, a Christian's ultimate loyalty and obedience is to God (Acts 5:29; *The Augsburg Confession*, XVI).

As a member of the worldwide Christian community, this church is challenged to take its part in facilitating communication among peoples of diverse cultures and political systems as the one people redeemed in Jesus Christ. In so doing, we are challenged to join in bearing witness to the One God whose ways begin and end in peace. Together with Christians throughout the world, we are a single living witness to the oneness of God's people and the unity which God intends for the human family.

CONCLUSION

God's loving "yes" in the creation and preservation of the world, in the cross and victory of Christ, and in the final victory of God over the powers of this age, is the substance of our present confidence and future hope. In praying "Thy kingdom come," we look forward joyfully to the coming of God's reign, and perform the works of hope and faithfulness. We take our place in the world which God loves, bearing witness to the Light which no darkness can overcome. We see in the worldwide longing for peace and justice evidence that God has not abandoned this world to the Evil One; and we therefore gladly join with all people of goodwill in the politics of peace.

This we do as redeemed sinners for whom, while we were yet God's enemies, Christ died. By the Spirit's empowerment we take up the ongoing political work of loving and reconciling enemies, making peace as becomes the blessed children of God.

ENABLING RESOLUTIONS

Resolved:

1. That the document "Peace and Politics" be adopted as an official social statement of the Lutheran Church in America.

2. That in adopting this document as an official social statement, the Lutheran Church in America expresses the grave urgency with which it regards the issue of world peace, and uplifts this as a topic of churchwide emphasis. To that end, this church emphasizes the understanding of the church as all the baptized people of God and enjoins all its members, laity and clergy, to become active in efforts to strengthen world peace and, in cooperation with others of goodwill, to seek even greater understanding of related issues and the expansion of efforts for peace;

3. That, continuing the call of the Eleventh Biennial Convention's resolution on peace and war, this convention calls upon the ordained ministers and congregations of this church to engage in extensive study of peace and war, using this social statement as a framework.

   It calls upon ordained ministers of this church to regularly

   a. preach and teach upon the duty of government to secure human well-being in community, and upon the Christian's special freedom and responsibility to exercise our life in Christ with God through political involvement for the good of the neighbor.

   b. preach and teach upon the peril of public idolatry, such as that which justifies one's own sin by seeing only the sin of another.

   c. preach and teach, as occasion warrants, upon the special peril into which, we confess, we all too often have fallen through a proud overreliance upon military might and technological prowess, at the expense of constructive policies for the securing of human rights and economic justice.

4. That this convention calls upon every member of the Lutheran Church in America to join with all Christians in taking up political responsibility as their faith and conscience demand; and to work faithfully, with all persons of goodwill, as God has been faithful to us in Christ, for the securement of human well-being on earth. Specifically, we are called to

   a. examine how we personally deal with conflict and seek alternatives to manage conflict constructively.

   b. work to build peace and understanding at home, school, church, and work.

   c. learn the process by which our local, state/provincial, and federal governments operate and how we can participate in decision-making.

   d. work with political parties and non-partisan groups in order to contribute effectively to the political process.

   e. exercise our right and fulfill our obligation to vote in elections at all levels of government.

   f. study the values and traditions of people of other cultures in the global village.

   g. address these and related concerns in the spirit of confession, penitence, and prayer.

5. That this convention calls upon congregations, institutions, and agencies of this church to sponsor for their communities free and reasoned discussion on that which makes for peace and justice, availing themselves especially of the resources in churchwide agency staff, church-related seminaries and colleges, synodical staff, and of persons whose occupations involve them daily in such concerns.

6. That this convention directs the churchwide program agencies and offices to develop programs appropriate to their several mandates in the bylaws of this church. These programs should be devised to equip the ordained ministers and

congregations to understand and apply the theological orientation and principles informing the social statement. Such programs should include

a. seminary and college courses.

b. continuing education for pastors, including counseling on the issues involved in this statement.

c. study conferences for parish leaders.

d. programs designed specifically to assist youth to grapple with these issues so that they might be enabled in their vocation as peacemakers.

e. provision of opportunities for individuals to communicate with appropriate government agencies.

f. opportunities for exchange and travel whereby individuals and congregations may learn more of different cultures, political systems, and national perspectives.

g. church school curricula.

7. That this convention encourages the Canadian members of this church to continue to explore their unique possibilities to mediate among nations, promote peace, and initiate steps leading to deeper understanding and better relations among nations and peoples in conflict.

8. That the Division for Mission in North America continue the work of theological study, issue clarification, and policy assessment begun in the preparation of this statement.

9. That the Division for Mission in North America, in conjunction with the Office for Governmental Affairs of the Lutheran Council in the U.S.A., advocate policies and actions as described in this statement, to agencies and officials of the United States government. This social statement shall be used as the basis and framework of such communications and advocacy. Similar advocacy efforts shall be made, through appropriate church channels, with governmental agencies and officials of Canada. Members of congregations of this church should participate in these continuing efforts.

10. That this social statement be sent to the heads of the world nuclear powers as the position of the Lutheran Church in America, as well as to the heads of Christian communions within those nations. It shall be accompanied by a communication from the bishop of this church urging concerted efforts to effect regional and international relationships, such as outlined in the 1975 Helsinki Accords, which would strengthen security for all, establish humanitarian concerns as a chief priority, and engender economic cooperation as a basis for comprehensive and stable relationships among nations, respectful of national concerns and individual freedoms.

11. That appropriate churchwide agencies and offices, especially the Division for Mission in North America, the Division for World Mission and Ecumenism, and the Office of the Bishop, be directed to initiate efforts leading to strengthened and common commitment with other Christian communions of the world in the unceasing work for peace with justice. These efforts should be marked by frequent consultation and communication, open and searching dialogue, and common commitment and activities related to the peacemaking role to which all Christians are called. These efforts will recognize a mutual accountability which is demanded of those churches and individuals who respond to the call to work for peace.

POVERTY

Adopted by the Third Biennial Convention, Kansas City, Missouri
June 21-29, 1966

Justice for the impoverished and dispossessed has been the concern of the people of God under both the Old and New Covenants. Under the divine imperative of prophetic faith, Christians today continue to seek justice for all whose lives are subject to abject poverty. Under the abundant mercy of the Father of Our Lord, Jesus Christ, Christians are constrained to minister compassionately to the needs of all their neighbors. Motivated by the love of God in Christ, the church has this double commission: to serve human need and to testify prophetically for justice in the ordering of society and the use of its resources.

Poverty is an age-old affliction of the human race. Concern for the poor, both through the economic arrangements of society and through the expression of personal responsibility, is a continuing theme throughout the Old and New Testaments. Today we find ourselves confronted by a radically new and potentially explosive situation in human society. On the one hand, the population explosion and modern technological developments threaten to create a class of human beings who are economically superfluous, and who find themselves increasingly sealed off from participation in the economic benefits of society.

On the other hand, the revolution in technology holds out, for the first time in history, the possibility of the virtual elimination of hunger and basic economic deprivation both at home and throughout the world. The contrast between plenty and poverty, on the domestic and on the world scene, becomes doubly scandalous in the light of this new possibility.

The possibilities for good inherent in God's new gifts to humanity in technology will not be realized without changes in some attitudes and in some economic arrangements. Today's situation presents vastly new dimensions of justice and confronts serving love with opportunities hitherto undreamed of. Realizing that no conclusive word can yet be spoken about new forms of social and economic order, or even of proper attitudes underlying them, the Lutheran Church in America sets forth the following ethical judgments in the conviction that they are in continuity with biblical concern for the poor, and are obedient administration of its understanding of God's grace and the abundance of nature.

1. We rejoice in the applied achievements of science and technology which make it possible, currently in industrially developed countries and potentially throughout the whole world, to provide basically adequate levels of living for all.

259

2. We approve of declarations of public policy in our own countries (U.S.A. and Canada) which seek to eliminate the paradox of poverty in the midst of plenty and further seek to open to everyone opportunities for education and training, for work, and for living in decency and dignity.

3. We believe that in nations where conditions of abundance exist, it should be the goal of the national economy to provide every able-bodied adult with the opportunity for meaningful employment sufficiently remunerative to secure, at the very least, the minimal necessities required in our society for living in decency and dignity. Further, where a full employment economy is not possible or not desirable, or where individual inadequacies exist, we believe our countries have the responsibility to move as readily as possible to assure income adequate to secure the minimal standard of living.

4. We believe that although the establishment of social justice is primarily a responsibility of governing authority, it is appropriate that innovative programs designed to counteract the causes of economic deprivation be enacted by any agencies having such responsibility.

5. We recognize that, in a time of population explosion, the problems of hunger and poverty cannot be solved without substantial attention to population planning. We affirm the responsibility of governmental and nongovernmental agencies to make available to the deprived the same knowledge and means of conception control already available to others.

6. We are reminded by the "revolution of rising expectations" of the universal dimensions of the present challenge to eradicate poverty. Any commitment to the elimination of domestic poverty must be accompanied by a commitment to seek justice in the reduction of the disparity between rich and poor nations by programs designed to assist the developing nations to raise their standard of living.

7. We encourage the congregations, the synods and the agencies of the church to be open to the kind of cooperation with public and voluntary agencies which as a part of the church's witness to God's love in Jesus Christ will enable them to participate in the struggle against poverty in measures fully consistent with the resources God has given us and our responsibility for the use of those resources.

The Lutheran Church in America commits itself to the struggle against poverty in full continuity with the biblical testimony about concern for the poor. While it recognizes that the forms of this struggle are subject to human judgment and are open to differences of opinion among fully committed Christian persons, it does not believe that commitment to the struggle is an open question for Christians.

PRAYER AND BIBLE READING IN THE PUBLIC SCHOOLS

Adopted by the Second Biennial Convention, Pittsburgh, Pennsylvania
July 2-9, 1964

In June, 1963, the Executive Council of the Lutheran Church in America adopted a brief statement on prayer and Bible reading in the public schools in the light of decisions on those matters by the United States Supreme Court (Engel and Schempp cases, 370 U.S. 421 and 374 U.S. 203).

The Biennial Convention of the LCA in July, 1964, received an interpretive memorandum attached by the Executive Council to the prior statement. The significance of the memorandum was in its fuller analysis of the Court's decisions and in the attention it gave to related proposals to amend the Constitution of the United States.

The convention ratified the statement of the Executive Council (in the words of the pertinent resolution) "as amplified and interpreted by" the memorandum.

The statement of the Executive Council (I) "as amplified and interpreted by" the memorandum (II) constitutes the official position of the Lutheran Church in America on prayer and Bible reading in the public schools and the question of constitutional amendment.

I. STATEMENT BY THE EXECUTIVE COUNCIL, 1963

We do not believe that much has been lost in terms of the specific points covered by the recent decisions of the United States Supreme Court in the school prayer and Bible reading cases. If the Lord's Prayer were to be recited in schoolrooms only for the sake of the moral and ethical atmosphere it creates, it would be worth nothing to the practicing Christian. The Lord's Prayer is the supreme act of adoration and petition or it is debased. Reading the Bible in the public schools without comment, too, has been of dubious value as either an educational or religious experience. The more we attempt as Christians or Americans to insist on common denominator religious exercise or instruction in public schools, the greater risk we run of diluting our faith and contributing to a vague religiosity which identifies religion with patriotism and becomes a national folk religion.

At the same time, in candor, these decisions must be seen as a watershed. They open an era in which Christianity is kept separate from the state in a way that was foreign and would have been repugnant to the minds of our ancestors at the time when the Constitution was written and ever since. They signalize the fact that the United States of America, like many other nations, is past the place where underlying Christian culture and beliefs are assumed in its life.

This event intensifies the task of the church. It heightens the need of the church

261

for strength to stand alone, lofty and unshaken, in American society. It calls for greater depth of conviction in all Christian men and women.

II. INTERPRETIVE MEMORANDUM, 1964

The United States Supreme Court has declared it unconstitutional for states to require religious exercises such as prayer recitation and the reading of the Bible without comment in the public schools. (Engel and Schempp cases, 370 U.S. 421 and 374 U.S. 203.) It is natural that the Court's decisions have created controversy and have aroused misgivings and questions on the part of those who have both an interest in the public schools and a concern for the religious and moral nurture of our children. To some it has seemed that the Federal Constitution should be expressly amended to nullify these decisions and otherwise restrict the application of the religion clauses of the First Amendment.

Criticism of the Court's rulings has been directed to the following points: that prayer exercises and Bible reading in the public schools have the sanction of historical usage, that to call these practices a form of religious establishment is to carry constitutional interpretation to an unwarranted extreme, that to invalidate these practices at the request of a minority is to deny majority rights, and that exclusion of such religious practices has the effect of conferring a constitutional blessing upon secularism as an official philosophy.

The Church is properly concerned about these questions. The validity, the meaning and the effect of the Court's decisions touch on matters of vital interest to Christians, both in terms of their responsibility under God for the good of the public order and their special calling in Christ for the sake of the Gospel.

It does not appear, however, that the church need be alarmed over the results reached by the Court in these cases. Persons of good will may have differences of opinion on the correctness or desirability of these decisions. At the same time believers and nonbelievers alike may share the view that in the end these decisions may have a wholesome effect in clarifying the role of the public school with respect to religious matters.

The Executive Council statement of June 1963 recognizes that from a religious point of view not much is lost as a result of the decisions of the U.S. Supreme Court in the school prayer and Bible reading cases. Recitation of prayers when prescribed by public authority easily becomes a formal, mechanical exercise that neither reflects nor contributes to genuine religious piety and reverence. Bible reading without comment may take on the form of a ritualistic exercise that contributes little to a genuine educational program or to understanding of the Bible.

Moreover, both the Lord's Prayer and the Bible belong to a particular religious tradition, and their use in religious exercises in the public schools does result in a religious preference and invites the risk of sectarian divisiveness in the community. In turn, any devotional use of the Bible designed to avoid or

262

minimize the sectarian aspect results in a distorted conception of the Bible and a dilution of its religious message.

Furthermore, any religious exercise designed to minimize the sectarian element, whether it be a nonsectarian prayer or Bible readings that ignore religious teachings, serves to promote a vague or a syncretistic religion that conveys none of the substance, the depth, and cutting edge of the historic Christian witness.

The nature of our contemporary pluralistic and democratic society requires a re-evaluation of practices which though sanctioned by historical usage had their origin at a time when the Protestant influence was dominant in the shaping of many public practices including the public school program. A due regard for all religious faiths and also for nonbelievers and nonconformists of all kinds makes it imperative that the public schools abstain from practices that run the risk of intrusion of sectarian elements and divisiveness. The public school serves a unique and valued place in helping to build a civic unity despite the diversities of our pluralistic culture.

It should also be noted that when the state deeply involves itself in religious practices in the public schools, it is thereby not only appropriating a function properly served by the church and the family but subjecting the freedom of believers and unbelievers alike to the restraint that accompanies the use of governmental power and public facilities in the promotion of religious ends. This consideration is particularly relevant in the case of religious exercises in the public schools. Children are required to be in school by compulsion of public law, the religious exercises are prescribed by public authority, public school facilities are used, and the teacher—the symbol of authority in the classroom—supervises the exercises. These factors combine to operate with indirect coercive force on young and impressionable children to induce them to take part in these exercises, despite a freedom to be excused from participation. Even persons with a genuine regard for prayer and the Bible may object to having their children engage in these exercises when they are supported by the compulsion of law.

Having said this, however, does not foreclose the legitimacy of having any reservations about the Supreme Court's decisions. The legal question whether the establishment clause of the First Amendment is properly interpreted to apply to religious practices in the public schools is a matter on which scholars disagree. It is quite valid to ask whether the Fourteenth Amendment should be used to make the First Amendment apply to every school community in the United States, regardless of the religious character of the local community.

A more serious question, moreover, goes to the concept of neutrality respecting religious matters, which played a central part in the Court's decision handed down in 1963. Clearly public school programs must be directed to secular purposes, and yet the schools cannot be absolutely neutral in regard to religious matters. Any education premised on indifference to the religious factors in history, in American life and in the life of the individual, is an inadequate education. Furthermore, the vacuum introduced by the exclusion of religion opens the door to the cult of secularism. The Constitution prohibits the establishment of all kinds of religion—whether theistic or secular in character.

Recognizing these considerations, the Court has wisely stated that schools may properly present programs for the objective study of the Bible and of religion. How successfully this can be done, without the intrusion of sectarian elements, remains to be seen. This points up the challenge to the churches and to the public schools to give serious attention to ways of studying the Bible and religion that will do justice to the religious factor and at the same time serve the larger neutrality which an even-handed interpretation of the Constitution requires. The LCA Commission on Church and State Relations in a Pluralistic Society is currently exploring this question and will report its conclusions to the Church in due time.

Christians should realize, however, that not too much may be expected of the public schools in dealing with religious matters. The schools must be careful to abstain from practices and teaching programs that involve commitment to ultimate truth or values. On the other hand, it should be possible for the public schools to teach respect for the spiritual and moral values that reflect the community consensus and which for most citizens have their roots in the Christian, and in the antecedent Hebrew tradition.

Our democratic society rests on certain moral assumptions. But even here the public schools must be careful. In teaching respect for the ethics of a democratic society, they cannot commit themselves to either a theistic or a humanistic philosophy respecting the sources and motivation for ethical conduct. The nurture of an informed, vital and relevant religious faith remains the responsibility of parents and the churches.

In view of these considerations it does not seem that anything of importance is to be gained through an amendment to the Constitution that would sanction prayer and Bible reading in the public schools. The Supreme Court has not held that there can be no prayers in public schools. Nothing in the Court's decisions precludes school authorities from designating a period of silence for prayer and meditation or even for devotional reading of the Bible or any other book during this period. Opportunity for voluntary participation in prayers of the student's own choice is not governed by these decisions which dealt only with situations where school authorities were directly involved in prescribing the kind of prayer and in giving direction to it. Moreover, the Court's recognition that the objective study of religion and the Bible in the public schools is consistent with the First Amendment gives promise of a constructive approach to neutralizing secularistic tendencies in public education.

Furthermore, the Supreme Court has not outlawed reference to God in public documents, proceedings or ceremonies. No constitutional amendment is necessary to assure the freedom of the federal and state governments to give appropriate expression to the religious factor in our history and in the lives of our people.

On the other hand, there is disadvantage in using the amendment process to deal with the present issue and there is risk in the results that would be achieved by it. The proposed amendments would represent only a piece-meal way of dealing with religious practices in public schools and in public life. It would be a use of the amendment process not to state general and fundamental principles but to sanction certain specific and detailed practices. This is, to say the least, a questionable use of the amendment process. Moreover, such an amendment would raise new problems of interpretation and could lead to unintended and unsuspected results in areas vitally touching on religious liberty. Finally, and this is most important, the proposed amendments in their substance would give constitutional sanction to distinctively sectarian practices in the public schools with all the risks involved of impinging upon freedom of conscience and belief and creating religious divisiveness in the community.

The Constitution should not be amended except to achieve large and important public needs and purposes consistent with the basic nature of our constitutional system. The current proposals for constitutional amendment do not meet these standards. Parents, churches and school authorities would be better advised to direct their efforts to programs for study of religion and the Bible in the public schools and to the formulation of types of programs which co-ordinate the secular educational programs of the public schools with programs of a strictly religious nature conducted by the churches themselves, rather than to seek constitutional sanctions for devotional exercises in public schools that have at most a minimal religious value, which invite the intrusion of sectarian influences into the public school system, risk the violation of the rights of religious freedom and are a potential source of conflict in the community.

RACE RELATIONS

Adopted by the Second Biennial Convention, Pittsburgh, Pennsylvania
July 2-9, 1964

The current racial revolution has thrust the church into a time of travail and perplexity but also of opportunity and hope. Injustice, which for a long time was either ignored, rationalized, or mutely borne, is now seen more clearly for what it actually is. Injurious discrimination based on race is a violation of God's created order, of the meaning of redemption in Christ, and of the nature of the church.

Implicit in such discrimination often are unbiblical views of God and of humanity. The church must oppose such false views with all the power of the truth of God: in its prayer and worship, in its theological thought, in its nurture of the personal life, in its institutional forms, and in individual and corporate action in society.

At the heart of the life of the church is prayer. In the Prayer of the Church, we find the great pleading and thanking voice of hundreds of thousands of Christians assembled each Sunday for the worship of God. Unless we mean what we say, and live as persons who intend to do what we mean, the holy gravity of our prayer itself condemns us.

In the Prayer of the Church we petition: *Sanctify and unite thy people in all the world, that one holy Church may bear witness to thee, the God and Father of all.*

Here we pray that God may heal—"Sanctify and unite"—the church in order that it may "bear witness" to the "God and Father of all" in whom alone the world finds healing. We pray that, our unity of communion being manifest, we may hold out to a broken world the salvatory meaning of God's parenthood.

This requires a unity that is visible and tangible.

It requires Christians to seek out and receive one another as brothers and sisters without regard to nation, race, or culture.

It means that a racially segregated church is institutionalized disobedience.

Having thus prayed for the integrity of our witness as a church, we pray for the nation and its structures of law and authority: *Preserve our Nation in righteousness and honor . . . Grant health and favor to all who bear office in our land, . . . and help them to acknowledge and obey thy holy will.*

When spoken in the Prayer of the Church, "righteousness" points to the "right" that God wills; "honor" implies being approved by God because of our obedience to that "right."

This petition indicates that the church supports the rule of law and the civil government which administers and interprets it. At the same time it means that the church must oppose any law or governmental practice which under the guise of rightful authority perverts justice. In particular it means that the church must oppose any force which would prohibit the expression of its inclusiveness according to "thy holy will."

Next we pray:

Give to all persons the mind of Christ, and dispose our days in thy peace, O God. Take from us all hatred and prejudice, and whatever may hinder unity of spirit and concord. These sentences are related. Our days cannot be lived in God's peace unless hatred and prejudice are removed from us. The prayer is realistic: it recognizes that we are guilty of harboring hatreds and prejudices which we are inclined to hold dear. Therefore, nothing less than a mighty, holy, act that can "take away" will do. We believe and confess there has been such an act in Christ! In blood and agony, God's decision has been made and sealed.

The problem of the relations between persons of different races, particularly between white and Black persons, is here exposed. To stand before God and pray, "take from us all hatred and prejudice," and then as a praying church to discriminate among persons on any such sinful basis is a contradiction of this prayer.

Finally we pray:
All these things . . . grant us, O Father, for his sake who died and rose again, and now liveth and reigneth with thee in the unity of the Holy Ghost, one God, world without end.

In prayer God's peculiar people acknowledge that they are freed for a strange new life before God and among their neighbors. The Prayer of the Church illumines the way of the church. Some things are no longer ours to decide. The decision has been made—and forever. In a time of travail and opportunity, perplexity and hope in race relations, the church needs to pray—and to act in accord with its prayer—"for his sake who died and rose again" and who reigns "world without end."

The substance of the church's action in all matters of racial discrimination is determined for it and stands as a permanent testimony each time the church prays or confesses its faith or proclaims its message. The forms of the church's action on the specific ecclesiastical, political, economic, and social expressions of racial discrimination are subject to human judgment and must be directed to specific times, places and circumstances.

In obedience to the Lord of the church and in repentant acknowledgment that urgent occasions require fresh resolutions, the 1964 Biennial Convention of the Lutheran Church in America. issues a renewed call to action to include the following elements:

1. No congregation, synod, agency, or institution of the church in its communion and varied ministries should discriminate against any persons on the grounds of race.

2. The publications of the church should present an objective picture of racial diversity and emphasize the Christian's responsibility in the struggle for racial justice. Editors should be realistic in their use of pictures and descriptive materials for such publications so as to reflect the inclusive character of the church.

3. The church, together with its congregations, synods, agencies and institutions, should support its concern for racial justice in all its business involvements and should give critical scrutiny to its own employment practices. In the calling of pastors and the employing of staff the congregations of this church should not make the race of the candidate a qualification for consideration.

4. The church, its congregations, synods, agencies and institutions should initiate programs and support occasions in which Christians acknowledge the imperative of worship, fellowship, and mission without regard to race.

5. The church, its congregations, synods, agencies and institutions should initiate and participate in efforts to bring about understanding at points of racial tension.

6. The church, its congregations, synods, agencies, institutions and individual members should support the enactment and enforcement of federal, state or provincial, and local legislation which seeks to guarantee to all persons equally, without racial discrimination
   a. civil rights, including the right to vote and full protection of law;
   b. access to education;
   c. opportunity for employment, promotion, apprenticeship, job training, and union membership;
   d. the right to rent, buy, and occupy housing in any place, and the right of access to means of mortgage financing;
   e. access to public accommodations.

7. Christians are committed to the rule of law as an expression of the moral law of God. Nevertheless, it must be recognized that laws have been and may in the future be enacted, or social customs may exist, which are believed to be in basic conflict with the constitutional law of the land or the moral law of God. In such circumstances, the church, its congregations, synods, agencies and institutions, including their representatives, as well as individual members, are recognized as free by all lawful means, including participation in peaceful public demonstrations, to urge repeal or invalidation of such laws or to effect change of such customs.

If and when the means of legal recourse have been exhausted or are demonstrably inadequate, Christians may then choose to serve the cause of

racial justice by disobeying a law that clearly involves the violation of their obligations as Christians, so long as they are
   a. willing to accept the penalty for their action;
   b. willing to limit and direct their protest as precisely as possible against a specific grievance or injustice;
   c. willing to carry out their protest in a nonviolent, responsible manner, after earnestly seeking the counsel of other Christians and the will of God in prayer.

In all of this, we are guided and supported by the normative teaching of the church in Article XVI of the Augsburg Confession: *Christians are obliged to be subject to civil authority and obey its commands and laws in all that can be done without sin. But when commands of the civil authority cannot be obeyed without sin, we must obey God rather than men* (Acts 5:29).

RESOLUTION ON CIVIL RIGHTS ACT
Adopted also by the 1964 Convention

WHEREAS, the Civil Rights Act of 1964 was signed into law on July 2, marking a historic advance in the long struggle to secure rights to which we, as Christians, believe all citizens are entitled; and

WHEREAS, countless organizations and individuals have contributed to this result, many of them at great personal sacrifice;

NOW, THEREFORE, BE IT RESOLVED, that the Lutheran Church in America record its appreciation for the action of the President and the Congress of the United States, and for the efforts of the countless private citizens who have contributed to the enactment of the Civil Rights Act of 1964; and

RESOLVED, that the Lutheran Church in America urge all citizens to join in compliance with the Civil Rights Act in letter and in spirit; and

RESOLVED, that the Lutheran Church in America call upon its members to take the lead in their communities to encourage obedience to this legislation, and to undergird by prayer and action those whose duty it is to enforce it.

RELIGIOUS LIBERTY
IN THE UNITED STATES

Adopted by the Fourth Biennial Convention, Atlanta, Georgia
June 19-27, 1968

"Religious liberty" is to be distinguished from "Christian freedom." "Christian freedom" is a theological term describing the gift of God which is received by faith and which cannot be destroyed by any earthly authority. It refers to the freedom of the believer from bondage to law, death and the demonic principalities which enslave everyone but are overcome by God's deed in Jesus Christ. "Christian freedom" may be experienced by prisoners or the oppressed and be unknown to persons in places of power.

"Religious liberty," on the other hand, is used in this document as a political term describing one major aspect of civil liberty in the United States. "Civil liberty" includes also such freedoms as those of speech, press and assembly, and is implemented by legislative enactments, which require for their effectiveness an organized civil community which is willing and able to enforce them impartially.

Christian faith asserts that religious liberty is rooted in our creation in the image of God and in God's continuing activity in the created world. Its validity in general society is based on the moral knowledge of all persons, which enables them to perform good deeds and pursue truth and justice. But we are creatures to whom God speaks and from whom God expects a response. This is essential to our humanity. To deny religious liberty and other civil liberties, therefore, threatens to dehumanize us all.

Christian faith asserts that God will not force anyone into communion with God. If, then, God refuses to impose divine will on humanity, then persons exceed their prerogatives if they try to use coercion of any kind on one another to obtain religious conformity. Religious liberty for all is thus not only a demand of civil justice but also an aid to our response to the Christian gospel.

Underlying all the issues of religious liberty are the divergent beliefs, feelings and attitudes of persons and groups toward each other. Strains develop from tensions at this level as well as from the conflicts which are in full view. Indeed, the constitutional guarantees which protect persons from overt acts of religious discrimination rest on and find their strength in a broad-based appreciation of the need for mutual respect among divergent persons and groups.

The record of the Christian Church and of individual Christians in fostering a climate of interreligious understanding has not always been exemplary. Far too often professions of loyalty to the principle of religious liberty have been betrayed by actions or attitudes grounded in prejudice. There have been times when the story has been one of vicious intolerance, suffering and death. Certainly some of the feelings which have contributed to these periods of tragedy are present in one form or another in church members today. They are aroused and perpetuated, not only by actual differences of belief or practice, but also by stereotyped impressions which people tend to have of those who differ from them.

AFFIRMATIONS

1. Religious liberty includes the right of a person, whether a believer in God or a nonbeliever,
   a. to be immune from coercion to participate in religious acts or affirmations;
   b. to worship in accordance with the faith and ritual of one's group, even in ways which appear curious or offensive to others, so long as the methods used are not legally defined as dangerous to the individual or the community; or not to worship if that is the choice;
   c. to witness to one's faith by the spoken and written word and by deeds of service; and to seek to win others to that faith in full recognition of their freedom to accept or reject;
   d. to worship or not worship in the home and to provide or not provide religious instruction to one's children.

2. Religious liberty includes the right of a church or religious organization as a corporate body,
   a. to conduct its internal affairs without interference by government or any other person or group, except where government is performing its legitimate functions of promoting such public interests as health, safety and justice;
   b. to organize for such purposes as conducting public worship, preaching and administering the sacraments, and engaging in social ministry, missions, evangelism and education;
   c. to give voice to its conscience on matters of public concern, whether from the pulpit, through formal resolutions or through other forms of communication;
   d. to hold and manage property and to engage in institutional enterprises which are deemed appropriate for the fulfillment of these purposes.

3. Religious liberty is not an absolute right; in every situation it must be weighed against other values before a decision is made. The religious liberty of a person or group may be limited by government only on the basis of an important and compelling public interest. Nothing less than a serious and immediately threatened violation of other basic human rights should warrant restrictions on religious liberty.

4. The exercise of religious liberty depends on specific legislative enact-

ments and their administration. This means that the way in which the civil community and its laws operate is of crucial importance to the actualization of religious and other liberties. Christians should strengthen and uphold government when it maintains in fact the freedom and welfare of all people in a just and equitable manner. The weakening of civil authority in a democratic society is more likely to undermine liberties than to produce them. Christians ought also insist on the active affirmation of the rights of all citizens as a check against the ever-present tendency to abuse of authority by the state or other structures of power.

5. Religious liberty is constitutionally guaranteed in the United States. Nevertheless, the prejudicial feelings and attitudes of individuals and groups may not only threaten the exercise of religious liberty but subvert its constitutional guarantees. The maintenance of religious diversity requires a general public recognition, not that all religions are equally valid, but that all enjoy equal status before the law. Such general public recognition, however, is possible only when persons and groups, without compromising their own convictions, respect the integrity of the convictions of others and avoid hostility when their efforts to win others to their positions are rejected. The church, admitting its failures in the past, should do all in its power to develop understanding among those with divergent points of view, to oppose prejudice and intolerance wherever they may be found, and to deal creatively with the real tensions which exist.

A CALL

In accordance with this statement the Lutheran Church in America

A. Lays upon the consciences of its members, as they witness to the gospel of Jesus Christ, the need to understand their own beliefs and convictions, to be sensitive to the beliefs and convictions of those who differ from them, to seek to win others to their position only by persuasion and example, and to resist the temptation to respond to rebuffs with hostility.

B. Affirms the right of everyone to free expression of his or her faith, especially in public worship and witness to others; and asserts its concern for every violation of religious liberty, wherever it occurs.

C. Acknowledges the crucial importance of the state in the realization of religious and other liberties and declares its support of the proper exercise of governmental power to that end.

D. Urges its congregations and their members to meet religious intolerance and hostility with understanding, and to provide concrete opportunities for communication among opposing points of view.

E. Commends agencies of the church which have developed programs and publications to help its people understand other religious groups; encourages them to continue and expand such efforts; and calls on all agencies carefully and continually to scrutinize their educational and promotional materials for references which tend to foster intolerance by disparaging other religious groups.

F. Declares its right and duty to address government and the general community, both through its members and through its corporate forms, not only in its own interest but especially in the interest of the welfare of all people.

G. Calls upon its members and congregations to speak and act specifically in application of these principles.

SEX, MARRIAGE, AND FAMILY

Adopted by the Fifth Biennial Convention, Minneapolis, Minnesota
June 25-July 2, 1970

Sex, marriage, and family are gifts of God in which to rejoice. Their essential goodness cannot be obscured by any crisis of our time.

As traditional moral codes are being challenged, there is a profound struggle to formulate bases of ethical judgment which have meaning for contemporary men and women. Powerful forces of social change, joined with discoveries in the medical and life sciences, influence all aspects of human existence. The church is concerned not only with specific issues and controversies, but with the basic Christian understanding of human sexuality.

HUMAN SEXUALITY

Who are we? We are responsible persons made in the image of God. God created male and female, making sexual interdependence serve the divine intention for life-in-community. Scripture portrays us as relational beings whose true humanity is realized in faith and love with God and neighbor.

True humanity is violated by sin, which is our broken relationship with God and each other. This alienation expresses itself in all facets of life, including sex, marriage, and family. At the same time God works in these broken relationships, healing and freeing the forgiven to devote their efforts to the well-being of others.

Human sexuality is a gift of God for the expression of love and the generation of life. As with every good gift, it is subject to abuses which cause suffering and debasement. In the expression of human sexuality, it is the integrity of our relationships which determines the meaning of our actions. We do not merely have sexual relations; we demonstrate our true humanity in personal relationships, the most intimate of which are sexual.

MARRIAGE

Christian faith affirms marriage as a covenant of fidelity—a dynamic, life-long commitment of one man and one woman in a personal and sexual union. While hereafter in this report the phrase "covenant of fidelity" is employed, and we recognize it as expressing a key insight about Christian marriage, in biblical language, it may also be helpful at times to express the same emphasis in other terminology through such a phrase as "mutual commitment to lifelong faithfulness" as a substitute for a "covenant of fidelity." Marriage is not simply a legal transaction which can be broken when the conditions under which it was entered no longer exist. It is an

275

unconditional relationship, a total commitment based on faithful trust. This union embodies God's loving purpose to create and enrich life. As the needs of the partners change, the covenant of fidelity must be renewed by God's grace and continually reaffirmed by husband and wife.

This view transcends the civil understanding of marriage as a legal contract. A marital union can be legally valid yet not be a covenant of fidelity, just as it can be a covenant of fidelity and not a legal contract. Such a covenant is also to be distinguished from an identification with the marriage pattern of any particular culture, from the idea that an established structure is normative for all times, and from the legalistic notion that because two people have had sexual intercourse they are bound together forever. The existence of a true covenant of fidelity outside marriage as a legal contract is extremely hard to identify.

Marriage is ordained by God as a structure of the created order. Thus the sanction of civil law and public recognition are important and beneficial in marriage, as checks against social injustice and personal sin. The marriage covenant, therefore, should be certified by a legal contract, and Christian participants should seek the blessings of the church.

The relationship between husband and wife is likened in Ephesians 5:21-23 to the relationship between Christ and the church. This depicts a communion of total persons, each of them living for the other. As with the covenant between Christ and the church, the promise of fidelity is fundamental. Therefore, Christians regard marriage as a primary setting in which to live out their calling from the Lord.

However, many persons are single for varied reasons. There should be no exaltation of either the single or the married state, one over the other. It is a matter for gratitude when the conditions of life make possible free and open choices.

FAMILY

The family has the function of nurturing human beings in relationships which are rich with creative possibilities. It provides the surrounding in which persons enhance rather than exploit one another, in which mistakes may be made and forgiveness realized.

The family appears in many forms in different times and places. It develops in response to the need of men, women, and children, whether married or unmarried, for a primary relationship in which they may have a sense of intimacy and belonging. There is no greater challenge today than in the family, for it is intended by God to be that basic community in which personhood is fostered. The family should not become centered on itself, but should be seen as a base from which its members move out to participate in society.

ETHICAL DECISION

The Christian's ethical decisions are made in the context of the relationships with God and other persons. Christians act knowing that we daily become alienated from God and daily need God's forgiveness. Under God's grace, however, we are freed to choose how best to serve one another in Christian love.

We Christians need more than love to guide us. In making decisions we should recognize that we and the other persons with whom we act are unique men, women, and children with particular gifts and responsibilities, living in particular places and relationships. Furthermore, we draw our guidance and strength from the Christian revelation, bringing to each situation the benefits of the accumulated wisdom and supporting community of the church.

Human life must be regulated by just laws because humans are finite and sinful. Such laws, enacted by reason and enforced by power, can never be the direct expression of Christian love. Nevertheless, Christians as citizens and the church as institution should join with others in advocating and supporting just laws. In this process, however, it is not proper for any church to impose its sectarian views on the general community.

SOME CURRENT ISSUES

The following statements are not to be thought of as categorical laws or "Christian" solutions to the problems involved. Nor are they intended to furnish easy answers to hard questions. They are offered as guidance to pastors and laity in their ethical decision-making.

1. Some Issues Related to Sexual Expression

Within the realm of human sexuality, intercourse is a joyful means of giving oneself in the mutual expression of love. It is within the permanent covenant of marital fidelity that the full potential of coitus to foster genuine intimacy, personal growth, and the responsible conception of children is realized.

Because the Lutheran Church in America holds that sexual intercourse outside the context of the marriage union is morally wrong, nothing in this statement on "Sex, Marriage, and Family" is to be interpreted as meaning that this church either condones or approves premarital or extra-marital sexual intercourse.

Scientific research has not been able to provide conclusive evidence regarding the causes of homosexuality. Nevertheless, homosexuality is viewed biblically as a departure from the heterosexual structure of God's creation. Persons who engage in homosexual behavior are sinners only as are all other persons—alienated from God and neighbor. However, they are often the special and undeserving victims of prejudice and discrimination in law, law enforcement, cultural mores, and congregational life. In relation to this area of concern, the sexual behavior of freely consenting adults in private is not an appropriate subject for legislation or police action. It is essential to see such persons as entitled to understanding and justice in church and community.

Sexual exploitation in any situation, either personally or commercially, inside or outside legally contracted marriage, is sinful because it is destructive of God's good gift and man's integrity.

The church recognizes the effects of social environment and cultural traditions on human behavior. It seeks, therefore, to respond understandingly to persons who enter into relationships which do not demonstrate a covenant of fidelity.

2. Some Issues Related to Marriage

It is the quality of interpersonal relationships within marriage that is the concern of the church. A covenant of fidelity can be broken in reality whether the union terminates formally through legal action or displays external solidarity. In ministering to persons affected by a broken covenant the church is called to assist them to perceive their problems more clearly and, hopefully, to experience forgiveness and reconciliation.

If the outcome is formal dissolution of the marriage, the church should continue to minister to all persons involved. To identify the legal action of divorce as sinful by itself obscures the fact that the martial relationship has already been mutually undermined by thoughts, words, and actions. Although divorce often brings anguish to those concerned; there may be situations in which securing a divorce is more responsible than staying together.

When the question of the remarriage of a divorced man or woman arises, the church and the individuals themselves will do well to concentrate upon the potential of the new rather than the collapse of the former marriage. A clear understanding of the dynamics which led to the breakdown of the first union helps a person prepare more adequately for the second. A divorced man and woman, of course, should fulfill all legitimate obligations to the members of the broken family.

A shared Christian faith contributes to the strength of a marriage. Even more, marriage and family provide a primary setting for Christian nurture and maturity. Before a man and woman enter into an interfaith marriage, each should strive to understand and respect his own faith and the faith of his partner. They should become intelligently informed about factors which can cause special difficulty.

Theologically, marriage between persons without reference to racial and ethnic differences and background is a witness to the oneness of humanity

278

under the one God, and as such should be fully accepted in both church and society.

3. Some Issues Related to Conception Control

The ethical significance of the use of any medically approved contraceptive method within a covenant of marital fidelity depends upon the motivation of the users. A responsible decision for or against having a child will include evaluation of such factors as the health of the potential mother, a reliable prognosis concerning the health of a possible child, the number and spacing of other children, the family's economic circumstances, and the rapid growth of population. People have a right not to have children without being accused of selfishness or a betrayal of the divine plan; and every child has a right to be a wanted child.

All persons are entitled to receive from governmental and voluntary agencies information about conception control.

4. Some Issues Related to Abortion

In the consideration of induced abortion the key issue is the status of the unborn fetus. Since the fetus is the organic beginning of human life, the termination of its development is always a serious matter. Nevertheless, a qualitative distinction must be made between its claims and the rights of a responsible person made in God's image who is in living relationships with God and other human beings. This understanding of responsible personhood is congruent with the historical Lutheran teaching and practice whereby only living persons are baptized.

On the basis of the evangelical ethic, a woman or couple may decide responsibly to seek an abortion. Earnest consideration should be given to the life and total health of the mother, her responsibilities to others in her family, the stage of development of the fetus, the economic and psychological stability of the home, the laws of the land, and the consequences for society as a whole.

Persons considering abortion are encouraged to consult with their physicians and spiritual counselors. This church upholds its pastors and other responsible counselors, and persons who conscientiously make decisions about abortion.

5. Some Issues Related to Family Life Education

There is need for competent education to understand sexuality and to prepare for courtship, marriage, and family.

This kind of education properly begins in the home, where parents teach their children not only by words but by their actions and expression of feeling. But children and young people also learn from other sources, such as the peer group, books, movies and television, which often convey incomplete or distorted information. Parents have the right to expect help from the church in their roles as educators in sex, marriage, and family, particularly in relating their Christian convictions to this task.

The church supports responsible family life education in the public school, so long as religious and moral commitments are respected. Helping young people grow into mature men and women is so important that every possible resource must be involved, including competent, voluntary agencies. But it is the public school that can furnish an education reaching most children and young people. Family life education in the school should include parents in its planning and execution. It should also offer courses for them, coordinated with those their children are taking.

The task of education in sex, marriage, and family requires that the home, the church, and the school prepare themselves for effective fulfillment of their appropriate roles.

A CALL

The Lutheran Church in America calls upon its pastors to reinforce the covenant of fidelity in their liturgical leadership, preaching, teaching, and counseling. It calls upon its members to study this statement and the booklet *Sex, Marriage, and Family: a Contemporary Christian Perspective;* and to give support to one another amid the painful ambiguities of making ethical decisions relating to sex, marriage, and family. It calls upon its agencies of education and social service to develop specific plans for helping synods and congregations incorporate the major emphases of this statement into their lives. It calls upon the church, both as a corporate body and as individual members, to witness to the civic community in behalf of just laws and policies affecting sex, marriage, and family, and in behalf of legislation that will improve the economic and social conditions which influence the lifestyles of people.

1978 LCA CONVENTION MINUTE ON THE SUBJECT OF ABORTION

Clarifying Minute to be appended to
the 1970 LCA Social Statement on Sex, Marriage, and Family
(Twelfth Biennial Convention, Toronto, Ontario 1984)

The 1970 convention of the church adopted the Social Statement on Sex, Marriage and Family. That statement provides basic principles on abortion based on theological grounds with socio-ethical considerations to be taken into account. Specific decisions are to be dealt with in counseling situations. (See also Report of the President, p.28, left column.)

The statement opposes

a. Abortion on demand— "Earnest consideration should be given to the life and total health of the mother, her responsibilities to others in her family, the stage of development of the fetus, the economic and psychological stability of the home, the laws of the land, and the consequences for society as a whole"; and

b. Use of abortion as an alternative form of contraception— " . . . the fetus is the organic beginning of human life, . . ."

The Division for Mission in North America provides helpful interpretation in its study book "The Problem of Abortion after the Supreme Court Decision."

The Committee on Memorials from Synods recommends that the above minute be transmitted to the Nebraska, Central Pennsylvania and Wisconsin-Upper Michigan Synods as the response to their memorials.

VIETNAM

Adopted by the Third Biennial Convention, Kansas City, Missouri
June 21–29, 1966

The deepening crisis in Vietnam is a cause of grave concern among all men of good will who seek the establishment of peace with justice and freedom. Especially troubling are the following aspects of the situation:

1. The rapidly mounting number of dead and wounded on both sides of the conflict;

2. The steady escalation of military commitments in Vietnam and, with it, the increased danger of a full-scale war in Asia;

3. The difficulty in achieving conditions which would make feasible the termination of military action in Vietnam in the near future;

4. The vast destruction of natural and developed resources;

5. The tragic diversion of attention and economic support from the assault upon domestic and world poverty to the growing war effort in Southeast Asia;

6. The turmoil and frustration among the people of South Vietnam in seeking to establish representative self-government.

Christians cannot be content to remain silent in the crisis of conscience that confronts them. They must be true to the conviction which is uniquely their own: that all men, regardless of nationality, politics, or ideology, are equally the object of God's judgment and loving kindness in Jesus Christ.

In facing the present situation in Vietnam, Christians must take cognizance of the fact that simplistic solutions are unrealistic. Attempts to bring easy answers to so complex a set of problems may only complicate them. Neither extended war nor immediate unilateral withdrawal by the United States seems to answer the problem. Continuance of the present limited war seems to be no solution. Consequently, it is important that every effort be made to bring all parties to the conflict toward a stance of openness and flexibility with a readiness to respond to whatever beginnings of solutions may emerge.

In view of the church's universal concern and its awareness that the situation in Vietnam defies simplistic solutions, the Lutheran Church in America calls upon its congregations and their members:

1. To engage in intensive study and free discussion of the Vietnam question, bringing to bear Christian insight upon all aspects of this crisis.

2. To pursue such study and discussion while exercising due caution against conclusions which:

a. Assume that ends justify means.

b. Overlook the dangers of the United States acting unilaterally rather than in cooperation with other countries through the effective utilization of international agencies such as the United Nations.

c. Absolutize international conflicts so that one's own position is seen as totally good, and the enemy's as totally evil.

d. Disregard America's traditional commitments to freedom of expression, and the right of dissent.

e. Ignore or underestimate international Communism's declared purposes of aggression, conquest and destruction of freedom.

3. To seek to foster within their communities a climate of political opinion characterized by such openness to new approaches as to foster a corresponding openness on the part of those holding national political office.

4. To stand in compassion and understanding beside those to whom the conduct of national policy is entrusted, to pray for them and to support them, though not uncritically, in their efforts to solve the dilemmas they face.

5. To be especially mindful of the spiritual and moral problems of men called to military service, including those who on grounds of conscience feel that they cannot participate in war.

Finally, the Lutheran Church in America commits itself to:

1. Continued works of mercy, relief, and rehabilitation in Vietnam through Lutheran World Relief; and

2. Joint efforts through the Lutheran World Federation, the National Council of the Churches of Christ in the U.S.A., the World Council of Churches, and particularly with the churches in Asia, in the quest for fuller understanding and possible solutions of the international issues related to Vietnam.

WORLD COMMUNITY
ETHICAL IMPERATIVES IN AN AGE OF INTERDEPENDENCE

Adopted by the Fifth Biennial Convention, Minneapolis, Minnesota
June 25-July 2, 1970

THE REALITY OF A WORLD NEIGHBORHOOD

To realize the oneness of the human family is an imperative. The technologies of communication, transportation, and weaponry are drawing humanity into an increasingly intimate neighborhood where the action of any nation or interest can lead to instantaneous and irreversible consequences for all. People are beginning to sense that if they do not soon devise some means of living together they will surely perish together.

The possibility of a massive extinction of life—through either nuclear holocaust or a general pollution of the environment—is matched by the possibility of a dramatic enlargement of the horizons of human fulfillment by means of humankind's burgeoning knowledge and skill.

Concern for human survival, fulfillment, and community flows from the very heart of the Christian faith. The church has long proclaimed both humankind's natural oneness "in Adam" and eschatological oneness "in Christ." The biblical writings attest to humanity's kinship with and stewardship over the earth which humans are not simply to "subdue" but "to dress and to keep" as well.

As a beginning of its response to the challenges of the present age of world interdependence, the Lutheran Church in America addresses the following judgments both to its own constituency and to all who must participate in the fashioning of a world community.

TOWARD A GLOBAL CIVIL ORDER

The classical Christian tradition views civil authority as a sign of God's loving activity of advancing human justice and well-being and of preserving humanity from its tendency to violence and self-destruction. Just government performs the double function of promoting the welfare of humanity and restraining wickedness.

As each age of history gave birth to institutions of civil authority appropriate to its needs, so this present age of global interdependence calls for transnational structures of law and authority within which human enterprise can be regulated to the benefit of all and disputes can be settled peacefully. It is of vital importance that there be established such world and regional

285

institutions as will encourage social, political, and economic pluralism productive of genuine human enrichment rather than perpetual conflict.

It is a hopeful sign that many nations are accepting legal obligations in connection with their participation in transnational organizations. These organizations should be regarded as emerging forms of world civil authority which, insofar as they promote peace and justice, are worthy of support by churches. Christians should be encouraged to exercise their vocation through international civil service.

The United Nations is the chief among these transnational institutions. Since the United Nations Charter emphasizes human dignity and freedom, membership in this world body should be universal. The world community will benefit if all nations have the opportunity to engage in continuous dialogue and co-operation which may prevent disputes among nations from escalating into wars. Exclusion of any nation willing to accept the United Nations Charter is not in the interest of world peace and community.

The work of the specialized agencies of economic and social development deserves increased support, particularly from the wealthy nations. The joint planning and action carried out through these agencies is useful in both the accomplishment of specific ends and in the provision of occasions in which nations may learn to perceive common interests and to co-operate toward common goals.

There continues to be a genuine fear, particularly within the developing nations, that the evolving international legal system will be simply an instrument whereby the more powerful nations can enforce their will on their weaker neighbors while themselves remaining free to obey or disobey the rule of law. This fear will doubtless continue until the greater powers show themselves willing to give more support to institutions of a genuinely multinational character and to abide by their rulings.

For the sake of strengthened confidence in the evolving structures of international law and institutions, nations holding self-judging reservations to the Statute of the International Court of Justice by which they reserve the right to reject the Court's jurisdiction should repeal these reservations.

HUMAN RIGHTS

The Universal Declaration of Human Rights, together with the Conventions related to it, is another sign of movement toward global civil order. Growing out of the general revulsion to the massive violation of human dignity during World War II, the Declaration bears witness to the fact that the rights of persons—civil, political, economic, and social—are no longer the exclusive concern of particular nation-states. Even though national governments retain legal sway over individual persons, they have become, to varying degrees, sensitive to the judgments of world public opinion regarding their treatment of their citizens.

However, the high ideals embodied in the Universal Declaration stand in tragic contrast to continuing violations of human dignity. These violations are not confined to one sector of the globe or to one ideological camp. They indicate a woefully insufficient sense of human worth on the part of nations.

The churches of every nation must be opposed to these abuses, and they and their members must find ways to work politically for a fuller realization of human rights. At the same time, they must examine themselves to discover to what degree they have contributed to dehumanization, and take such actions as repentance and justice may demand.

THE INTERNATIONAL PUBLIC DOMAIN

Rapidly growing technology is making demands on the world's resources which, if permitted to continue without regulation, may result in extensive depletion and pollution. It is no longer possible for one nation to consider its use, or abuse, of resources within its own borders—for instance, air and water—as its exclusive concern. The time has come for all nations to cooperate in the coordination of conservation efforts within their respective territories, as well as to establish the rule of law governing resources of oceans, polar regions, and outer space—"the international public domain." The latter task, a beginning of which has already been made, includes the establishment of agreements which protect international resources from uncontrolled private or national exploitation, the guarantee that such resources shall not be used for warlike purposes, and the development of genuinely international agencies empowered to enforce the agreements.

As possible reservoirs of new resources, the oceans, polar regions, and outer space could generate economic support for international organizations aiding developing countries. Creative use of the international public domain should also include the devising of means of more effective communication among peoples. Imaginative use of communications satellites could contribute to increased international understanding at both the popular and governmental levels. A world communications organization might be established for the purpose of supervising such a global communications system.

SECURITY AND WAR PREVENTION

It is clearly time for a rethinking of the meaning of national security. In view of the overkill capacity now possessed by the super-powers, national security can no longer be defined in terms of either nuclear superiority or even nuclear stalemate. The common threat which such weapons hold for all humanity teaches that their continued development can only undermine security. It is now necessary both to create an international legal framework within which arms control can be brought about and to help nations perceive that their safety must be conceived in more than military terms.

A beginning has been made in the construction of the necessary legal framework. This effort should be intensified, should become increasingly multinational in character, and should include all weapons of mass destruction. In the meantime, the United States should be encouraged to undertake such unilateral initiatives as may contribute to a climate more hospitable to the limitation of arms.

It is of vital importance that all nations give sustained attention to the inappropriateness of massive arms as a means of maintaining national security, a critical appraisal of their arsenals in the light of such considerations, and a restudy of national needs and goals with a view toward the reallocation of resources for peaceful purposes.

The classical Christian tradition takes full account of the human tendency to destructive aggressiveness and the component of force required by political authority for the purpose of maintaining peace within and among nations. At the same time, it recognizes that any true and lasting peace cannot be purely the maintenance of existing power relationships. Indeed various aspects of the existing power relationships may help to sustain and contribute to the maintenance of dehumanizing and unjust structures that stagnate and resist the growth and development of human rights and justice. True peace must include justice for all; and violence can often be a symptom of unrealized justice. In such cases violence must not be merely viewed as a break from orthodox dissent but also as a manifestation of frustration and despair experienced by oppressed people. Peace will be established not through the suppression of human aspirations but rather through the provision of structures within which they can flourish. In addition, this suppression is contrary to the freedom given to everyone and can only result in sowing the seed of greater disunity and ultimate violence and destruction. The history of free people reflects a tradition of liberation. This grants people the strength, freedom and right to challenge oppressive systems in their struggle for justice and social progress.

The present Christian attitude toward armed violence must of necessity be a two-sided one. On the one hand, it must recognize the suicidal character of nuclear war among the Great Powers; on the other, it must accept the fact that while injustice persists there will continue to be violent conflicts within and among nations.

The churches must work, therefore, for a lessening of the nuclear peril and the realization of greater degrees of justice for the poor of the world.

The peacekeeping function of the United Nations should be revived and strengthened and should receive support from the Great Powers which, on their part, should pledge their noninterference with the international police function.

THE DEVELOPMENT OF PEOPLES

There can be no full or abiding peace without justice for all the world's people. The prophets of old warned that until the poor were treated as full members of the community rather than the objects of exploitation, there could be no security from the wrath of God or humankind. The nation which lived by injustice sowed the seeds of its own overthrow.

It is the Christian community within the affluent countries that is, by virtue of its prophetic heritage, called to set forth the obligations of the wealthy and the rights of the poor. It is scandalous that the industrialized West uses so little of its great wealth for the economic and social development of the newer nations. It is now time to mobilize support for increased aid policies which will insure a larger degree of justice to the developing nations. Having supported the overseas ministries of evangelism, education, and mercy, the people of the church must now, without abandoning these tasks, undertake the *political* task of securing that massive aid necessary for meaningful development.

The use of development aid by the Great Powers to achieve short-run political ends is to the disadvantage of both donor and recipient. Short-term aid commitments do not contribute to a climate of trust in which sound planning can be done. Aid given on the basis of purely political motives can, in fact, compound the problem of world poverty.

It is important that development aid be channeled in increasing amounts through multilateral agencies and committed for periods of sufficient duration to insure trust and responsible planning.

Poor nations should not be kept outside the world economic mainstream, excluded by policies advantageous to the more affluent nations. Unfavorable terms of trade should be removed in order to encourage participation by these nations in the world economic community and free them from any status as economic, if not political, colonies.

In their own work in the new nations, the churches must strive constantly to develop such relevant programs as may complement those under public auspices. In the new nations the indigenous churches must challenge their governments and people toward a higher level of well-being for all. If such churches request help to develop skills for the political task, the churches in the affluent countries should be ready to share experiences and resource persons.

THE CHURCHES AND WORLD COMMUNITY

Underlying all this is the fundamental premise that, as a corporate entity within a given nation, a church body has the God-given responsibility of generating support for national policies which contribute to the building of a world community. It is imperative that the Lutheran Church in America in both the United States and Canada begin the generation of such support by means of (1) more intensive study of international issues; (2) representation to the respective governments in support of multilateral development assistance, greater support of the world organization, and further efforts at arms-limitation; and (3) joining with other organizations and persons of good will in pursuit of these ends.

Although the church ideally transcends race and nation, frequently it has in fact generated or condoned policies in sharp contrast to that ideal. It is the duty of the organized churches working together to create occasions for the meeting and sharing of perceptions between people whose respective nations may be locked in deep conflict and to provide channels of communication when others are cut by political and ideological division.

Sensing the urgency of the times, the Lutheran Church in America recognizes these roles as central to its God-given mandate and pledges itself to redoubled effort in the building of world community.